*Welcome aboard G.W. and Bonnie...
Hope you enjoy our voyage together!*

*Weldon and Dee Parker
8-5-85*

SOL SEAKER...

down the

MAGICAL

MISSISSIPPI

Weldon ♥ Dee Parker

Cover Photograph·Ray Lippert
Drawings·Weldon Parker

Sun Seeker Books ✱ Clearlake, California

A Sun Seeker Book

For information or additional copies, write:

Weldon Parker

P. O. Box 4246

Clearlake, CA 95422

Our appreciation goes to all who reviewed the manuscript at its various stages of completion. A special thanks to the following, whose criticism and encouragement spurred the authors forward.

Lois Erickson
Earl and Helen Strohbehn
Wes and Alberta Stone
Jane Leatherman
Dorsey Kinnamon
Eloyce Arrants
Fran Hawkins
Lonna Smith
Ralph and Bev Miller
Mae and Bill Rice
Peggy Davis
Verna and Orville Parker
Sid and Shiela Tiedt

Our deepest gratitude and love go to the many river friends who so willingly shared a part of themselves with these two strangers. This sharing helped create the **magic** which made possible, **SOL SEAKER: DOWN THE MAGICAL MISSISSIPPI**.

Contents

Contents

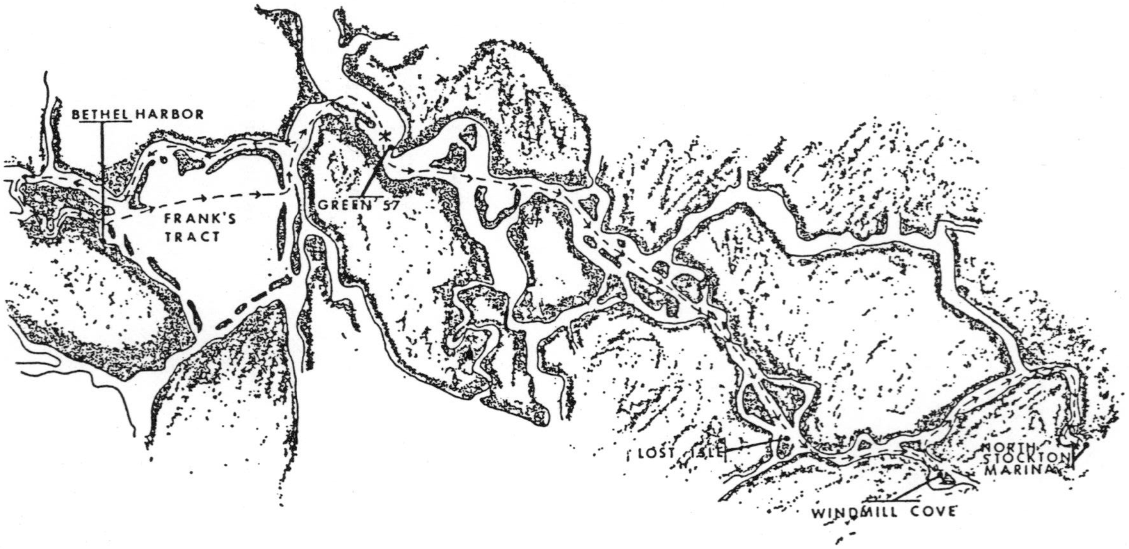
BETHEL HARBOR
FRANK'S TRACT
GREEN 57
LOST ISLE
NORTH STOCKTON MARINA
WINDMILL COVE

CH-1

1

SHAKEDOWN CRUISE

As we pulled into Raoul's Marina, a Catholic Priest eyed the stern of our boat. Was he surprised to see a boat from Clearlake, California making port at the tip of Grand Isle some sixty miles south of New Orleans, where the Barataria Seaway joins the Gulf of Mexico? Or was he interested in the name of our boat - **Sol Seaker**?

"I like the name of your boat," the Priest said, as we secured the lines. I know it means "Sun Seeker", but when said aloud it could mean something else."

"That's not coincidental," I replied. "My wife, Dee, and I have spent almost three months coming down the Mississippi from Minneapolis. We sought both the sun (sol) and people (souls) along the way."

"Did you find what you sought?" he mused.

"Yes we did!" we said in unison as we looked at each other. "Yes we did!"

It had started more than a year before. The day was warm, the breezes gentle as wife, Dee; son, John; and I prepared to back **Hey Babe**, our newly acquired twenty-six foot cabin cruiser, out of a guest slip at Bethel Harbor in the San Joaquin delta area east of San Francisco Bay. The engine idled quietly at seven hundred RPM's. "A bit too fast," I thought, "but it will slow when I put her in gear."

With John and Dee on the bow, I shifted to reverse. The lever seemed stiff, perhaps due to my unfamiliarity with the boat. We moved backward. At the proper instant I shifted to neutral and let her drift a bit more before shifting into forward and turning to leave the harbor through a narrow opening between the uncovered guest slips and a long metal building containing covered berths. The boat moved more rapidly than I had expected. I quickly shifted to neutral; At least I thought I was shifting to neutral, but soon realized that I had in fact shifted beyond neutral and was again in reverse.

1

As the boat moved backward, Dee yelled, "Look out! The antenna is about to hit the power lines."

I grabbed the whip antenna and pulled it down to a horizontal position with one hand while trying to shift to neutral; then forward, and steer the boat with the other. My crew shouted new directions and warnings as they unsuccessfully attempted to prevent **Hey Babe** from colliding with the dock.

When finally headed in the direction of the narrow aperture, I realized that the current, caused by an incoming tide, was swinging the bow toward the metal covered berths. I turned the wheel too late to avoid a second collision - happily a glancing blow which pushed the bow into the opening. Suddenly we were free of all obstacles.

Embarrassed, I pulled into the gas dock for fuel and water for our weekend shakedown cruise to Stockton. Although still having some difficulty with the speed and shift controls, I made a moderately successful maneuver into the dock.

Finally underway, we successfully crossed Frank's Tract without mishap. In False River I pushed the throttle forward - 1200 RPM 1600, 2000, 2500. We turned right into the San Joaquin River and headed toward Stockton. Red navigational markers on our right and green on our left assured us that we were headed in the right direction. Although we had never had a formal course in navigation, we were familiar with the phrase "red right returning" - the red markers should be on the right when returning from seaward toward an inland port.

In the river, I increased **Hey Babe**'s RPM's to 3300. As we skimmed along at thirty miles an hour, we settled back to enjoy the scenery. The breeze felt cool and invigorating, and the height of the flying bridge made it possible for us to look over the low levees to the fields and trees beyond.

Approaching green day marker 57, it happened - the motor sputtered, popped, and died, leaving us adrift in the middle of the shipping channel. A westerly breeze began pushing us toward the rock levee on the east side of the channel. I tried to restart the engine only to find that both batteries were dead.

"Where's the anchor?" John asked.

"I think there's one down in the engine compartment," I replied. "Get ready to drop it over when we drift outside the shipping lane."

2

In a few moments John called back, "I found the anchor. We've got a big problem." He held up the anchor to show me that there was no rope attached. A quick search through the boat produced a few short pieces. As he tied these together, Dee removed the mooring lines from the bow and stern cleats. With every available rope attached, John dropped the anchor overboard, hoping the rope would be long enough and strong enough to halt our five thousand pound boat's relentless movement toward the rocky shore. We were in luck. It held!

Dee had insisted we bring along our Citizen's Band radio. As we clipped and spliced wires to hook up the radio, the big question in our minds was, "Will the dead batteries have enough power left in them to operate the radio?" They did.

Everyone knows that channel 9 is the emergency channel. Since we were not sure how long our anchor ropes would hold, I designated our situation an emergency and began calling on channel 9. "Break, break on channel 9." No answer. More insistently; "Break, break on channel 9, anyone on channel 9?" No answer.

"If you really want anyone to hear you," John said quietly, "you'd better depress the button on the microphone before saying 'break, break.' You're speaking into a dead mike."

I flushed red as I paused to think through the steps for transmitting and receiving - "depress the microphone button; say, 'break, break for channel 9; release the microphone button; wait for an answer."

I executed the steps, then waited and waited and waited. Static. Finally a weak, garbled female voice joined the static. I thought I heard, "What is your problem?"

Depressing the button I said slowly, "I'm in a disabled boat located at green marker 57 on the deep water channel three miles east of Frank's Tract. Over."

"This is . . . buzz . . . hiss . . . crackle . . . Give . . . crackle . . . location. Over."

Depress button. "I'm near green marker 57 on the San Joaquin River about 3 miles east of Frank's Tract. Over."

". . . Crackle . . . buzz . . . your location. What state . . . crackle . . . hiss . . .in? Over."

Was this some kind of joke, or was she really asking what state we were in? I calmly asked, "Where are you located? Over."

3

"This . . . buzz . . . crackle Anchorage . . .
laska . . . What state . . . buzz . . . crackle in?
Over."

"A state of shock! I think I'd better try to raise
someone on a local channel. I'm in California. Clear
on 9."

During this time John was stationed on the rear
deck of the boat. He had lined up marker 57 with a
distant telephone pole and was keeping watch to see if
Hey Babe was holding on her makeshift anchor rope - the
anchor was still holding.

Dee began to wave at people in passing boats hoping
to get one to stop, but all she got were friendly waves
in return.

I continued my calls for assistance by starting at
channel 1. Depress button, "Break, break on channel 1."
Release. Wait. No answer. I moved to channel 2. Depress,
"Break, break on channel 2; "anyone on channel 2?" Release. Wait. No answer. Channel 3, no answer. Channels
4, 5, 6, 7, 8, no answer. Channel 9.

"This . . . buzz . . . crackle . . . Alaska . . .
call . . . crackle, fizz . . . for you? Over."

Channels 10, 11, 12, 13. No answers.

"Break, break on channel 14, anyone on channel 14.
Over."

"This is the **Yellow Rose** on channel 14. Over."

A huge sigh of relief was heard from all aboard **Hey
Babe**. "**Yellow Rose**, this is **Hey Babe**. We're having
engine trouble. Over."

"Yes, **Hey Babe**, this is the **Yellow Rose**, Coast
Guard Auxiliary, give me your location, the nature of
your problem, and tell me what I can do to help. Over."

Our rescuers turned out to be Tex and Ellen Howle
of Kelseyville, California. The Howles had trailered
Yellow Rose to the Delta for a weekend of pleasure boating. Fortunately for us, the Coast Guard Auxiliary is
never off duty, and are dedicated to helping boaters in
trouble. Using his Marine Radio, Tex called Gary, the
broker who had sold us **Hey Babe**. A mechanic would be on
his way as soon as possible.

We thanked the Howles for their help, signed their
report, and promised to take a Coast Guard Auxiliary
class at our earliest opportunity. When they were sure
we were okay, they left us to wait for the mechanic.

With time on our hands while we waited, we observed. We observed tugboats, trawlers, houseboats,

skiffs and cruisers moving effortlessly through the gently ruffled waters. We also observed the strange behavior of a fly and a lady bug. An observation which occupied much of our time.

When we first noticed them on the deck of the flying bridge, the lady bug was sitting very still as the fly walked cautiously up to her (assuming the female gender) from behind. He (assuming the male gender) nudged her with his fly's equivalent of a nose. Apparently puzzled by the hard shell of this strange but beautiful creature, he backed off a bit, then moved around to her left side, slowly approaching and nudging her again. Again he backed away, confused. He then circled her several times, occasionally moving in to sniff or nudge. After five or six circuits, he seemed to lose interest.

Suddenly he turned and, with renewed attraction and growing determination, again approached the lady bug. After several unsuccessful attempts to satisfy his passions, and obviously frustrated by the indifferent lady bug, the fly again walked away.

Just as he turned for a new effort, the lady bug spread her wings and flew away. After returning to the spot and searching for several minutes, the fly also took wing.

As we continued to wait, we wondered how we could have been so amateurish as to start out without a more thorough check of the boat. It wasn't our lack of experience with boats. We've owned six boats. In fact we still own six boats.

Our first boat was a compromise. Dee wanted a sailboat and I wanted a rowboat for fishing. Our compromise was a ten foot aluminum put-it-together-yourself jon boat kit with optional sail package. It took John and I three days to get it assembled, at which time I "launched" it on the front lawn. As I sat there in the stationary boat, feeling the force of the wind in the blue nylon sail, I was oblivious to the snickers and stares of neighbors as they drove past.

In the water, our compromise boat was not the most graceful swan on the pond. But it did attract quite a lot of attention, especially from twelve year old boys as they whizzed by in their El Toros.

Not long after we got our sail-and-fishing boat we added boats 2, 3, and 4 - homemade, folding, plywood and canvas kayaks. Each of these new boats was made from a single sheet of 4' x 10' marine plywood cut lengthwise into four equal strips. The strips were rounded on the ends and a piece was cut from two of them to form a "cockpit". When the four strips were bound together with canvass, two diamond shaped spreader boards were inserted in front of and behind the cockpit. A flat seat board in the cockpit and two homemade paddles completed the kayaks.

After some exciting kayak trips on the beautiful Russian River in California, we purchased boat number five, a nineteen foot outboard runabout which we use for ocean and lake fishing. Twenty years of boating; however, hadn't prevented us from getting stuck in the San Joaquin River on boat number six, **Hey Babe**.

When Gary's mechanic arrived, he towed us to protected waters on the lee side of a clump of tules. As he adjusted the timing, checked the alternator, and replaced the batteries, we watched a loaded ocean freighter round the bend from the direction of Stockton, and pass about a hundred yards to the east of us - almost the exact spot our engine had failed.

The sun was dropping below the northern edge of Mount Diablo when we were on our way again after being disabled for four and a half hours. Little did we realize that the engine problem was just the beginning of a weekend we'd rather forget.

It was dark long before we reached our intended overnight destination, Lost Isle. We were grateful for a clear sky and a bright moon, although it was not a moonlight cruise we had envisioned for our first voyage.

The lights on the red and green navigational aids shown like the landing lights at an airport, outlining the way down the channel toward Stockton. With the engine running smoothly, Dee took her turn at the helm. We all peered intently into the inky waters ahead. Suddenly Dee slowed and veered to the right. She had spotted a strange dark object in the water. A floating log? The top of a submerged rock? She continued at this slower speed. Soon we all began to see dark objects. **Hey Babe** was kept on a zig-zag course to avoid hitting them. Stopping to inspect one of the objects, we found it to be a mass of floating water hyacinth, posing no great threat to navigation.

We increased speed again and began to search for a sign that would tell us we were at Lost Isle. Unfortunately, we had passed Lost Isle while we were busy dodging water hyacinths; and, for the time being at least, Lost Isle would remain lost.

We finally spotted a narrow opening on the right bank and a small lighted sign identifying it as the entrance to Windmill Cove. We nervously maneuvered through the opening which, by moonlight, seemed much narrower than it really was. Dee turned the helm over to me, apparently forgetting that it was I who, some six hours earlier, had bumped into the docks at the beginning of our ill-fated voyage.

Once again I proved my masterful ability at the helm by putting **Hey Babe** bow first into the dock directly in front of a sign which read, "All Boats Stern In." With John on the dock pulling and Dee shouting directions we finally got **Hey Babe** into a "side in" position, the bow pointing toward the cove exit for a quick get away in case someone objected.

Safely moored - or whatever is the correct term for being left-side-in at a stern-end-in-only dock, we headed for a door beneath a restaurant sign. The restaurant was closed for the night, a circumstance which gave us the opportunity to try out our on-board alcohol stove. After several exciting flare-ups, the front burner finally settled down to a one-sided orange-blue flame which sputtered and hissed at regular intervals.

Dee triumphantly broke out our emergency rations - a can of corned beef, some left over summer squash, a loaf of french bread and a very seedy watermelon. She heated the corned beef and squash and we sat down to our first feast aboard **Hey Babe**. As we ate, we agreed on two things - we didn't like the name **Hey Babe** and we were tired, tired, tired!

The night passed with only a few interruptions - several boats loaded with very boisterous and very drunk individuals came and went from the harbor; the bar stayed open until 2:00 A.M., telling us something about the relative value of nutritious food and strong drink in our modern society; each of us made two trips to the bathroom (I later learned to call this the head), the excitement and the gentle rocking of the boat having a unique effect on the urinary system. The final interruption came at dawn when Dee screamed, as a large cat stared at her through the windshield just above her pillowed head.

I don't know if it was this final event or an accumulation of experiences that affected Dee's sanity,

7

but we later found her talking to a dead cricket. When John asked, "Why are you talking to that dead cricket," she replied, "Oh, I thought it was a cockroach."

A few minutes later she was observed talking to the leftover watermelon seeds. We didn't have the heart to tell her that these, too, were not cockroaches.

The morning was fair and clear. No one seemed to care that we were parked incorrectly and the restaurant was now open for breakfast, solving the problem of possible starvation.

Before resuming our cruise, I practiced docking and undocking. There were few boats in Windmill Cove giving me plenty of room to maneuver. Dee and John stayed on the dock to observe and voice such encouraging admonitions as, "Your going too fast! Slow down! Reverse, reverse! I think you need to come in at a flatter angle! Look out, you're going to hit!"

The shift lever at the bridge helm was still very hard to move and didn't seem to hit forward, neutral and reverse at the proper locations. As I made my first approach, accompanied by the aforementioned encouragement, I shifted from forward to neutral. Okay! Then I shifted from neutral to reverse. Not Okay! **Hey Babe** continued to move forward from its original momentum. No matter how loudly Dee yelled, "reverse, reverse," the damned boat refused to reverse.

I yelled back, "The lever is pulled as far as it will . . ." At that instant I hit the dock a blow that was softened only because both Dee and John risked personal injury to fend off the bow with their hands.

Securing the boat to the dock again, John and I inspected the shift mechanism and found a severely bent cable. After considerable effort we straightened the cable enough to make it work. With renewed confidence I again circled the boat. This time I made an indefectible approach, speed and angle both perfect. At the proper instant I shifted to neutral, then reverse. The boat responded flawlessly. Before I reached **the dock** the boat began to back away. I had forgotten **to return** the shift to neutral. By the time I realized my **error,** I was several feet away and still going backwards.

I tried again. The shift lever moved easily - too easily. There was no forward, no neutral, no reverse. The cable had become disconnected - stripped threads.

John took over as chief mechanic, reattaching the cable. It held through some trial shifts, but there was no more practice time as we still had several miles to go to a North Stockton marina where we would pick up John's ex-wife Kathy and daughter, Amber.

In Fourteen Mile Slough John took his first turn at the helm. As he rounded a sharp hyacinth choked bend, he met a large trawler on our side of the channel. The trawler's skipper was also dodging water hyacinth. John turned in closer to the right bank. As he did so, the propeller encountered several tons of broken concrete, dumped as rip-rap along the bank to prevent erosion. A sixteen inch aluminum propeller is no match for a bed of broken concrete, and **Hey Babe** began to shake as the emaciated propeller chopped unevenly at the water

We limped into the harbor to find Kathy and Amber waiting on the dock. Kathy took me to a store to buy a large wrench, as none of mine were big enough to fit the nut holding the propeller. With new wrench in hand and outdrive raised, I went over the stern. Standing on top of the outdrive, I held onto the railing with one hand and leaned down as far as I could, barely able to reach the nut with the wrench. Aware that one slip and the wrench and I would both be in ten feet of muddy water, I slowly loosened the nut. The strain on my fifty-one year old left arm was causing a great deal of pain, but I didn't dare stop. When the nut was removed the propeller stubbornly refused to come off the shaft. In desperation and exhaustion, I replaced the nut a few turns and gave it three sharp whacks with the end of the wrench - a trick I learned from my father. Success! I handed the damaged prop to John and he handed me one of the two spare props. As I slid it in place my arm reached the end of its endurance. With some effort I climbed back aboard and turned the wrench over to John, something I should have done sooner since he is much younger, taller and stronger than I.

John quickly completed the job and, once again, **Hey Babe** was ready to go. My left arm, however was not. It was several days before the pain subsided, and I think my left arm will always be a few millimeters longer than the right one.

With everyone aboard, we were again underway, staying well away from the banks, particularly in the turns. In Fourteen Mile Slough we encountered a would-be water skier having difficulty getting up on his skis. As I started to slow down, the boat veered sharply toward the left bank. I quickly reversed the engine, backed into

9

mid-channel, and crept past the would be skier, puzzled as to why **Hey Babe** had decided to make an unscheduled left turn. I increased speed slowly, always ready to stop if the steering again became erratic.

Next we met a successful water skier; who, as water skiers often do, headed straight for us to give us a thrill, not knowing that we had already had more than our share of thrills. In an impromptu poll, we voted to banish all waterskiers to a remote part of the galaxy where they could give each other thrills, and leave us sedate pleasure boaters alone.

Still hoping to find Lost Isle, we headed west on the deep water channel. There it was! Unfortunately, we didn't have enough time to stop for the picnic we had planned. Instead we circled the island and headed back to Stockton.

As **Hey Babe** reached full speed, she began to veer left again. Slowly I corrected course by turning the wheel to the right. All the way to Stockton, I found that I had to continually move the wheel to the right to keep the boat on a straight course. Something was definitely wrong. Perhaps our tip-toe through the concrete had damaged the steering mechanism.

When Kathy and Amber were safely back on dock, we drove full-speed from the inside helm, where the steering worked perfectly. At Bethel Harbor, John and Dee headed for San Jose in John's car while I remained behind to see that the boat was back on the trailer and properly stored. Again there was a problem - the marina was closed. I made the boat fast to the end of the dock, leaving a note and hoping someone would put **Hey Babe** safely back in dry storage.

Driving the one-and-a-half hours back to San Jose, I was thankful that the shakedown cruise was over. Everything that could go wrong had gone wrong. But then I guess that's what a shakedown cruise is for. When I arrived home, Dee had learned that a Coast Guard Auxiliary boating class would be starting the next week at Prospect High School.

We would be there.

FLY AND LADY BUG

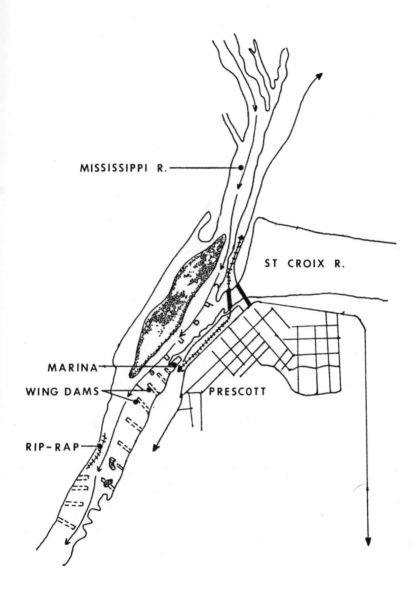

MISSISSIPPI R.

ST CROIX R.

MARINA

WING DAMS

PRESCOTT

RIP-RAP

CH–2·3

2

MIDNIGHT MONSTER

SJS PROFESSOR   RETIRES
LAUNCHES TWAIN-TYPE TRIP

"A decades old love affair ended recently at San Jose State University, but a new romance has begun. After twenty-three years in the university's education department, Weldon Parker retired.   At his farewell party his students hugged and kissed the man they say taught them how to teach from the heart.   Parker said his 'retirement' is just the beginning of a new labor of love: a three month cruise down the Mississippi River on a twenty-six foot cabin cruiser with his wife Dee. Parker, 52, plans to write a book about the experience."

So stated the article in the San Jose News.

My decision to retire at age fifty-two had, indeed, involved saying good-bye to a thirty year love affair with teaching. It was a difficult decision, emotionally and financially, for both of us.   I'll never know how Dee endured the months of indecision, but she was always there, ready to support whichever inclination prevailed at the moment. When the final choice was made, we sold our fourplex and small patio home hoping that the money from these and my small monthly retirement check would sustain us.

Moving our furniture to our small vacation home at Clearlake broke the final ties that bound us to San Jose State University. Including my student years, I had been affiliated with the University for thirty-four years - almost two-thirds of my life.

Dee had been engaged in her "hobby" of selling real estate for several years, but high interest rates and a national economic recession had virtually stopped all real estate activity. She was willing to take a break.

In addition to this major decision, a number of minor decisions and activities occupied our thoughts and actions.

In the boating class we learned boat handling,

11

navigation, rules-of-the-road, repairs, marine radio operation and the all important terminology which separates the true boater from the uneducated landlubber. We learned that the bow is forward, the stern is aft. Scuppers are the little holes that allow the water to drain off the deck into the river instead of into the cabin. We learned that the bilge is the lowest part of the boat, and that buoys are divided into two major types - "cans," usually black, are to be kept to the left when returning to port; "nuns," usually red, give rise to the phrase "red, right, returning." We still do not understand how a "buoy" can be a "nun." We learned that port is left (port has four letters, left has four letters), and starboard is right, and the most important lesson - ropes, when used on or about a boat, cease to be ropes and become lines. There are anchor lines (also called the rode), bow lines, stern lines and spring lines.

Shortly after our shakedown cruise on the **Hey Babe,** we began the long, sometimes frustrating, sometimes humerous task of picking a more suitable name for our boat. Our nineteen foot fishing boat, **Anhinga**, was so named by our daughter, Kathy. She selected this name because it was the name of a large dark colored bird we had observed deftly spearing bluegills in a pond in the Florida Everglades. She thought that if we named the boat **Anhinga** we too would have good fishing when we were aboard her. It worked.

What we needed was the perfect name for a boat that we planned to trailer to America's waterways where we would live aboard, cruise, fish and meet new people. We first thought of names that related to boat living - like **Tepee Canoe, Sea Shanty,** and **Harbor House.** But these weren't quite right.

Dee, who loves the sun, insisted that our new boat somehow reflect the idea that we would use it under sunny conditions whenever possible. Thus we considered **Sunday Seas, Sun Dee Seas,** and **Sun Dee Sun.** None of these struck THE responsive chord.

I offered two names with more subtle reference to the sun, **Fanny Tanner** and **After Burner.** But was booed and hissed by Dee, son John, daughter Kathy and son-in-law Ted. I was even less successful with two names that hinted at retirement years, **Sun Seaty** and **Sea Nile.** We became convinced that at the proper time the perfect name would emerge. It did.

12

For several years Dee and I had taken vacations in Mazatlan, Mexico. This year we had to forgo our trip because of the numerous demands on our time created by retirement and moving. During the week that we would have been in Mexico, Northern California experienced a depressing rain and wind storm. Early one morning, while we were still in bed, Dee said, "I wish we were in Mexico where the sun is shining. Maybe we should have bought one of those condos we saw at Islas Del Sol."

We looked at each other. "Sol," we said together. "Let's use the Spanish word for sun."

With gestaltic enthusiasm Dee exclaimed, "How about **Sol Seeker**? Only let's spell Seeker, **S-e-a-k-e-r**."

Dee was thinking of the sun and the sea, but I immediately sensed a further, if more subtle meaning. One which made the name doubly appropriate. The Spanish word **sol** is pronounced the same as S-o-u-l.

We had decided that our first voyage would be down the Mississippi River. If we were going to travel the nation's waterways, why not start with the most important, best known, most written about and most controlled waterway of all, "Ole Man River" himself? Our purpose in this voyage would be threefold; to experience first hand the moods, machinations and meanders of this great river; to follow the sun southward on it's annual trip through the autumnal equinox toward the winter solstice; to discover the inner sols or souls of the people we would meet along the way while refreshing our own souls in the process.

The name, **Sol Seaker**, was perfect. Now all we had to do was acetone off **Hey Babe**, install the new name and try to live up to the high goal that it implied.

The spring months passed swiftly. After a round of office cleaning, retirement parties and well wishes we trailered **Sol Seaker** to Clearlake for some final outfitting. There, where most boats are in the fourteen to sixteen foot variety, our neighbors dubbed our twenty-six foot boat the **Queen Mary**.

Early on the morning of August 15, I drove **Sol Seaker** up the placid waters of Cache Creek and out into Clearlake. I was awed as usual by the beautiful reflections in these tranquil waters. As a great blue heron broke the stillness with his raucous call, I began to ask myself why we were leaving such a beautiful spot to travel the unknown stretches of some distant muddy river. I was sorry that Dee wasn't with me in these

13

quiet moments, but one of us had to drive the car and trailer to the launching ramp at Redbud Park while the other drove the boat. Dee said she preferred to drive the car because she wasn't as experienced at handling the boat. But I knew that she always gave me the more glamorous jobs while she retained the more mundane for herself. Also, she didn't trust me to back the trailer into the water.

Old "sol" was just topping the eastern hills as, without fanfare or audience, the two of us loaded the boat on the trailer and began the overland portion of our first **Sol Seaker** voyage.

At KOA campgrounds we used **Sol Seaker** as a camping trailer. In one a group of campers had a hearty laugh as we backed boat and trailer toward the bank of a narrow, shallow river. They thought we were going to launch the boat, but we were only placing **Sol Seaker** close to a picnic table to use as a boarding platform.

What a relief when we crossed the Continental Divide. From there on it was down hill. Every stream was, like us, searching for the Mississippi River. Some day during the next three months we might actually be floating on the same molecules of water that were presently buoying a group of "tubers" floating alongside the road on the Yellowstone River of Montana.

We marveled at the expanses of beautiful sunflowers in North Dakota and Minnesota. Like soldiers at attention, each with its face turned toward the sun, they stood waiting for someone to yell, "forward march."

It was 6:30 in the afternoon when we rounded the final curve on Highway 10 near the small village of Prescott, Wisconsin, located at the junction of the St. Croix and Mississippi Rivers, about twenty-five miles southeast of Minneapolis-St. Paul. The last two miles had been narrow and wound through dense woods and past lovely homes. Here and there were signs - "Apples for Sale".

Rush hour traffic from the twin cities was lined up behind us as we passed a beautiful swimming beach on the St. Croix River and slowly crossed the narrow steel bridge. A train moved cautiously onto the parallel Burlington Northern Railroad bridge. From our vantage point we could see that both the Mississippi and St. Croix were lined with lush green forest.

Crossing the bridge we turned off Highway 10 onto Main Street. Commuter cars sped by, grateful to have

14

these snail paced travelers out of their way. We drove
to the launching ramp that had been recommended by Don
Fluetsch, one of several people with whom we had corres-
ponded before starting our trip. "Sternwheel Don", as
he calls himself, lives in Cassville, Wisconsin. On a
trip to Minneapolis last spring he had checked on
several ramps and suggested this one in Prescott. Jeff,
a student who works at the ramp after school, asked if
we were planning to launch our boat today.

I said, "No, we're just looking at the ramp. We
want to have the stern drive checked before we launch
the boat, we've trailered it all the way from California
over some bumpy roads."

"Is there a good restaurant nearby?" Dee wondered.

"There's two restaurants in town, The Captain's
Table and The Steamboat Inn. The Steamboat Inn is fancier but they both have good food."

Dee and I looked at each other, thinking, "What
appropriate names for restaurants for our first meal on
the Mississippi."

"Which is closer?" Dee queried.

"The Captain's Table is right up there." Jeff
pointed to the back of an old brick building which
fronted on Main Street.

"The Captain's Table it'll be," I replied. "Can we
leave our car and trailer parked here while we eat?"

"Are you sure you're not going to launch your boat
today? 'Cause if you are I need to collect $3.00 before
I go home."

"We promise not to launch today. All we want to do
is eat, check in at the Prescott Marina and get some
rest," I replied.

"It's okay to park here. The marina's right over
there." Jeff pointed to a large metal building just
beyond a high fence. "But they're closed for the day."

The Captain's Table was empty except for one couple. We selected a booth near the door which gave us a
view of the entire room as well as a peek into the
kitchen. We were disappointed that the dining room did
not afford a view of the river. On the wall near the
table occupied by our fellow diners was a picture of a
sternwheel steam packet - the trademark of Mark Twain's
Mississippi. On another wall was a large portrait of a
riverboat captain.

"We really are here," Dee whispered as our waitress
Robin appeared, dressed in faded jeans and sneakers, her

hair in two long European braids. We ordered New York
strip steaks with mushrooms, a real bargain at $3.75,
and a glass of Jacques Scott Rose Lambrusco. As we sat
waiting for our food to arrive we overheard parts of the
conversation between the other couple. Actually it
wasn't a conversation, as the woman did all the talking.
She had been to a funeral.

"I had to close my eyes real tight so I wouldn't
cry. Know what I mean? 'Cause if you start to cry then
everyone in the whole damn place starts to cry. Know
what I mean? She was a nice person. That's the trouble
with the world. Even if you think someone's nice, you
don't tell them they're nice. Know what I mean? We
need to tell people that we think they are nice before
it's too late."

Our attention was diverted to two women in their
sixties who had just entered the restaurant. The ener-
getic and outspoken one, a large blond, wore a once
fashionable green dress draped with a fox fell. The
quieter one was dressed in a gray pants suit. They
looked around. The blond spoke, "Shall we sit in our
regular seat?" Their "regular seat" was under the portrait of the riverboat captain.

Our food came and we began eating hungrily, our
attention no longer on the other diners. Sometime later
we again took notice of the talkative blond when, after
finishing her soup, she rose, walked over to the picture
of the steamboat, leaned forward, and began to inspect
its every detail. She peered intently for some minutes
walked back, sat down, and asked her companion if she
remembered when the **River Queen** came to Stillwater. Her
companion replied in the affirmative. The talkative
lady then stood again, looked straight into the eyes of
the captain's portrait and asked in a voice for all to
hear, "Were you the captain of the **River Queen**?"

She waited as if expecting an answer. Perhaps she
got one, for she nodded and said "hmmm" half under her
breath as though she had just completed a conversation
with a real person.

After dinner we moved the boat and trailer inside
the large fenced boatyard where we parked close to the
river in order to be away from any activity that might
occur in the morning before we were awake. With some
difficulty we climbed aboard. We missed having the
picnic tables that had served as steps to get us aboard
in the campgrounds.

The evening was cool but humid. We sat for a few minutes on the transom watching the placid river glide by. We wondered if the red and black buoys marked the "wing dams" we had read about in our Corps of Engineers chart book. The river here looked easy. If the entire Mississippi was like the small part we could see, our voyage would be a "piece of cake". When several mosquitoes began to find their target, we moved inside, thankful that we had made screens for the windows.

It was Dee's turn to read aloud from "Go South Inside", a book about boat travel on the Intracoastal Waterway between Chesapeake Bay and Miami, Florida. If all went well on our Mississippi River trip, we planned to do the Intracoastal Waterway at some future time. We had decided not to trailer **Sol Seaker** back to California until we were through using her in the eastern half of the country.

Dee finished a chapter then fell asleep, and I was beginning to doze off when I heard a sound that brought me back to a state of full wakefulness. It was somewhat like the whine of a diesel locomotive struggling to pull a fully loaded train up a steep hill. It was coming from the direction of the railroad bridge. As I continued to listen the sound grew louder and closer. Suddenly a blinding light flooded the inside of the boat with daylight. I bolted upright, my first thought was that unknowingly we had parked on the railroad track and a train was bearing down on us. The light disappeared.

Peering out the cabin window toward the source of the sound, I was relieved that no train was heading for us, but the sight I beheld gave me little comfort. On the river next to us a dark mass moved slowly by. A fixed red light and a blinking amber one at the front of the mass gave it the appearance of a giant monster. As the monster advanced downriver, the glaring white light flashed on again, playing across the top of the moving object, illuminating great rusty steel hulks topped by an assortment of pipes, braces and barrels. The beam originated somewhere upstream. The entire erie mass continued to move relentlessly by.

Dee was wide awake and seated beside me. Although our mouths were open, we were speechless for several moments. Dee spoke first, "Oh my God!"

We watched as the bow lights disappeared downstream behind a tree. Upstream the source of the bright light, a huge towboat, came into view, slowly pushing the

17

barges ahead of it. As the towboat came alongside I gasped, "There's no way you're going to get me on the river with one of those things."

Dee responded, "Let's go do the Intracoastal Waterway! NOW!"

This experience with our first river towboat wasn't the only excitement of that introductory night alongside the Mississippi. After our pulses and adrenaline flow had slowed, we once more neared that happy state of slumber when a police car drove into the lot and parked near the large metal "Two Rivers Boatworks" building. A policeman was out of the car shining a light on an open window in the building. We wondered if we should make our presence known, as we heard the policeman radio the dispatcher asking her to phone Thomas to come down with the keys. We now saw that there were two policemen. One walked up and down the parking lot with a flashlight which he pointed at our boat for a few moments, perhaps noting that the registration was California - CF 3334 GR. We expected to be hailed, but no, he turned and went back to the police car. Thomas arrived in about thirty minutes. One policeman waited outside at the ready while Thomas and the other policeman inspected the inside of the building. Apparently all was well. They closed the window, exchanged good-byes and left. No one seemed to care that a strange twenty-six foot cruiser from California was parked a few yards away.

Once again we tried to get to sleep. By now it was 1:00 A.M. Before we dozed off, there again came the persistent whine of what we now knew to be a river towboat. This time the noise was louder than before and was coming from downriver. There were two reasons for the louder sound. This tow was pushing against the current and it was larger and longer than the earlier one. In the darkness, broken only by the bow lights and the occasional piercing flash of the spotlight, it seemed to take hours for the barges to pass. The sound of the powerful engines lingered on the air long after the tow had rounded the bend more than two miles upriver. Dee and I realized that no one could really know the modern Mississippi River until he had encountered the power and sound of a Mississippi River towboat passing in the night. We wondered if we were really ready for daily encounters with the size, power and sound of these behemoths of contemporary technology.

18

Except for five or six Burlington Northern trains
which crept   by on the other side of the Two Rivers
building and one noisy moth trying to escape through a
closed window. the rest of the night, what little there
was of it, passed without incident.

At sunrise a third tow pushed downriver with six
open barges filled with a black granular substance that
we concluded to be asphalt, probably being transported
to a construction site downriver. This tow wasn't as
large or loud as those that passed in the night - or the
light of day had given us a new perspective.

CAPTAIN OF THE RIVER QUEEN?

3

PTOOEY

During Breakfast at the Captain's Table, where Robin was again our waitress, we reviewed the night's events. We also remembered a fortune cookie I had been served at the end of a meal of spicy Kung-Pao Chicken, Mu-Shu Pork and Sauted Vegetables in our favorite Chinese restaurant in San Jose just a week before we left California. With surprise I had read:

Leave your boat and travel on firm ground

Never before had I seen a fortune so specific and so easily related to our planned activities. As Dee read her fortune, **Soon you will be on top of the world,** I realized that I, in fact, had two fortunes stuck together. I peeled off the ominous one and read the one behind it: **Soon you will be on top of the world.**

Unanimously we decided to ignore the ill-omened fortune and go with the two favorable ones.

With the night's events fresh in mind, we wondered if perhaps we had been a bit hasty. Further support for these doubts came from other happenings of the past two weeks.

Before leaving home we had watched two television movies related to boating. One was about modern day pirates harassing two sailing couples off the coast of Florida. The other depicted a shipwreck in which twenty-eight people shared a life boat designed to hold only nine. During a long ordeal several people died.

On our trip to Wisconsin we had stopped at Dee's parent's home in Woodburn, Oregon, where our car was broken into. Among other things the thieves had stolen our new marine radio. In Portland we heard about a tragedy on the Columbia River. A barge had hit a sailboat. One man was still missing. In Miles City, Montana a man told us about a wheel coming off a boat trailer and almost hitting his car. A woman told about a friend who had bought a new boat on Lake Superior and started across the lake with four people aboard. Later the boat had been found, upside down. One person was trapped in the cabin. Two were found in life jackets floating together. All were dead. The fourth person was never located.

Leave your boat and travel on firm ground

Fortunately, Robin reappeared to inform Dee the cook was out of bell peppers for her Denver Omelet. This new turn of events stopped our runaway imaginations and gave us a concrete problem to solve. After substituting mushrooms for bell peppers, Dee asked Robin how she was able to work the dinner shift which lasted until 10:00 P.M. and make it back in time for the 5:30 start of breakfast.

"The double shift is only temporary. I hate getting up so early in the morning, but I need the money for car insurance and rent."

We noted that in addition to being a waitress, Robin cleaned tables, washed dishes and ran the cash register. Sometimes she was so busy that customers would walk to the kitchen and say, "I'll leave the money by the register."

Outside the restaurant we met sixty-seven year old John Filkins. John was talking with two men; one had a strange device consisting of a six inch metal box with several metal finger like projections hinged above the open side. The box was attached to a handle. On the handle was a lever which, when moved, opened and closed the metal fingers. "Bet you don't know what this is," the man said to us.

We studied the contraption carefully and confessed that we hadn't the foggiest idea what it was.

"It's a cherry picker."

He demonstrated by holding the machine high above his head in the branches of an imaginary cherry tree. He moved the lever to open the fingers, and carefully raised the box up to a hypothetical cluster of cherries. Moving the lever again he closed the fingers around the cluster. Lowering the handle slowly, he picked every cherry without losing or bruising a single one.

Noting that we were strangers in town, John asked if we were the ones who had arrived with the cabin cruiser. We nodded. "Well, I'm John Filkins. I'm in charge of the launching ramp for the city. Jeff called yesterday to tell me you were here. He was worried someone might break into your boat while you were at dinner, so he stayed around until he saw you coming back. He was also a little worried you might launch the boat without payin' so he wrote down your car license number."

As we returned to the boat, Dee remarked, "I don't think I'd try to launch our boat without paying. John and Jeff seem to be efficient keepers of the ramp."

As we climbed aboard, a car stopped beside us. "Is it okay for us to park here?" Dee asked.

"After your long trip? Sure you're fine there. I'm Doug Griffin and I have some bikes for you. They arrived yesterday."

Doug, tall, blond, tan, and sturdily built moved here two years ago from California with his wife and two children. He enjoys the slower pace and uncrowded conditions of Prescott. In addition to managing the marina, Doug sub-leases the boat repair shop and boat supply store. He also rents boat slips and hauls, winterizes and stores boats.

The bikes Doug was referring to were Bumble Bikes we had ordered about a month before leaving California. Two weeks before we were to leave two tiny motors arrived, neatly boxed, but without the bikes. There was a note which said the bikes would arrive in a few days. Three days before our scheduled departure, the bicycles had not arrived.

Dee had called the toll free number in Florida. A lady on the other end said "Yall mean yall ain't got yore bikes yet? They's shipped from New York. I'll call and see if they's been sent an' call you back this evenin."

"What's your name," Dee asked, "In case we need to call you?"

"Dale Spencer."

When Dale called, I answered the phone. The news wasn't good. The bikes were ready to ship, but hadn't gone out yet. It would be a week before they would get to Clearlake. I explained that we didn't have a week. Then it occurred to me that perhaps we could have them sent to the Prescott Marina. With calls to Prescott and back to Dale the arrangements had been made.

"I haven't ridden a bicycle for years," Dee said. "I'm going to have to practice riding a couple of days with the pedals before I try using a motor."

I could tell she was apprehensive. She didn't like any kind of motorized cycle.

22

Since Jerry, the mechanic who would check our boat engine, would not be at work until noon, I began to assemble our bikes. Like most unassembled "toys" the job was much more difficult than expected. Before I finished even one, Jerry arrived, so I paused to explain that I wanted the outdrive checked, and lubricated.

My continued work on the bikes began to draw the attention of everyone who came by. We met Katie and Cy of the motor yacht **Makay**, Harold from the houseboat **Third Love**, and Dr. O'Dean of the yacht **Lemon Twist**. All remarked that the bikes would be ideal on a boat trip. Dee whispered to me, "Maybe we should call the Bumble Bike Company to see if we can get a commission for orders. I bet we could sell lots of bikes between here and New Orleans."

When the bikes were completed, we pedaled them to a station for gas and a bottle of two-cycle motor oil. With the tank full of the oil-gas mixture my tiny engine sputtered to life. As I rode up and down the marina yard, everything was fine until I stopped. I couldn't remember to turn down the hand throttle before squeezing the clutch lever which lifted the drive wheel off the tire. The result was that each time I stopped, the little engine raced on at high speed much to the amusement of a considerable group of spectators.

After Doug and Jerry tried the little yellow beast with the same results, I didn't feel so bad. These tiny motorized folding bikes would be perfect for the trip - if we could ever master them.

"You all agree that the bikes will be good land transportation, now tell us what you think about our boat for this trip?" asked Dee.

Doug and Jerry looked at each other. Doug said, half apologetically, "Well, it is a little small."

Dee looked crushed. In the delta our boat had been average size. On Clearlake she was the **Queen Mary**. Across Montana and North Dakota we were towing a battle ship. Here on the Mississippi she was "a little small".

Jerry said, "Most people who travel the river have two engines just in case they have a problem with one."

That evening the metamorphosis through which our lives had been going during the last year hit us with full intensity. Drained of energy we climbed into our snug bed just as the uppermost edge of "old sol" disappeared behind the tree lined western shore of the river. Sleep came soon and soundly.

23

The next day Dee carefully backed boat and trailer into the water while I undid the winch cable. As she eased the trailer forward, **Sol Seaker** floated lazily on the still waters of the Mighty Mississippi River. I took the boat for a test run while Dee paid John Filkins $3.00, then drove car and trailer back to the marina.

Jerry and Tom panicked when they saw me open **Sol Seaker** up for a short run downriver. Jerry asked Dee, "Does he know about the wing dams?"

Dee assured him that I did. When I returned to the marina Tom directed me to a covered berth a few slips from his own boat. What a joy to be afloat. No more climbing a shaky ladder to a deck seven feet above ground.

As we relaxed, discussing up-coming activities, we were suddenly interrupted by a loud rush of water. Our first thought was that the engine compartment was being flooded, then Dee realized that the sound came from the boat next to ours. She went aboard and knocked on the door asking, "Is there anyone home?" No answer.

We later learned that the boat had a leak. The owner had installed two automatic pumps. Every twenty-five minutes enough water got into the bilge to trigger the pumps. For the next several days and nights there came that same noisy rush of water every twenty-five minutes.

That afternoon we gave our Bumble Bikes their first real workout as we toured Prescott, a town built on three levels.

The lower level runs along the Mississippi to the bridge which marks the confluence of the Mississippi and St. Croix rivers. Along this level are Leo's Marina and gas dock, The St. Croix Winery, several small stores, a launching ramp, a grain and feed dealer, a wholesale petroleum dealer and The Prescott Marina. The Burlington Northern track is also on this level. Here, too, are a few well-cared-for homes overlooking the river. Most are older, but there is one modern A-frame with large view windows. An older white house has a beautifully kept lawn adorned with three elaborate bird houses high atop metal poles. A large yellow cat, tethered on a long leash between the house and the birdhouses, stalks each bird that ventures to the lawn in search of food. Sometimes he runs at a bird only to be jerked backwards as he comes to the end of his rope.

On the second level, about fifteen feet above the

lower level, is Main Street, lined with old brick buildings housing small stores, service stations, bars, and
offices. Across from the drug store is a medical clinic
with a nurse on duty at all times. At the end of Main
Street, near the bridge, is the town's most elegant
restaurant the, Steamboat Inn.

From the second level a long steep hill reaches
upward to the third level on the rolling plain above the
river. Several streets run straight up the hill. These
are intersected by a series of cross streets running
along the face of the hill. Along these cross streets,
between levels two and three, is Prescott's residential
area. To the west, beneath majestic trees, are older
homes on large fenceless lots. To the east and at the
top of the hill are newer homes on smaller lots. Several businesses, the school and post office are located at
the top of the hill. From the upper level the land
stretches north and eastward in rolling glacial mounds
deposited during the great ice ages. This glacial ter-
rain is now covered with wood lots and fields of corn
and soya beans.

At the St. Croix Winery we met Mel. Our tour of
the one room winery; with its small grape crusher, apple
crusher, several heavy plastic wine tanks and five or
six oak barrels for aging red wine, took only a few
minutes. In the center of the room a young man hand
labeled bottles of newly made cherry wine. Mel escorted
us to the tasting counter where bottles of grape and
apple wine were ready for tasting. As we sipped Mel
told us he had lived in Healdsburg, California, my own
hometown. While there he worked for Sebastiani Winery
and was still a representative for them in Minnesota and
Wisconsin. Mel knew Jim Pedroncelli, owner of Pedroncelli Winery and a classmate of Dee's at Geyserville
High School in the late 1940's, and the Bagnani family
who had owned Geyser Peak Winery across from Dee's girlhood home.

Dee told Mel that the picture of her girlhood home
was now the logo on Summit Wines, one of the brands
produced at the Geyser Peak Winery.

"Where do you get the grapes for your wine?" I
asked Mel.

"They're grown locally."

"I thought it was too cold here for vineyards to
survive."

"It is. In the fall we prune the vines severely,

25

then pull them down flat along the ground and cover them with a thick layer of dirt to insulate them from the cold."

This new information made us appreciate even more the fine wine from Mel's tiny St. Croix Winery. After tasting several wines and some excellent Wisconsin cheese we bought bottles of Soft Apple and Niagara, then headed our Bumble Bikes back toward the marina.

At the launching ramp we saw John. Although we had met John earlier we were not prepared for the real John Filkins that emerged as we straddled our bikes and visited with him through the open window of his car. John liked to sit unobserved in his car and, . . ."catch the cheats who try to launch their boats without payin' (ptooey)."

We moved a little farther away from the window as John punctuated his comment with an exclamatory stream of brown spit.

"We're on the honor system most of the time," John continued. "The rule is $3.00 in the envelop, write your car license number on the outside, and place it in that locked box over there (ptooey)".

A near miss as Dee moved to one side. John continued, "Ever once-in-a-while I check the license numbers on the envelops against the cars and boat trailers in the parking lot. That way I can tell who ain't paid (ptooey)."

At that moment two men drove up to the ramp trailering a small runabout. John said, "I bet they're gonna try to get away without payin' (ptooey). I can tell they's cheats."

After launching the boat one of the men stayed at the ramp while the other parked the car and trailer. The man got out of his car, hesitated a moment, then walked over to the 'honor system' box. John eyed him intently as he took an envelop, put something in it and dropped it in the slot. As he headed back toward the boat, John jumped out of the car and went straight to the locked box. He unlocked it, removed the envelop, then began yelling at the two men as they prepared to leave the dock. "Hey, come back here! You didn't put your car license on the envelop."

The boat started away from the dock. John looked inside the envelop. Now, really excited, he ran toward the dock more like a twenty year old than a sixty-seven year old. "Come back you sons-a-bitches, come back!"

The men stopped the boat and asked in a guilty voice, "Is there something wrong?"

"You know there's something wrong damn it! You only put $2.00 in the envelop and you didn't put your car license number on the outside!"

The rest of what John said to the men was lost in the noise of a passing houseboat, but the waving motion of his hands and his pointing first at the boat, then at their car, then the envelop and finally the money box, clearly conveyed the message. We knew John was really angry because he never once took time to spit.

When he returned, John said, "I can always spot the cheats (ptooey)."

"Did you get your three dollars?" asked Dee.

"You damn right I did! I should have charged him eight!"

"One day," John continued, "two young men challenged me (ptooey). Challenged me they did. With the Coast Guard boat settin right out there. (ptooey)." He gestured toward the river. "I'm a fighter (ptooey). Always did like to mix it up (ptooey)! So I said to these kids, 'pay up or else'. That's when one of them smart ass kids hit me. Well let me tell you, wham, wham and it was all over (ptooey)."

"What happened?" asked Dee.

"Beat the piss out of them, I did (ptooey). Then I called to the Coast Guard out there, 'You can pick 'em up or drown 'em, I don't care!' They both got took to the Hastings Hospital (ptooey). The Coast Guard wanted me to file assault charges but I figgered they'd had enough. They wouldn't be botherin me again (ptooey)."

John went on to tell us that different groups had tried to run the launching ramp, but each one had gone belly-up; so the city kept coming to him. "First year they paid me a thousand dollars for the season, but when they saw the big profit I made they gave me a five hundred dollar bonus (ptooey). The next year they paid me $2,000. This year $2,500. I made the city $11,000 last year. This is my last year though. The public likes me. They know I'm tough but fair (ptooey). Now I can tell you folks are good folks. You folks are fair. If I'd seen you launch your boat and you hadn't put money in the box, I couldn't care less. I would have knowed you just made a mistake (ptooey). But I knowed them guys was cheaters."

John continued, "I don't know if you two are rich

people or not. I don't think you are. But I know you're nice people. One of the nicest couples I ever met (ptooey). When you come back for your car, you call me if you need a ride to a motel. Or I'll come over to Hastings to pick you up at the bus station (ptooey). The Greyhound don't stop at Prescott (ptooey). You call me. I'll do it free. Won't charge you nothin' (ptooey). In fact you can have my bed. I got two bedrooms and one has a single bed, so you can have my bed (ptooey). If you come back after the first frost you ought to go up to my cabin in Northern Wisconsin. Oh, the colors are beautiful on the hard maple trees after the first frost (ptooey)."

"When we come back, why don't you go up there with us?" Dee asked.

"Oh, I can't", John said, an air of melancholy about him. "I have to watch this ramp 'til November. But you could go. But I've got to tell you - outside privy. Bet you never had one of those."

"Dee hasn't, but I was in sixth grade before I lived in a house with indoor plumbing'" I told John. "And we've both done a lot of camping where there were outdoor privies."

"Well, my wife and I figured it was best - didn't have to worry about pipes freezing and everything. All we had was an outside hand pump for water. I haven't been up there since she died three years ago. The kids use it though."

These final comments were made in a quiet and re-flective tone and there was no wet punctuation at the end. John obviously still felt the loss of his wife and couldn't face going to their "retreat" alone.

Before we went back to the marina, John made us promise to drop by to see him before we headed down-river. He wanted to see Dee riding her bicycle on engine power.

If we had been looking forward to a restful first night on the water, we were to be disappointed. After braving a severe rainstorm to drive fifteen miles to see "On Golden Pond," we returned to the marina to find several young people spending the night on the boat next to ours. One boy was in a sleeping bag on the bow of the twenty-two foot boat, and two boys and a girl were inside.

Shortly after we arrived, two more girls came down to the boat to say they were having trouble sleeping in the car. They entered the boat and one boy left to go up to the car. Later he returned and the three girls left. Now there were two boys in the boat and one on the bow.

One of the boys inside said, "Boy can she French kiss. I've never had a girl French kiss me like that before."

"Did you go all the way?" The other boy asked eagerly.

"Go all the way? Who wants to go all the way when they can get French kissed like that?"

Their voices trailed off into inaudible whispers giving us the few moments of quiet we needed to drop off to sleep.

LAUNCHING SOL SEAKER

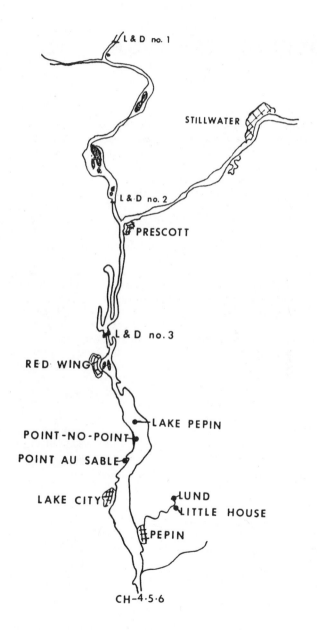

L & D no. 1

STILLWATER

L & D no. 2

PRESCOTT

L & D no. 3

RED WING

LAKE PEPIN

POINT-NO-POINT

POINT AU SABLE

LAKE CITY

LUND
LITTLE HOUSE

PEPIN

CH-4·5·6

4

LOCKING THROUGH

The next day we had our first on-the-water encounter with a towboat. Doug had suggested that we
might want to make our first run up the deeper and less
trafficked St. Croix River. The trip was beautiful.
Bordered by tree lined cliffs dotted with view homes and
private docks, the waters of the St. Croix are not muddy
like the Mississippi, but have a rusty hue from the
iron mining country through which the river passes. A
series of sandbars provides beautiful spots for the
popular weekend activity of sandbarring.

Groups of friends beach their boats side-by-side on
a favorite sandbar, keeping the boats secure by attach-
ing long anchor lines to the stern cleats. The anchors
are made fast on the beach about ten feet above the
water's edge. The lines form a V from the stern, such
that the anchors are about thirty feet apart on the
sandbar. A bow line is attached to a stake driven in
the sand directly in front of the boat. A bow ladder
makes for easy movement between boat and sand.

Food is prepared in the galleys or on charcoal
grills. Activities range from fishing and swimming, to
softball, volleyball, sand castle building, cards, sunbathing, roasting hot dogs and drinking. Whatever the
daytime events, the evening is spent around a roaring
bonfire made from the abundant supply of dead wood along
the shore. When the kids are in bed, the adults usually
share the latest "dirty" jokes or gossip.

Our seventeen mile trip up the St. Croix was on a
Friday afternoon. Already the favorite sandbars were
being staked out by early arrivers.

On our way back downriver we met the towboat **Sioux**
pushing her six barges of asphalt. This first real
meeting with a towboat was much less terrifying than our
on-land encounter. We had seen the **Sioux** on several
occasions as she came down the Mississippi from St. Paul

to a point just below the Prescott Marina. Here she
used a channel behind Prescott Island to turn her barges
around so she could make the run up the St. Croix River.
We wondered where she was taking all that asphalt.

That evening was the traditional Friday Fish Fry at
The Captain's Table. The buffet contained nine kinds of
salad and all the fish and chicken you can eat for
$4.75. The tiny restaurant served three hundred
people, and Robin finally had a night off from her
double-shift duties.

We turned in early for a long night's rest, but the
relief and romance of finally being in our own boat, on
the river, alone, led to activities which delayed our
slumbers.

On Saturday we slept late, then went to the marina
store to look for items we might need for our trip downriver. Cy, who was also in the store, asked, "Do you
have a good spotlight?"

"Just a small 50,000 candlepower," I answered.

"You really should have a light that will shine
half a mile so you can see the reflectors on the buoys
at night. Mine is 300,000 candlepower. It works fine.
Lots of people have remote control spotlights, but I get
by fine with my hand held light. You really should have
a bigger light. Why don't you come over to our boat
about 3:00. Katie will be back. I'd like to show you
my light and I can tell you about the lower river -
where to get fuel and places to tie up or anchor out for
the night. There aren't many marinas on the lower
river. Not like up here. Fuel can be a real problem.
Bring your charts so you can mark the locations."

At 3:00 we boarded the **Makay**. Along with zucchini
bread and a Coke, Cy and Katie gave us the benefit of
their recent trip upriver. Soon our two chart books
were filled with valuable notes on restaurants, marinas,
gas stops. danger areas and overnight anchorages. We
were shocked to learn that below Cairo, Illinois it was
sometimes more than two hundred miles between gas stops.
This posed a problem we would certainly have to solve
when we got to the lower river since **Sol Seaker** had a
range of only 150 to 170 miles.

As we left Cy said, "Tonight is prime rib night at
the Starlight. All you can eat for $9.00."

Dee answered, "After last night's fish fry I'm not
sure I can handle another all-you-can-eat dinner for
awhile."

31

Later that same day we drove to Hastings to take a look at lock and dam number two. The locks and dams are numbered starting with number one at Minneapolis and continuing through number twenty-seven just above St. Louis approximately eight hundred miles downriver.

We arrived at the lock just as the **Sioux**, with three empty barges. locked through going upstream. We then watched two small pleasure boats enter from up-river, be lowered eleven feet, and leave to continue downriver. Five pleasure craft were locking up as a family from St. Paul joined us on the observation plat-form. Although they lived less than twenty-five miles from three of the Mississippi River locks, they had never before seen a locking operation.

Above the lock the dam created a broad, still pool. Sky and water were just beginning to take on the sepia-pink tint of sundown which we would see frequently and come to call "Mississippi Mauve."

By the time we returned to Prescott, the mauve of sunset was being replaced by a calm, gray dusk. The prime rib began to sound good, so we stopped at the Starlight. selecting a window table from which we could watch the last touch of color leave the St. Croix.

As we ate, Cy, Katie and Harold entered the res-taurant, but didn't see us as they sat at a table near the door. We couldn't finish even the first serving of our all-you-can-eat prime rib dinner. With doggie bags in hand we stopped by our marina friends' table only to learn that on prime rib night they were eating spaghetti and fried chicken!

Later when we were in bed, Dee said, "You know, I'm beginning to feel like we belong here in Prescott."

"I know what you mean. If we don't leave pretty soon we may stay until we're driven out by the first snowstorm."

The incessant drumming of rain on the corruga-ted metal of our covered berth woke us early. Occasional gusts of wind rattled the metal and blew spray against the cabin window.

Dee turned on the marine radio. "This is NOAA weather radio operating at 162.55 MHz. The forecast for Minneapolis and the surrounding areas - rain this morning with gusty wind and possible thunder storms, clearing this afternoon."

We snuggled deeper and lay for a long time, drift-ing in and out of sleep as we listened to the rain and wind make a kind of rhythmical music against the metal roof. When we finally got up, the rain had slowed to a drizzle and the wind had dropped to a light westerly breeze. After a quick breakfast of scrambled eggs prepared on a small electric hot-plate Dee calls our "fifth burner," we decided to brave the drizzle and head up-river toward Minneapolis. We drove from the inside helm. About a mile below the Hastings Lock I called the lockmaster on the radio, channel 14.

"Lock and dam number two this is the pleasure craft **Sol Seaker** calling. Over."

"This is lock number two to the...er...ah... pleasure craft calling. Over."

"This is **Sol Seaker**. We're about a mile below you heading upriver. When can we lock through? Over."

"Yes. er **Soul Seeker**...ah...we have a tow locking down now. As soon as he's through you can join the other pleasure craft that are waiting to lock up."

"This is our first time in a lock. We can use all the help we can get. This is **Sol Seaker**, W.R.W.2683, clear on 14."

"You'll do fine. Lock two clear."

We waited about thirty minutes with our engine idling as we drifted near two other boats also waiting to lock up. "I'm glad there are some other boats," Dee said. "Let's let them go in first, then we can see how they do it."

While we waited, I re-read the "Locking Through" pamphlet provided by the Corps of Engineers, and Dee changed into her tennis shoes in preparation for her traverse around the four inch wide walkway between the stern deck and the bow. I recalled that the first time she had negotiated this narrow path she clung tenacious-ly to the hand railings. Now she trotted around to the bow with the ease of a cat walking a backyard fence. I remembered, too, our early attempts at docking **Sol Seaker** (**Hey Babe**). Dee would stand on the bow ready to jump off the instant we touched the dock. The first time she tried this, I hit the dock too hard causing her to catch her foot on the bow rail. She fell forward in a heap triumphantly hanging on to the bow line. The next time I thought I was stopping too far away from the dock so I eased into forward just as Dee prepared to leap. The sudden movement of the boat caused her foot to catch the rail but this time it threw her backwards on the deck. Black and blue from these mishaps, she

33

stated emphatically, "We have to find a better way to dock this damn boat, or I'm not going to live long enough to enjoy it!"

At that time we decided it was my responsibility to dock the boat gently so she could step off leisurely and make the lines fast. A lesson that took a long time to learn.

After Dee had been on the bow for a few minutes, I realized that it would work better if she held a stern line and I held a bow line from the flying bridge. Dee agreed and returned to the stern. It was at these stations that we would accomplish thirty-five lockings over the next two and one-half months.

We both grew more nervous as we watched the towboat prepare to leave the lock. Dee made a quick trip to the potty, an action that became routine pre-locking procedure. When the green light flashed, we were the third boat in. A beautiful houseboat followed us into the lock. The lockmaster handed us one end of attached ropes by extending them to us with a long pole. As the water rose in the lock, we moved our hands up the ropes keeping the boat near the wall. Using our boat hook, I held us a few inches away from the wall in an effort to keep our fenders from getting scruffed. I was not entirely successful as the breeze would push first the bow then the stern in against the lock wall.

Later, in strong winds and more turbulent locks, we would find it impossible to keep our fenders clean. On those occasions we would be happy that the fenders were there to protect the boat from severe damage.

After the lockmaster handed ropes to the houseboat behind us, he came back to us. "You're from California?" he asked.

"Yes," we said in unison.

"You're doing fine," he said. "Do you plan to use your surfboard on the Mississippi?" he asked, indicating our folding dinghy.

We laughed. "That's not really a surfboard, it's a folding boat," Dee said, pointing to the opening on one side where the boat folded out, creating a space for two seats to snap into place. "It's our dinghy. We're going all the way down to New Orleans and we thought we'd best have a dinghy in case of emergency."

"Goin' to New Orleans, huh? Well I hate to tell you this," he said in all seriousness, "but New Orleans is that-a-way." He pointed back the way we had come.

34

"You're headed for Minneapolis. Do you have river charts?"

We assured him that we knew the way to New Orleans, that we had river charts, and that we were going to Minneapolis so we could tell our friends that we went from Minneapolis to New Orleans. We were afraid no one would know where we started if we said we went from Prescott to New Orleans.

"What should we know about locking through on the locks downriver?" I asked.

"Most of them are just like this one. The lines will be provided. Not all the lockmasters will hand them to you, so you need to be ready to reach over and get them. There's a big lock at Keokuk. It drops about forty feet. There you'll need your own rope, about twenty feet. They have floating barrels in the lock wall that you loop your rope around. Don't tie it to the barrel, just hook it over so you can let go of one end and pull it back when you're ready to leave the lock."

A loud horn blew one long blast. We both jumped. Without realizing what was happening, we had been raised eleven feet to the level of the pool above the dam, and the gates were open. From here we could see the same broad expanse of water we had seen the day before. It looked as though you could go anywhere with the boat; however, there were red and black buoys marking a rather narrow channel.

As we pulled away the lockmaster said, "I envy you your trip. I get four days off next week. I'm going to get my canoe and see how far downriver I can get. Someday I'd like to do what you're doin'."

After we cleared the lock, Dee took the controls downstairs out of the continuing drizzle, and I made a beeline for the head. While I was indisposed, a voice came over the radio, "**Sol Seaker**, this is **C Castle** beside you. Do you have 70 on your radio?"

I could hear Dee saying, "I don't know! Weldon! Do we have 70?"

"Yes," I replied as I emerged from the head, "just turn the dial."

"This is **C Castle** on 70. We heard you talking to the lockmaster about your trip. We'd like to hear more about it. Also, we want you to know that there are lots of stumps out there on the right. Be sure you stay between the buoys. One day we saw some people in a new

35

boat come out of this lock and head full speed right
into that stump field. We shouted but they couldn't
hear us. Suddenly they came to a stop. Luckily they
only wrecked their propeller. They could have torn the
bottom out. Over."

"Thanks," Dee said. "We wondered why the buoys
were there. Over."

"We're going up to St. Paul. We're berthed at the
Watergate Marina. Would you like to follow us there?"

"We sure would," said Dee, relieved to have someone
show us the way.

Having someone to follow freed us to enjoy the
scenery, although it was obscured by the mist. Above
lock and dam number two the channel meandered back and
forth between small, tree covered islands, sandbars and
wide expanses of shallow stump field water with names
like Spring Lake, Baldwin Lake and River Lake. At mile
827 the river narrowed and we began to enter the industrial zone of St. Paul.

On the left at mile 833 we passed acres of smelly
South St. Paul stockyards. On our right was Pig Eye
Island, where the river narrowed more. We began to see
an occasional empty barge moored along the water's edge.

At mile 836 we made a sharp bend past a large sew-
age disposal plant. Here the river was lined with
dozens and dozens of empty barges waiting to be filled
with beans or corn for their slow passage down river to
St. Louis, Baton Rouge, or New Orleans. As they waited,
small towboats added additional barges until each would
have a full complement of fifteen. This maximum size is
governed by the size of the locks. A towboat with
fifteen barges requires a double locking. The boat
slowly pushes into the lock. The first nine barges completely fill the lock. An elaborate system of cables
and winches holds the barges together. In a double
locking the tow is split so that nine barges stay in the
lock. The towboat with the remaining six barges backs
away just far enough to allow the gates to close. After
the first nine barges are lowered and removed, the lock
is refilled with water to receive the remainder of the
tow. The entire process of a double locking can take as
much as one and one-half hours.

Between miles 836 and 842 were many commercial
docks for loading grain, sand, gravel, asphalt and petroleum products. Here the river was lined with clusters of small brightly painted towboats waiting for

calls that would send them off to move a barge to a waiting tow or loading dock. Beyond the barges and docks we could see parks and picnic tables, and here and there a fisherman.

The domed state capital at St. Paul was sandwiched between tall, modern office buildings, presenting a contrast between old and new. Beyond the 35 E Bridge, the scene changed completely. All evidence of commerce was left behind and trees once again lined the river. At mile 844 the river split. To the left was the Minnesota River. We followed the **C Castle** to the right and into the quiet and secluded Watergate Marina.

After the thirty-three mile trip, we shared a bottle of St. Croix wine with Matt and Margot Crawford. Matt is in advertising. They use the **C Castle** as a cottage, often staying aboard in the marina for the entire weekend. This weekend; however, the Crawfords had taken a trip to Stillwater on the St. Croix.

Matt pointed to the steep, limestone cliffs that ran along the north side of the marina. "For years", he said, "they mined silica sand in those cliffs. The purest sand you can find. They used it for making glass for automobile windows and windshields. After they quit mining here, the large, horizontal mine shafts just sat empty. Some are huge rooms with level floors. A few years ago the marina owner got the idea of storing boats in the mines in the wintertime. Our winters are so cold here that all the boats have to be pulled out of the water and winterized. They drain all the water from the tanks and bilges, put anti-freeze in toilets and everything. Well, those caves stay at about fifty-two degrees all year round. He put a big door at the opening and pulled the boats into those large rooms. He would then go in and check on the boats every few days. One day in mid-winter the door wouldn't open. Moisture in the caves and seeping out of the rocks had frozen the door shut. Now he has big ventilation fans in the door. It works beautifully now."

After the Crawfords headed home, we searched for a marina bathroom, but found none. We also found that our electrical cord did not fit the marina outlets. We had both a standard plug and a thirty amp adapter, but Watergate uses a twenty amp system.

After a long walk to town for a Mexican dinner, we returned to a very quiet marina. Although surrounded by a metropolitan area of more than half-a-million people, we were isolated from both sight and sound by the high limestone cliffs, a dense growth of trees and a spit of land which separated Watergate from the river. We didn't see another human until eight o'clock the next morning, when we were shocked to learn that the fee for our overnight dockage was $13.00. We had no electricity, no bathroom and no shower, just two cleats for our lines and a walkway to shore. At Prescott we had all the conveniences and a covered berth for $7.50 a night. When Dee expressed her surprise at the exorbitant fee, the man at the marina office said, "Well, that's still better than the Holiday Inn."

My only reply was, "At least the Holiday Inn provides a place to take a pee!"

We had enjoyed our visit with the Crawfords, and the peace and quiet of Watergate, but were happy to leave. We felt like we had been taken. Two and a-half months later we would still feel like we had been taken at Watergate, for this was the highest overnight fee we paid, anywhere.

The day was clear, warm and beautiful. We cruised upriver to the base of lock and dam number one, where the river was a deep brown color and filled with floating stuff, mostly twigs and leaves from the trees which closed in on both sides of the narrow channel. But here and there a plastic bottle, beer can or condom floated by. In a four mile stretch we counted two dozen cigarette butts, six plastic drink bottles, five used condoms, four beer cans, three plastic bags, two rubber gloves. Dee laughingly sang, ". . . and a partridge in a pear tree."

At the base of lock number one, we turned **Sol Seaker** downriver for a warm, leisurely trip back to Prescott. On the way we met three tows. The first two were small and posed no problem, not even a potty trip for Dee. The third was a different story.

I was at the bridge helm. The towboat was large with fifteen barges, coming upriver around a bend. Cy had told us that we should always meet a tow on the inside of the bend even though it might look like the wrong place to be. "Just remember," he had said, "that when the head of the tow turns toward you, the stern will be turning away from you. When you get past you will be safe from the stern wash, which will be pushed away from you."

As the barges approached, turning to the right, I

38

stayed to my left. It did look frightening. There appeared to be only a few feet between the right side of the barges and the line of red "nuns" which marked the safe channel. Would we fit? There was a lot more room on the other side of the river. At the height of my indecision, the captain of the towboat gave two sharp blasts on his horn. Panic! No way could I remember whether two blasts meant "pass to port," "pass to starboard," or "get the hell out of my way!"

The front of the tow continued its relentless swing in our direction, as Dee ran below to radio the captain. Before she could complete the call, panic caused me to do the unpardonable. I cut across the front of the tow heading for the right side of the river. For a few moments we were hidden in the captain's blind spot in front of the barges. I could almost hear his sigh of relief as we emerged on the other side.

Over the radio Dee heard the captain say, "You're okay now."

There was a distinct note of vexation in his voice, and he raised his hands in a gesture of hopelessness as we drew even with the towboat.

Leave your boat and travel on firm ground

As soon as we were safely past, and Dee had taken her potty break, I gave her the helm and headed for the potty, then for the reference books where I learned that two blasts means, pass starboard-to-starboard. What idiots the towboat captain must have thought we were! And he was right! I immediately took out pieces of paper and drew diagrams to illustrate both meeting and overtaking situations and wrote next to them the appropriate horn signals. I taped a copy to each helm and vowed that from now on, if there was any doubt, we would call the towboat captain for advice long before the situation became critical.

When we emerged from the downstream gates of lock two, we felt that we were ready. Tonight we would celebrate with an elegant dinner at the Steamboat Inn. With its polished wood trim, red table cloths and red crystal chandelier, we could imagine that we were dining aboard one of those plush nineteenth century steamboats. Tomorrow we would head down "Ole Man River" to our first stop, Red Wing.

They say that "tomorrow never comes." For us this certainly seemed to be true. We awoke to heavy rain and a NOAA weather report of continued rain. Instead of going to Red Wing by boat. we drove down to check out the two marinas. Dee liked the downtown marina with its floating boat houses attached at each corner to wooden "gin" poles. It is said that before refrigeration people tied their gin bottles to these poles and lowered them into the water to keep them cool. I preferred the smaller and more serene marina at Colville Park a mile below town.

That night, after reading a chapter in Chris Markham's "Mississippi Odyssey," we dropped off to sleep about 10:30. It was still raining very hard. About 11:30 we were jolted awake by the loudest clap of thunder we had ever heard. What followed was an hour-long spectacular display of thunder and lightning. Every few seconds, the corrugated metal roof of our slip vibrated and rattled. The entire area was daytime bright as bolt after bolt of lightning split the clouds directly overhead. We knew the lightning was close because there was no interval between flash and thunder clap. They were as one. We closed all windows against the wind-blown rain and snuggled deep into our bed.

LOOKING THROUGH

5

ANCHORS AWEIGH

Tomorrow finally came.

On Wednesday, September 1, at 11:07 A.M. we were underway at last. No bands played. No streamers or confetti were thrown by well wishers. There were no crowds at the pier to see us off. In fact our departure went totally unnoticed except for the marina turtle who slid off his log as we backed **Sol Seaker** from her slip and headed toward the harbor exit. Ahead of us lay two thousand miles of twisting, turning, sometimes treacherous river - a river so great that it drains nearly one-third of the continental United States.

Would we, as some of our friends had suggested, soon become bored with this river? Would the days, like the current itself, begin to run on endlessly in an unbroken sameness. Would we tire of the cramped quarters and unnatural togetherness of our tiny floating home? Would we long to get away individually in some unavailable secluded corner? Would we become lonesome for home, family and friends? These were some of the questions which might have run through our minds had we not been so thrilled to be on our way at last. Even the lack of bands, banners and good-byes, one usually associates with the beginning of a great voyage, couldn't dampen our spirits on this warm, sunny day.

Without a word, we squeezed each other's hands - a squeeze that said, "I'm happy to be sharing this moment and this experience with you."

Perhaps it was fitting that the beginning of our voyage was delayed by weather until today, for September first also marked the official first day of my retirement from teaching. A new adventure! A new life!

As we cleared the harbor entrance, we made a sharp turn to starboard to avoid the submerged wing dam extending from shore to a red nun marking the limit of the nine foot deep channel. Without this marker, there would be no way of knowing that a treacherous rock dike

41

lay only a few inches below the surface. This wing dam was but the first of thousands we would pass on the 811 miles of the Upper Mississippi.

Before the lock and dam system was installed, wing dams were the sole means of funneling the river into a central channel to keep navigation open during periods of low water. Now the dams were the bane of commercial and pleasure craft alike. Every year towboats, barges and pleasure boats run afoul of wing dams because of displaced markers or just plain inattentiveness. We vowed to be super cautious!

At center channel we turned downriver, with our engine speed set at about eight to ten miles an hour. For the next two and one-half months, our boat would be our home.

Sol Seaker is a twenty-six foot Fibreform cabin cruiser with flying bridge. We board our floating home by way of a rear deck measuring about six feet by six feet. The deck floor consists of three removable panels giving access to the bilge and engine compartment below. A two hundred thirty-three horsepower Mercruiser Sterndrive utilizing a three hundred fifty-one cubic inch Ford engine drives a sixteen inch propeller. Unlike many sterndrives, our engine is equipped with a closed cooling system which works on much the same principle as an automobile radiator. The difference being that the automobile fan and radiator are replaced by a heat exchanger which uses water instead of air to keep the radiator coolant at the right temperature. The advantage of a closed system is that outside water (lake, river or ocean), which can contain harmful sand, silt or salt, is never pumped into the engine itself.

Below the deck, on each side of the engine, is storage room for tools, spare engine parts, extra propellers, lines, oil cans, and anchors. Also below deck and in front of the engine is a seventy-five gallon fuel tank.

When we stand on the stern deck and face toward the bow we look into the main cabin through a sliding glass door and a small window. The cabin is reached through the door and down three steep steps. The flying bridge is reached by a three step aluminum and teakwood ladder to the right of the sliding glass door.

As we enter the eleven-foot long cabin we must take care not to bump our heads while descending the three steps. On our right is the galley, consisting of an alcohol stove (three burners and oven which are covered with a folding orange Formica top when not in use); a small storage area for food, pots and pans (beneath the oven); a tiny 15 x 16 inch sink (with both hot and cold water); a drawer for silverware; and a two and one-half cubic foot refrigerator (complete with two six inch ice cube trays).

Next to the galley, also on the right, is a ten inch wide clothes closet which we use for storing an assortment of dishes and food items.

On the left across from the galley is the head. Inside is a tiny aluminum basin which is almost inaccessible beneath an overhanging section of the fiberglass hull. The basin faucets double for the small shower by means of a flexible metal hose and a device for diverting the flow of water from basin to shower. Since our ten inch closet is filled with foodstuff, the shower doubles as closet for both hanging and soiled clothes. It is also a storage area for a bag of assorted medications and beauty aids. The throne is a portable potty which must be removed from the boat and carried to a dumping station much more often than we would like.

Between the galley and head is an eighteen-inch wide aisle (too narrow to be called a hallway). Five feet of the eleven foot cabin are taken up by the aforementioned galley and head. The next six feet contain the dining-area, living-area, inside helm and storage for folded clothes, shoes, books, typewriter, television, radio, charts, cameras and all the other liveaboard paraphernalia.

On the right side is a narrow couch – usually piled with crackers, fruit, cameras, binoculars, shaver, books, glue, purse and bottles of diet cola. Next, also on the right, is the helm with wheel, controls, instrument panel, compass and marine radio. The helm seat has a removable back which can be fitted beneath the wheel to turn the entire six foot area into a narrow bunk.

On the left is the dining area consisting of a small table and seating for two. Beneath one seat is a hot water heater which works on either 110-volt shore power or the heat of the engine when underway. Beneath the other seat is more storage. With table removed, this area can also be used as a couch or as two narrow bunks, one above the other.

From this point forward, the sides of the boat curve inward to join at the bow. This triangular area,

43

known as the cuddy, is seven feet long and forms one large bed seven feet wide at one end narrowing to two and one-half feet toward the bow. The entire bed is two feet above the floor of the cabin providing space under the five removable cushions for a thirty-five gallon water tank and storage for heavy coats, life jackets and other seldom-used items. The bed is so situated that at night we can look up through the slanted windshield to the sky above. And, as Dee learned on the shakedown cruise, cats can look in.

Over the main cabin is a flying bridge about eight feet long and six feet wide. Up here are two seats and the outside helm. It is this helm that we use in all but rainy or cold weather; for, from here we have an unobstructed three hundred sixty degree view of the world around us. When we are forced to drive from inside, the windows make us feel as though we are seeing the world on a television screen. But here on the bridge the world is real and alive. Beneath and in front of the bridge steering console is storage for such items as fishing gear, oars, cushions and canvass.

At best **Sol Seaker** is an efficient and compact floating travel trailer. At worst she could become a crowded, cluttered, calaboose. Time would tell which it would be for us.

It was from the vantage of our flying bridge that we, with navigation charts in hand, guided **Sol Seaker** effortlessly down a gently flowing, tree lined Mississippi River.

At Prescott the river is roughly a quarter of a mile wide, but wing dams, wooded islands, sandbars and rip-rap create a safe channel of only two hundred to four hundred feet. To the east, close by the waters edge, run the busy Burlington Northern tracks. To the west wooded islands and marshland form a part of a vast area of wildlife management and wildlife refuge extending along much of the Upper Mississippi.

At mile 807 we passed a tiny sand island that is a favorite picnicking spot for several Prescott families. Downriver a small cruiser was nudged up to a sandy beach on the Wisconsin shore. Had they spent the night, or were they just enjoying a day of fishing in this peaceful, pristine setting? From time to time we caught glimpses of houses nestled among the dense growth of trees. A few could have been farm houses, but most were small, seasonal cottages - accessible only by boat.

Even at our slow speed, we were overtaking a huge
Minnesota Transport Company boat which, with the aid of
the current, was pushing fifteen heavily laden grain
barges.   Although still a mile behind the tow, **Sol
Seaker** began to undulate to the rise and fall of its
sternwash.

We had two alternatives, to stay behind the tow, at
a snail's pace, all the way to Red Wing, or pass it. Cy
had told us that when overtaking a towboat we should
always call the captain to let him know we were behind
him and to seek his advice regarding the safest passing
side.   I tried several times to reach the captain on
channels 13, 14 and 16, to no avail. Our charts showed
us that the river was reasonably straight for the next
several miles. Passing appeared safe enough on either
side. We decided on the "two whistle" side. I drove
Sol Seaker toward the towboat, moving to our left as I
did. When we were even with her stern on the port side
I pushed the horn button twice. Dee burst out laughing
as our horn gave two weak burps, sounding more than
anything like the final gasps of a dying bullfrog.
These "blasts" were hardly audible to us. They could in
no way have been heard by the towboat captain over the
roar of his two churning diesels.

Passing a towboat is a different experience than
meeting one. When meeting a tow, once you have established the passing side the ordeal is quickly over due
to the combined speeds of your boat and the towboat.
When overtaking and passing a tow, you must subtract the
tow's speed from your speed in order to arrive at the
passing speed. We were going about eight miles an hour,
the towboat about six. At these two speeds it would
take us almost eight minutes to pass this monster.
After about two nerve-wracking minutes of inching past
the first rusty hulk, I increased our speed to eighteen
miles-per-hour. It still seemed like an eternity before
we finally drew even with and passed the front barges.
As we glanced over our shoulder at the slowly retreating
bows of the front barges, three abreast, our hearts
stood still.

"What if our engine stopped now," I thought, but
dared not utter the words aloud. A look at Dee's face
revealed that I didn't need to say anything for she was
already thinking the same thoughts. I slowly inched the
throttle forward until **Sol Seaker** was at full speed,
about thirty miles an hour. By my pounding heart. and

deep breathing one might have thought I was trying to
outrun this metal terror on foot rather than in a speeding boat.

We maintained top speed for several minutes before
venturing another backward look. We both sighed as we
saw that the giant barges had retreated a safe distance.
I throttled **Sol Seaker** back to a more comfortable speed.
If someone had asked us what the Mississippi River
looked like between miles 804 and 801, neither of us
could have said.

Just beyond mile 801 we could see the tiny picturesque Wisconsin village of Diamond Bluff set on sloping,
wooded land between the river and a magnificent white
limestone cliff. The river widened somewhat providing a
perfect spot for water skiing and boating.   Several
waterfront homes had large houseboats moored to private
docks. Two tiny marinas and a launching ramp provided
access, gas, food and boat rentals.

On the first of September Diamond Bluff looked like
the perfect spot to retire and take life easy. Unfortunately it isn't always the first of September in Diamond
Bluff. Two Californians might find it a bit frigid on
the first of February.

As we passed Diamond Bluff an outboard towing a
water skier whizzed by on our port side. In a few moments the skier returned to speed by on our starboard
side and travel about a half mile upriver before turning
again. **Sol Seaker**'s wake was providing just the right
waves to add a little excitement to the otherwise smooth
waters.

Below Diamond Bluff the river formed a lazy reverse
S, with lock and dam three at the end of the lower
curve.   A mile out Dee called the lock on channel 14.
We were not as lucky as we had been at lock two. "I've
got a double in now, cap. Soon as I git the front nine
down I gotta come back to pick up the back six and tow.
When they git hooked up an' clear the lower end I gotta
bring some pleasure craft up. I'll take you down soon's
the pleasure boats clear the lock."

"I understand. About how long do you think it will
be?" Dee asked.

"Oh, I'd say thirty to forty-five minutes.   Maybe
an hour if they have any trouble hooking together. Keep
your radio on 14."

About a quarter mile above the lock we pulled over
to a safe spot outside the main channel and dropped

46

anchor. "What will happen when the towboat we just passed arrives to lock through?" Dee wondered.

"I don't know," I replied. "The guide to locking through says they have priority over pleasure craft."

We didn't have to wait long to get our answer. The radio came to life with a slow southern drawl. "I'm 'bout a mile above you commin' down with a double of corn headed fer Baton Rouge," said the voice. "Wonderin' when I can lock through. Over."

"Well, Cap, you're gonna' have a little wait. I've got a double just hookin' up now. When they clear I got some pleasure craft commin' up, then a little pleasure craft goin' down. Then I'll come back and git you. It's gonna be thirty to forty-five minutes."

"That's fine with me," came the measured reply. "I got me thirty days to make the trip."

"Come on up on the wall, Cap, but leave enough room for the upriver pleasure craft to clear the locks."

"Roger. I'll bring her on the wall."

While we continued to wait, the tow inched up to the six hundred foot wall, coming to rest without so much as a bump. Deck hands quickly made lines fast to huge iron bollards. The engines throbbed quietly.

We marveled at how the man in the tall pilot house, almost a quarter of a mile behind the lead barge, could stop his twenty thousand ton mass of steel and grain at exactly the right spot, while we often had difficulty docking our small craft without at least one jarring jolt.

Over the radio came the voice of the lockmaster trying to contact the captain of the towboat. From our vantage point, we could see the captain sitting in his chair looking straight ahead over his string of barges. He didn't move as the lockmaster continued to call.

I weighed anchor and moved **Sol Seaker** closer to the idle towboat waving my arms in an effort to get the captain's attention. He continued to stare straight ahead.

"The light just turned green," Dee called.

I had been so intent on signaling the towboat captain that I had failed to see the gates open and four pleasure craft emerge from the lock. Quickly I turned toward the open gates. On one last glance backward I noticed that the captain was picking up the receiver of his radio-telephone. Apparently the lockmaster had finally succeeded in getting through.

47

It was strange being alone in this cavernous one hundred by six hundred foot lock. We grabbed the waiting ropes, bounced against the rough, stained concrete wall a couple of times and began our slow nine foot descent to the level of the river below the dam.

As we emerged from the lower end, we noted that the current was much swifter here, a pattern which held true for all of the Upper Mississippi. The river is narrower and faster below each dam, gradually slowing and widening as we approached the next. The wider area above each dam is called a pool, and each is numbered to correspond with the dam. We had just left pool three and would enter pool four before reaching lock and dam four some forty-four miles downriver.

When we caught up with the tow that had locked down ahead of us, she was stopped near mid-channel as the captain cautiously jockeyed her around the "sharpest bend on the Mississippi" and got her in line to pass between the piers of the Highway 83 bridge which spanned the river at Red Wing. As we passed the tow we could see the highway bridge ahead. On our starboard was the boat harbor with its famous "gin poles." Beyond, several large grain elevators towered above the town's business district. Over everything Barn Bluff, a promontory that had been sighted almost three centuries ago by early French explorers, dominated the scene. At the base of Barn Bluff the "Pretty" city of Red Wing had grown.

More than a hundred years has passed since Chief Red Wing greeted the first white settlers to this area. Little did he know that a century later his name, if not his culture, would be perpetuated in this thriving community of agriculture, industry, recreation and civic pride.

We passed beneath the bridge and continued the mile and a half to where Brad Beetsch, the high school aged son of marina owner Dick, helped us "walk" our boat around behind the gas dock to a convenient location near the ramp. Up the ramp was Colville Park.

"This looks like a great place to ride our bikes!" I exclaimed, as I looked out over the huge park complete with swimming pool, picnic tables, tennis courts and acres of lawn and paths.

As soon as **Sol Seaker** was secure, I unloaded our yellow Bumble Bikes and walked them to the top of the ramp where I met Dick who had just completed his day's work as coach and teacher at Red Wing High School. Eying the tiny "chainsaw" motors mounted above the rear wheels, Dick said, "If your bikes will make it, you should ride up to Memorial Park. It's about the most beautiful view of the river anywhere."

Our bikes did make it, although I had to give a pedal assist to mine. Dee said it was because of my extra weight, but I contended that my bike had a weaker engine.

The view was spectacular. We absorbed as much as possible, took pictures and headed back down the steep and winding road. On the second curve I realized that my handlebars were loose. When I turned them the bicycle had a tendency to continue straight ahead unless I went at a very slow speed. I went at a very slow speed.

When we stopped at a lower overlook, Dee found that she was having the same problem. It was then that Dee recalled the Florida lady's admonition, "Be shore yall always take the 'ranch' with you when you're riding the bikes in case yall need to make any adjustments."

We didn't have the "ranch" with us, so we rode very slowly to the bottom of the hill. Dee waited while I rode back to the boat for the "ranch." After simple adjustments to each bike we continued toward town. Curious heads turned as we buzzed down the street, several people asked where we got our unique bikes.

After an early dinner we returned to the marina where we met Dick's wife Barb, an elementary school secretary. We joined Dick and Barb in comfortable chairs on the dock and shared our last bottle of St. Croix wine before the early evening mosquitoes drove us inside our bug bombed boat and sent the Beetsch's home.

We were greeted early the next morning by a warm September sun streaming in **Sol Seaker's** windows. We dressed in shorts, ate a quick breakfast and headed our bikes toward Red Wing for a day of shopping and sightseeing. Our journey took us to a shoe factory, clothing outlet store, pottery stores, museum and Barn Bluff. Dee bought "Dee Gees" jeans and we bought a watermelon and "mushmelon" from a pickup vendor and meat at a market. At 5:00 P.M. we turned our overloaded bikes toward the marina and "home."

By six, cars began to fill the parking lot near the marina. People were lining the bank hoping to catch a glimpse of the sternwheeler, **Mississippi Queen**, which was due to pass Red Wing at seven on its upriver journey to Minneapolis.

49

Dee and I, still in shorts, walked down the riverbank beyond the crowds. Seven o'clock came and went,
but no **Queen.** At 7:30 some of the people began to
leave. As the sun sank low in the west, the air turned
cool, chilling our sparsely clad bodies. We were ready
to head back to the boat when we spotted something nos-
ing around the bend. As it came into view, we were
disappointed to see that it was only a towboat pushing
fifteen empties upriver.

We strolled toward the marina watching the barges
pass. A chance glance back downriver was just in time
to catch sight of a long gang plank moving slowly around
the bend. A bow came into view. As the **Queen,** made her
grand entrance, the glow of the setting sun bathed her
royal highness in amber and pink, and the calliope
played a rousing river tune!

The next morning a restless breeze stitched the
river surface into tiny pleats, as we passed Sawdust Bar
and entered three-mile wide, twenty-two mile long, Lake
Pepin, formed by a natural dam of silt and sand deposited years ago by the Chippewa river.

The gently ruffled waters of Lake Pepin offered a
new freedom, as the broad deep lake made navigation aids
unnecessary. And there were no threatening wing dams or
hidden sandbars to occupy our attention.

We did, however, begin to experience a strange and
disconcerting phenomenon. The shoreline, now almost a
mile away to our starboard, appeared to be moving as
fast as we were. More accurately, we and the shoreline
seemed to be standing still.

"This feels weird!" exclaimed Dee. "We're moving
but we don't seem to be going anywhere. Go faster!"

I pushed the throttle forward. Slowly the heavily
laden boat climbed onto a plane and sped along at almost
thirty miles an hour. Still the shoreline followed.

I set my eyes on a point protruding from the Minnesota shore. Several minutes passed, but the point got
no closer. Later we learned that the point we were
trying to reach is called "Point-No-Point." On the Minnesota side, Lake Pepin curves gently for more than
five miles along an unbroken wooded shoreline. What we
were seeing was the "point" at which we could see no
farther around the curve. As we moved we were seeing
farther and farther, but Point-No-Point was receding at
the same speed we were proceeding.

Suddenly the shoreline straightened revealing a new

point, Point Au Sable. The sensation of suspended
animation was broken. We passed the Methodist Camp,
catching, a glimpse of the church steeple and the sleepy
village of Old Frontenac, which occupies the site of a
French fort built in 1727. The village is now surrounded by Frontenac State Park.

At the waters edge were unusual boat docks made of
metal frames topped by a wooden deck. On the end that
protruded into the river were automobile wheels, complete with tires, mounted at the bottom of two vertical
metal supports. The wheels were rolled into the river
to a point where the wooden deck became level. Cables
attached to the shore end were made fast to nearby
trees. These portable piers could be moved in concert
with the rise and fall of the river. In winter they
could be stored high on shore.

At Lake City, we went immediately to The Chamber of
Commerce to thank Darlene for the nice letter she had
written in response to our written inquiry. Although
she was about to leave for lunch, Darlene took time to
show us replicas of the very first water skis, and tell
us that it was here, in Lake City, that the sport of
water skiing was born. In 1922, eighteen year old Ralph
Samuelson, the "father" of water skiing strapped two
pine boards to his feet and after extensive experimenta-
tion, "got up" on his skis. This event ushered in a
multi-million dollar industry and a sport enjoyed by
millions all over the world.

Another Lake Citian, Dennis Francis, at age twenty-
six, celebrated the fiftieth anniversary of water skiing
by skiing 1,842 miles from Coon Rapids, Minnesota to the
Gulf of Mexico, in fourteen days.

Leaving the Chamber of Commerce, we met Mr. Peterson selling roasted peanuts on the street corner. We
bought some peanuts and inquired about a locksmith, the
post office and a place to eat. "The locksmith's just
two blocks down and the post office is past there around
the corner," he answered. "Across over there's the
Pepin Inn. I'll tell them two Californians are coming.
They'll be ready for you."

As we headed for the locksmith, Dee mused, "I wonder what he meant by, 'they'll be ready for you.' And
who is Mr. Peterson?"

The locksmith was out to lunch so we got stamps at
the post office and walked back to the restaurant. Mr.
Peterson was still on the corner. "They're waiting for

51

you," he said cheerfully, "don't have many Californians stop in Lake City."

"Who is Mr. Peterson?" We asked our very pleasant waitress.

"He owns a hardware store and a mortuary. If he doesn't get your business now, he'll get it later. He's selling peanuts for the Kiwanis Club."

During lunch we agreed that Lake City, like Red Wing, was very civic minded. There were memorials and parks everywhere, and the people we met showed pride in their community. Also, like Red Wing, Lake City appeared to be a neat, tidy, conservative town.

By contrast, Prescott had been casual, earthy, and a bit less tidy. All three towns were pleasant, but we decided Prescott was more like us - "casual" and "less tidy."

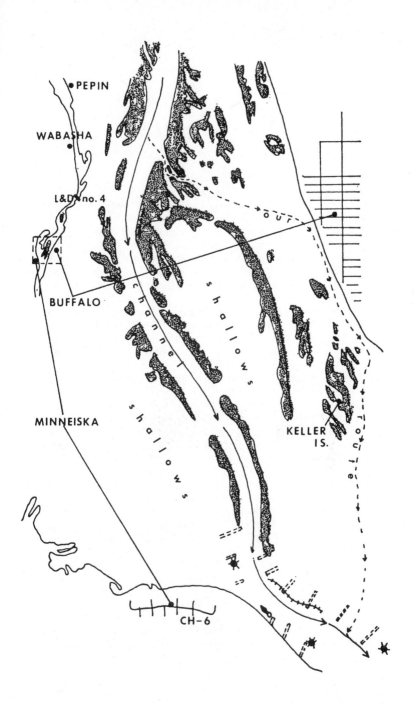

PEPIN

WABASHA

L&D no. 4

BUFFALO

MINNEISKA

channel

shallows

shallows

shallows

out

outle

KELLER
IS.

CH-6

6

MORAINE, MORE RAIN

A crisp, north, stern-wind pushed us toward the village of Pepin, Wisconsin, seven miles down and across the lake. Even before entering the harbor, we knew we were going to like Pepin. The houses and shops were well separated and "homey" looking. A beautiful crescent shaped beach lay above the long rock jetty which separated the western end of the harbor from the lake. Over the jetty we could see the tall masts of dozens of sailboats.

At the sparsely stocked marine store we inquired about a slip, and were directed to F7, a two boat slip, the downwind half of which was occupied by a sleek sailboat. Realizing that an error in docking could cause **Sol Seaker** to blow into the sailboat, I maneuvered cautiously. Error! We blew into the sailboat, luckily without a scratch.

Our folding bicycles drew not only attention but also an invitation to have a before dinner drink with Don, Donna, Eleanor, Lois, Del and Ned aboard Ned's sailboat. Ned is one of the many doctors from the Mayo Clinic in Rochester who have boats along this section of the Mississippi.

After our drink, we returned to **Sol Seaker** where we met Scott arriving for a weekend aboard the bumped sailboat. "I want you to know I get a little noisy sometimes after a bottle of rum. I have some friends coming later. I hope we don't get too loud for you," Scott said in greeting.

Later, when we emerged from the Friday fish fry at the Pepin Hotel, we heard an unpleasant sound coming from the direction of our slip. Scott, on his deck with his friends, was blowing into a long red air horn.

As we approached, they headed for dinner. Tired from our day's voyage, we were soon in bed. Later, I was aware of Scott returning to his boat, and giving one long blast on the horn, as I drifted into dreamland.

"Fog!" Dee poked me. "You won't believe what I see, fog!"

I looked out. The marina had taken on a mystical quality. Tall masted sailboats faded in and out of the slowly moving fog. I grabbed my camera and, still clad in pajamas, stepped out onto the damp dock to take pictures of the ephemeral sight. Almost instantly the fog began to dissipate. Before we had finished our breakfast, the sky was bright with the promise of a perfect day for our bike ride to the Laura Ingalls Memorial, "Little House in The Big Woods," about eight miles from Pepin.

The ride proved to be all we had expected, and more. To really see and appreciate the rolling farmlands along the Mississippi River in Western Wisconsin, one must leave his automobile at home and ride a bike. A speeding automobile blurs the wildflowers, cornstalks, beans, birds, frolicking dogs and curious cows. The powerful automobile also flattens out the undulations of the moraine so that the rise and fall is scarcely detected. Our tiny motorbikes served to emphasize those undulations. With engines off the downhill gravitational pull kept us constantly braking to maintain a safe speed. With engines on we struggled to slowly reach the crest of each rise.

We stopped to peel back the husk of a ripening ear of corn and smell the freshness inside. In one field a harvester was at work, its large, pointed fingers cutting and stripping the corn. The stalks fell into a shredding machine where they were chopped into bite size silage for winter cattle feed.

Although it was a warm, early-September day, the morning fog, the nighttime "nip" in the air, the harvesting activity and a flock of blackbirds preparing to head south gave indications that summer was almost over and the cold of winter was on its way. But before winter came, there would be autumn and a few days of Indian Summer, locally called "the fifth season."

As we passed a roadside mailbox, a large black dog of indeterminant breed and a tiny chihuahua emerged from their hiding place in the tall grass. The sound of our motors was not the familiar one of their awaited master, but it aroused their curiosity. Although they, like many farm dogs, expressed an interest, there wasn't a bark or threatening gesture.

The Laura Ingalls Memorial, which occupies the

vantage of a pleasant hilltop, was a welcome stop.
After eight miles on our bikes, we were ready to dis-
mount and walk around, as a bit of numbness was beginning to set-in on our sitting-ends. The log cabin is
back from the road and surrounded by well manicured
lawns.   A display of pictures and information includes
records of Laura's school work and of her father's par-
ticipation in town elections.

     In addition to posterior discomfort, the long ride
generated a great thirst.   We brought cheese and
crackers for lunch, but were looking forward to some
cold pop to help wash them down. According to our map,
the village of Lund should be nearby. We asked directions of two boys who were mowing the memorial lawn.

     "It's a mile down the road," one answered.

     "We're looking for a grocery store," said Dee.

     "The only store in Lund is a cooperative store for
the local people," replied the other boy.

     "All we want are some cold drinks. Can't we get
some there?"

     "Well, if that's all you want, you can get that,"
said the first boy.

     That was all we could get in Lund. The store was
closed, but there was a "coke" machine in front of the
tiny co-op market. The machine didn't have diet drinks,
so we settled for Mellow Yellows, downing them immediately.   A look around Lund disclosed a gas station
(closed), a fire truck, several houses and two churches,
one a beautiful, tall, steepled brick structure on a
promontory just around the next bend out of town.   We
found a sunny spot on the grass at the back of the
church out of the freshening breeze.

     Taking the cheese and crackers from the cracker
box, I felt inside for the knife Dee had packed.   No
knife. "You must have lost it on the way," she scolded.

     "Surely I would have heard it drop," I defended.

     Fortunately the sun-softened cheese could be cut by
inserting the corner of a cracker then pushing and saw-
ing. Usually the cracker "knife" broke in the process,
but occasionally we were triumphantly successful in
cutting the cheese without damaging the cracker.

     As we sat on the grass, backs against the wall of
the church, a small car roared up the long driveway. "Oh
no," we thought, "the townspeople have spotted us and
we're in trouble for eating on the church lawn."

     But the man in the car hardly glanced at us as he
55

continued around the building, back down the long drive, onto the main road and away.

Dee saw a note on the front door of the church saying, "Pastor, we waited for you until 11:30 and you didn't arrive. We have gone into town to call you. If you arrive before we get back please wait." We were hoping the pastor would return so we could see the inside of the church. But, except for the man in the speeding car, there wasn't a person visable in the entire town of Lund. At 12:00 we heard a siren go off, but when we rode back through town we couldn't find the source of the sound.

Stopping back at the "coke" machine we found that we were five cents short of having enough change for one drink. Our thirst would have to wait.

The trip back to Pepin was more downhill than up. As we dropped toward the river, we rode side-by-side talking, listening to the countryside, and looking for the knife I had lost. We found the knife, not on the road, but back at the boat on the counter where Dee had left it. With my tongue I pretended to moisten the index finger of my right hand and slowly made a tally mark in the air. "That's one for me!" I said.

From outside, the Harbor View Cafe looked like a quaint old fish-and-chips place; inside the atmosphere was loud and boisterous. All tables were full and a croud of waiting diners jammed the bar area and doorway. There were no reservations and no waiting lists, yet the young ladies in charge seemed to keep everyone in mind. After standing for awhile, Dee and I found two recently vacated bar stools, where we sipped white Sebastiani wine while waiting for a table. We got the table we wanted, an intimate one near the back where we could people watch, hold hands, and play kneesies.

Dee's Coque Vin with pearl onions and new potatoes was fit for a queen. And my Hungarian Goulash with pearl onions and German red cabbage was a treat to the palate. These entrees were preceded by delicious spinach salad and a fine mushroom soup with sour cream and tarragon. Although stuffed, we topped off our gourmet meal by sharing a fresh raspberry tart and a piece of frozen Kalua and cream pie. In San Francisco such a meal could easily have cost $50.00 for two. Here the price was $21.00, including wine and dessert.

Of all our meals out, we agreed that for gourmet elegance the Harbor View took the blue ribbon award.

After dinner we planned to dance to live music at the Pepin Hotel, but the combination of our long bike ride, large meal, relaxing wine, and a scheduled morning departure, caused us to opt for an early bedtime.

The predictable, unpredictable happened, we awoke to a cool, rainy morning. Sailboaters and fishermen sat around hoping the storm would pass quickly. This was Labor Day weekend, a time for sailing and fishing, not for sitting inside watching water drip from the mast.

At 10:30 the skies partially cleared and, on cue, the marina came alive with people preparing to head out into the lake. Although there were lingering clouds and strong breezes, we assumed that the natives knew what they were doing, and joined the preparations by unplugging our shore power, switching back to battery power, checking oil, coolant and engine belts, securing all loose items and sniffing to make sure no gas fumes had escaped into the bilge area. I flipped on the "blower" for a few minutes to clear any undetected fumes, then started the engine, while Dee cast off the lines.

As we left the protection of Pepin Harbor, we felt the full force of the northwest wind. The lake was alive, each wave topped by frothy meringue and blowing spray. Here and there a sailboat split the turbulence while leaning precariously in the wind. We were jarred and jostled as we made-way toward the center of the lake, taking the waves on our stern quarter.

About three miles out, a wind-driven rain began to fall. Thunder shattered the air. To the northwest heavy dark clouds moved rapidly in our direction, issuing forth jagged bursts of lightning.

Should we turn and run the three miles back to the shelter of Pepin Harbor? Or should we speed up in an effort to beat the storm to Wabasha, four miles downriver? Staying ahead of the storm seemed more sensible, so we increased our speed as much as possible.

The wiper blade had difficulty keeping up with the ever increasing downpour. Ahead, fishermen in small skiffs scurried toward Read's Landing on the Minnesota shore trying to beat the rapidly approaching storm. When we and the rain drew even with Read's Landing, boats were beached everywhere, their occupants having taken refuge in cars, tents and cottages. We slowed, hoping to see a pier at which we might dock and wait out the storm. There was none.

"Sometimes the storms are so dark you can't see the channel markers," Cy had warned us.

"It's best to find a safe spot and anchor until the storm passes," Doug had added.

I moved toward shore in preparation for dropping the anchor, then realizing we might be in the way of some small boat that had not yet made it to safety, we decided to look for a safer spot. As we rounded the bend at Drury Island, we could see Wabasha a couple of miles ahead. The channel was clear of boats so we made a run for the Wapasha Resort, where we took the last spot at the gas dock. Making **Sol Seaker** secure we quickly joined the dozens of other "drowned rats" who had found refuge in the upstairs dining room.

It was 11:47. Busy bartenders were preparing dozens of "Bloody Mary's," but no one was buying them. We soon learned why. At exactly 12:00 rcon the Sunday curfew on alcoholic beverages was lifted and the drinks disappeared into the hands of eager customers.

Barb Beetsch had told us that there were two things we should do in Wabasha. ". . . Eat a 'slipperyburger' at Slippery's and visit the restored Anderson Hotel."

We asked a couple sitting at a window table if they knew the way to Slippery's. "No," said the lady, "we trailered our boat up from Iowa to go fishing. That's it down there." She indicated a fourteen foot jon boat. "We've been camping on a sandbar. This morning we packed the tent in the car. I'm glad we did or it would be drenched. We only caught one fish before the rain started."

I went downstairs to the boat to get our umbrella, then into the bait store to ask the young man if it was all right to leave our boat at the gas dock until the storm passed. "Sure you can leave it there, nobody'll be comin' in for gas in this storm."

"Can you tell me how to get to Slippery's?" I continued, prepared for a walk in the rain.

He gave me a quizzical look then stated, "This **is** Slippery's!"

This fact was verified by a look at the upstair's menu where we saw in large letters SLIPPERYBURGERS $1.30. We both ordered Slipperyburgers and chili, just the combination for a cool, stormy day.

As quickly as it had started, the rain stopped, and we headed toward the one hundred twenty-four year old Anderson House, Minnesota's oldest operating hotel.

58

Along with four ladies, we toured several rooms which were authentic nineteenth century. The authenticity included lumpy mattresses placed on antique wooden bedsteads and covered with colorful handmade quilts. Papered walls, braided rugs, lace curtains and antique dressers holding porcelain pitcher and basin completed the austere interiors. Even the bath was authentic - down the hall. The floors were so slanted that just staying in the lumpy bed might prove difficult.

We decided that the Anderson House was a nice place to visit, but for sleeping we would take the cuddy-bed in our own **Sol Seaker**.

Later that day we pulled into the Alma Marina looking for an overnight berth. The first people we saw were the four ladies from the Anderson House and their husbands. They had left Wabasha before us in their two eighteen-foot boats headed for La Crosse, some sixty miles and five locks downriver, where they had left their cars and boat trailers. About three miles out of Wabasha one of the boats developed a problem in the sterndrive. The other boat had towed it to Alma.

They were trying to figure out how to get their cars and trailers up from La Crosse, as Dee and I rode our bikes to Alma two miles away. While we were eating dinner at the old Burlington Hotel, the same four ladies entered the dining room. After dinner we stopped by their table to ask how things were going. "The people at the marina are very nice," said Joan Edwards. "They loaned the men a car to go to La Crosse and they loaned us a car to come here for dinner."

Judy Bridgford asked me what I did.

"I taught at San Jose State University for twenty-three years," I replied. "I retired this year."

"San Jose State!" exclaimed Jean Kenny. Then turning to Judy she said, "Don't you have a relative teaching there?"

Judy thought for a moment then said, "No, at Fullerton State."

"I mean Gary Johnson," said Jean.

"You mean Gary Johnson in Counselor Education?" I asked.

"Oh yes," said Judy, "He's a second cousin."

"I know Gary very well. In fact we've taught together in the School of Education for many years."

"It's a small world isn't it?" said Dee.

Next day we moved **Sol Seaker** to a delapidated dock

59

across the tracks from the old Burlington Hotel. We hauled our bikes up steep rickety steps, over two sets of tracks and some rocks, before reaching the street. We rode to Buena Vista Park (pronounced Buna Vista), for what was supposed to be, ". . .the most spectacular view on the river."

The ride gave our bikes their toughest workout yet, but the view was worth it. We watched as two boats sped toward the Alma Lock directly below us, their trailing V's breaking the glassy smoothness of the water's surface. As they slowed and entered the open gates, a third boat rounded the bend a mile upriver. Traveling at full speed, he was obviously hoping to reach the lock before the gates closed.

It was a curious race, the two lead boats moving at a snails pace through the "no wake" zone toward the waiting ropes as the larger boat rounded the final buoy and sped toward the lock. When he reached the "no wake" area he suddenly throttled back and stopped dead in the water. A wave from his own wake caught the stern and pushed him forward. Other waves repeated this action, and by short spurts, he was propelled toward the lock wall.

From our vantage we could understand why the manual warned against approaching a lock at high speed. There was a real danger of your own wake propelling you into a lock wall or another boat with enough force to do serious damage or cause injury.

Close to the dam several small fishing boats were plying the fast water below the partially opened tainter gates, and a small gray houseboat made continuous trips back and forth across the river, taking fishermen from Alma to a fishing pier at the far end of the dam.

We could make out the town of Wabasha, eight miles upriver. In this area the main channel is narrow, but the marshy wildlife area known as Nelson Bottoms extends a mile on either side of the channel. Reportedly this area has some of the best fishing and hunting to be found anywhere in the country.

After our bikes were stored, we studied our charts. The name "Buffalo" intrigued us, but the charts showed the town to be more than a mile away from the main channel at the lower end of Pomme De Terre Slough.

"Shall we see if we can make it to Buffalo?" Dee asked.

"Sure," I said with feigned confidence.

60

The backwater could be entered at three different locations, mile 748 near Indian Point, mile 746.5 at Roebuck's Run and mile 745.7 at Sand Run. We selected Sand Run, as it would require the shortest travel through shallow unmarked waters.

We entered Sand Run at idle speed, depth sounder reading seven feet. As we moved farther into the backwater, the sounder showed six feet, five, four, three.

We scanned the surface ahead hoping for clues that would indicate the deepest route. There were no clues. We need three feet of water to navigate safely without raising the outdrive, two and one-half feet with the outdrive raised. The sounder read four feet, five feet, four feet. We seemed to have found an adequate channel.

Ahead were three openings from Sand Run into Pomme De Terre Slough. We selected the middle one. Halfway through the cut, logs extended into the water from both right and left sides, and a clump of cattail grew just left of the center. Ahead a large white egret stood almost at the center of the cut in water less than a foot deep. We steered to the right of the egret. He flew away, removing one of our landmarks.

Four feet, three feet. We raised the outdrive and angled toward the logs on the right side. The sounder continued to read three feet as we passed halfway between the logs and the spot vacated by the egret. The sounder read four feet, five feet, seven feet.

"Thank God that egret was there!" I said. "Otherwise we would have been aground just about where he was standing."

We had always liked egrets, now they were officially our favorite bird.

We took a leisurely run along the shoreline of Buffalo, looking for a place to stop for a stroll around town, but the rickety piers were much too small for us. The water around Buffalo was more reminiscent of a placid Louisiana Bayou than a scene along the Mighty Mississippi in central Wisconsin. "Do you suppose there really were buffalo here," Dee wondered.

Now, three miles into the backwaters, we had to decide whether to return the way we came or continue through the shallows, returning to the channel below the village of Minnieska. The way we came, it would be six miles to Minnieska, but less than two miles if we could make it through the uncharted waters ahead. We decided to go ahead.

61

To be successful, we had to skirt low reed and weed covered Keller Island (which was really fourteen or fifteen separate tiny islands), avoid the stump fields of Spring Lake, and find our way through the wing dams and rip-rap that lay between us and the main channel.

Ahead, birds stood in the shallow waters. Ahead, also, randomly placed sticks marked something - but what? Deep water? Shallow water? Good fishing spots? A submerged log? Our sounder read three feet. With outdrive raised we picked our way cautiously through the brown water. The sounder continued at three feet. We were past Keller Island and staying well west of the stump field. Through binoculars we could see several channel markers, now less than three-quarters of a mile ahead. North of one of them was a safe opening between two wing dams. If we mis-identified the markers we might run into a wing dam or cross over some prop-eating rip-rap.

Correct identification proved more difficult than expected. According to our chart, the daymark that should have been the safe one was the third from the right. According to our compass heading, it was in the wrong location relative to the village of Minnieska, now clearly visable on the Minnesota shore. We finally realized that on this page of the chart book north is oriented toward the side of the page rather than the top. By turning the chart book sideways the picture became clearer.

We headed toward the safe opening. The sounder began to read four feet, five, seven, ten. We re-entered the channel, lowered the outdrive, and headed toward Fountain City - our next overnight stop.

LITTLE HOUSE IN THE BIG WOODS

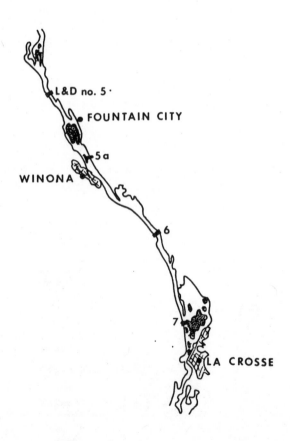

L&D no. 5

FOUNTAIN CITY

5 a

WINONA

6

7

LA CROSSE

CH-7

7

FOUNTAIN CITY

We often ·build mental images of persons or places before we actually see them. These preconceived pictures are usually quite far from reality. Sometimes our preconceptions have become so genuine to us that the reality is disturbing, even disorienting.

I experienced such a disorientation several years ago when I first caught sight of Niagara Falls. I had seen many pictures of the falls, so their actual configuration was not a surprise, but their orientation in relation to the rest of the world created several minutes of real confusion. In my mind's eye I had always seen Niagara Falls flowing out of Canada into the United States, from north to south. When I saw the falls actually flowing from the United States toward Canada, I literally could not believe my eyes. My family thought I was insane as I repeated over and over again, "This is all wrong. The falls are flowing the wrong way."

The name Fountain City had conjured up images of small tree-shaded parks and free-flowing fountains. Our view of Fountain City from the river revealed nothing to destroy these images. The village was squeezed into a narrow strip of steeply sloping land between the river and the inevitable limestone bluffs. Its closely packed buildings could easily have hidden the parks and fountains of my imagination. As we approached by water, both Dee and I were struck by a feeling of familiarity, as though we had seen Fountain City before. Finally it hit us. "Heidelberg," we said in unison.

It was a fact that several brick buildings on the upper level dominated the town much like Heidelberg Castle dominates the City of Heidelberg when viewed from across the Nekar River. Of course, Fountain City was a miniature by comparison. We cruised slowly past town looking for the right place to take a picture that would capture this similarity. We then turned and slowly retraced our watery path, taking several pictures along the way.

So intent were we in our picture taking that, at first, we had failed to see four people in a moored boat eagerly waving to us. We waved a return greeting and tied up at the dock amidst invitations to, "join us for a drink."

Our hosts were Rosie and Bill, and Teddie and Jim of Winona. Bill, a printer by trade, wore the bright green pants that seem so popular among men in this part of the country. Their curiosity had been aroused first by the strange surf board and bicycles on our deck, and then the words "Clearlake Calif." on the transom. They were eager to learn how **Sol Seaker** had brought us here from California.

As we sipped strong screwdrivers we shared our story with them. Like many people, they envied us, saying they wanted to make the same trip - someday.

Politely refusing a second drink, we took our leave, heads spinning from so much alcohol on empty stomachs. Taking the path that runs beneath the Burlington Northern tracks we entered The Fountain City of reality - not fantasy.

The real Fountain City is a thoroughly charming place, having escaped the neon lights and plastic food stands that are the commercial weeds of many towns and cities in this last half of the twentieth century. The variety store, Our Own Hardware Store, the tiny family-run grocery store and the Red Lantern Antique Shop all spoke of earlier days. Only here and there could one spot progress on the move. On the waterfront, a young man from northern Wisconsin was remodeling an old house. At the south end of town a small low-cost housing project was nearing completion. On the upper level, an old brick school house, one of the components of our imaginary "Heidelberg Castle," bore the inscription, "School Apartments, 1979," where the original construction date had once appeared.

With all its charm and quaintness, The Fountain City of reality was not the Fountain City of my imagination, for the only fountain to be found in the entire town was a drinking fountain located in a tiny park at the "Y" just south of the older part of town.

64

When Dee and I started planning this trip we had wondered how we would get acquainted with people along the way. Fortunately, we never found this to be a problem. Everywhere we went people were ready to talk, to share. On our first stroll around Fountain City we met six people, all of whom could have been the subject of an interesting story. First, we met the man who was working on the wood and glass addition to his old house.

Dee said, "We saw your building from our boat. It looked so different from the other buildings we just had to take a closer look. It reminds us of buildings in California."

"It's a lot of work," he answered. "The old house was in bad shape. I had to jack up the front and put in a new foundation. I've got most of that done now. When I get this addition finished it'll act as a passive solar system in winter. Should help with heating bills. Say, do you like tomatoes?"

"Sure," Dee answered.

"Well, come back here." He led us to the rear of the house where several vines were loaded with large "beefsteak" tomatoes. He gave us four.

A block farther down the street we entered the Red Lantern Antique Shop. We do a lot of antique-looking but very little buying. Dee was struck by a small poorly made ceramic figurine of a young man and woman fishing. A piece of broom straw served as the fishing pole. The small piece, which was made in occupied Japan after World War II, was designed to sit on the edge of a shelf or table. The price was $18.00. Dee passed.

We turned right at the next street and started up a steep incline toward the upper levels of town. On each side of the street were deep, cemented ditches. On the right, part of the ditch was paved over to form street-side parking. The remainder of both ditches was open, except where wooden or cement bridges gave access to driveways and garages. There was a protective railing on the sidewalk side of the left ditch, but the other ditch had no protective railings at all. Both ditches were dry, but if they ever had water in them they would be very dangerous, especially the side that was paved over. If a child or animal fell into the ditch above the paved area, it would be swept under the pavement with little hope of survival.

65

On the next corner two elderly men were talking. One had a bucket of recently caught fish. The other, Al, was holding an antique-looking crockery pot. "We're curious about these deep ditches along the road," I said. "What are they for?"

"Drainage," Al answered. "Sometimes we get lots of rain. This is the only way the water can get from them bluffs to the river. Sometimes both ditches are completely full."

Dee and I looked at each other, feeling a sense of concern about what would happen if a child fell into one of those ditches in a raging torrent.

The man with the bucket of fish left.

Al continued, "I was a butcher for 42 years. Now I live right up there. I do wood carvings. I go along the river looking for special roots, then I carve them into all manner of things - mostly animals."

"Could we see some of your carvings?" Dee asked eagerly.

Not ready to invite us to his apartment, but anxious to show us his handiwork, Al said, "I'll be right back." He walked the quarter of a block to his apartment. We waited. Several minutes passed and Al hadn't returned.

As we were about to leave he returned with a troubled look on his face, and three carvings in his hands. Two of the carvings were tiny buffaloes, lifelike in every detail except the mouths, which were half-open slits similar to that of Rolf the Muppet dog. The third carving was a cartoon-like dinosaur painted white with multi-colored polka dots. This too, had the open mouth. We admired the carvings and took a picture of the largest buffalo.

Al said, "I looked for an old coin I have, a half-dime, but I couldn't find it. I have some other coins too, but they aren't where I keep them. My grandson and his friend have been staying in my apartment while I was on a trip. Just got back last night. Guess I'll have to ask him if he's seen my coins."

"Could we see some more of your carvings?" I asked.

By now Al had decided it would be safe to invite us in. On a small chest was a menagerie of camels, elephants, squirrels and turtles all exquisitely carved from the lightweight river roots. Most were realistic

looking and highly polished, but a number were dressed
in polka dots or stripes. All had that same simple
half-open Rolf mouth.

While Al was pleased that we were so enthusiastic
about his work, he continued to look troubled. "You
know, I had about twenty-five hundred dollars worth of
old coins in a drawer. Maybe my grandson took them to
my daughter's house for safekeeping."

Dee and I looked at each other, both wondering if
Al's grandson's friend or some friend-of-a-friend might
have taken the coins. Before we left, we asked Al if he
would sell one of his carvings. He declined. "I used to
give them away to my friends," he said, "but it's
gettin' harder and harder to find the roots, so I'm just
gonna keep these."

Although disappointed, we understood his reluc-
tance. As we were leaving, Al asked, "Have you been in
the hardware store over there? One of the biggest col-
lections of arrowheads in these parts. That store's
been in the same family for over ninety years. A young
couple from Minneapolis just bought it. They're
throwin' stuff out. That's where I got this pot." He
pointed to the pot he had been carrying when we first
met him.

Dusk was approaching as we cupped our hands to peer
through the big front window of Our Own Hardware, trying
to get a look at the collection of Indian artifacts that
lined the upper walls on both sides of the narrow old
building. We didn't see Gary and Judee Brone until they
opened the front door.

"Come in," said Judee.

"Oh, we don't want to bother you," replied Dee.
"We just wanted to see the Indian collection."

"We're just finishing up. Come and look around."

Judee's tousled auburn hair framed a round flushed
face with large full mouth and a ready smile. She wore
baggy red slacks and her blouse was covered by a loose
fitting smock coat. Gary had the same red hair and a
matching, neatly trimmed, moustache and beard. His
cheeks were pink and thin, and he too flashed a ready
smile.

The collection of Indian artifacts contained hundreds of spear points, arrowheads, scrapers, stone
knives, stone axes and grinding tools. "They belong to

67

the original owner," Gary stated. "He's ninety years
old now and in a rest-home. But he still remembers
where each point came from. Of course they are only
catalogued in his head and when he dies the information
will be lost forever."

"That would make our archeologist son very sad,"
Dee replied. "He has a thing about cataloging everything; says that's the only way the information can be
transmitted to future generations. He's right of
course, but I'm still unhappy that he took a beautiful,
tiny arrowhead I found on Monitor Island in Clearlake,
and placed it in the laboratory at Sonoma State College
where I'll never see it again."

Judee and Gary were eager to show us the rest of
the store which would be theirs when they signed the
papers the next day. The wall behind the counter along
the right side of the narrow store was backed by old
fashioned wooden drawers holding who knows what. Down
the center aisle were display tables of assorted hardware items, including enameled cooking pots and small
thin-walled wood stoves out of the 1930's. Along the
left wall were tools of all sorts.

The dark walls, dark well-worn oiled wooden floors
and high pressed-metal ceilings appeared to be original.
The tiny, single, bare light bulbs that shown here and
there, gave hardly enough light to illuminate the merchandise. At the right rear was the proprietor's corner,
a raised platform holding the safe, a huge desk, a wood-
stove and a high stool where the owner could sit, pipe
in mouth, and keep an eye on the entire store.

As Dee's eyes roamed over this quaint old store,
she spotted a small green hand pump on a high shelf. "Is
that for sale?" she asked. "I've been wanting one of
those to put on our back deck at home."

"That belongs to the previous owner," Judee replied. "Tomorrow I'll ask him if he will sell it." Judee
caught my glance toward a rack of guns in one corner. "I
don't want to sell guns," she said. "But it's duck
season here. Everybody hunts, so I guess we'll have to
sell guns. Our son wants one, but I feel sorry for the
ducks."

"I hunt ducks - with a camera," I replied.

"I hate guns and hunters," Dee said hastily. "I
save bread to feed the ducks in the marinas."

Well, we're against nuclear arms," Judy replied, "and I don't like guns, but I guess we'll have to keep our prejudices to ourselves or lose business."

Judy had directed a pre-school and Gary had been a counselor for schizophrenic children in Minneapolis before the two of them decided to leave the big city and bring their own children to this tiny, picturesque river town. Neither had been in business before and it was with mixed feelings of anticipation and trepidation that they were embarking on this new venture.

"We'll come back tomorrow to buy something when the store is officially yours," Dee said as we left.

The dock where we were moored was only a few feet from the Burlington Northern tracks. Here, unlike Prescott, the trains went by at full speed. During the night, no fewer than eight trains roared past with deafening noise and unsettling vibration. Sleep came in irregular intervals. In the morning I tried to catch up on writing our previous days activities, while Dee went to town. It's best that she tell her experiences in her own words.

DEE: I got off the boat and walked carefully along the rickety dock. Jumping over a tiny stream that was trickling under the bridge, I thought of how the Great Mississippi was built from just such trickles as this. Beyond the bridge I could see the deep ditches. I noticed that a car was parked on the covered area. The cement looked thin and I wondered if the owner was concerned about the car breaking through.

Heading south on the main street, I passed the drinking fountain. Up from there was the bank, one of the town's few new and modern buildings. Norwegian bells rang as I opened the bank doors. Inside a display case held an albino deer and an albino squirrel. As I stood looking at them, I recognized a voice and turned to see Judee and Gary. We greeted each other as old friends.

"What are you doing here?" I asked. "I thought you'd be in your store."

"We're here to sign the papers," Judee said. "It will be ours at 12 noon."

"Is the store closed?" I asked.

"No it's open, the owner is there. He's going to

69

be helping us out for a few days until we know what
we're doing," Gary said. "Why don't you stop by to ask
him about the pump."

"That's a good idea," I said, as the bank officer
motioned them toward his desk.

I cashed a traveler's check and headed toward the
Red Lantern Antique Shop. Last night I had dreamed
about the fishing couple figurine, remembering the times
when Weldon and I sat side-by-side fishing. I would put
my arm around his shoulder, just like the figurine girl.
I really wanted that figurine to sit aboard **Sol Seaker.**

The price was $18.00, but today I would bargain for
it. Sometimes my bargaining makes Weldon nervous, so I
welcomed this chance to enjoy one of my favorite activities. The shop owner said, "You can have it for $15.00."

"Great." I said, then looking at his old bottles,
I asked if he collected antique bottles.

He confessed he didn't know much about bottles. I
gave him some of my information - accumulated during the
times our son had coerced us into bottle collecting. I
wished Weldon was with me as he is more knowledgeable
than I, and he would have enjoyed the discussion.

With figurine in hand, I headed to the Hardware
store. The owner was sitting in the proprietor's corner
puffing a pipe - a part of the antique decor. "I saw
your pump last night and wondered if I could buy it," I
said.

"You'll have to ask my sister," he said sharply.

"How can I get in touch with her?" I asked.

"She's in Winona, won't be home 'til evening."

"I'm on a boat and I'll be gone by then."

He didn't seem to care. What a contrast to the
friendliness of Judee and Gary. They certainly should
increase the store's business.

I was eager to get back to to the boat to see how
Weldon was doing with his writing. Instead of writing,
he was fishing.

WELDON: "You caught me," I said. "But I haven't
caught any fish.

Later, we took a long walk through town. We stopped by Al's again. to see if he had found his coins, and
if he might have changed his mind about selling one of
his smaller carvings. He hadn't found the coins. We

70

didn't ask about the carvings, hoping he would volunteer to sell one. He didn't, but he showed us a carving we hadn't seen before - a cane with an exquisitely carved dog's head, Rolf mouth, of course. Al "allowed" that some day he might need to use the cane, but not yet.

Circling past the "Heidelberg Castle," we stopped at Our Own Hardware. Judee was alone. She told us about her seven year old who had skipped a grade, but now seemed unhappy in school even though he did fine academically. "He's smaller than the other kids in his class here," said Judee. "Being the 'new kid' in a conservative rural school doesn't help."

I suggested she watch the situation very closely. Skipping a child in school for purely academic reasons often retards the child's social and emotional development, especially if the child is small for his age. "If it looks like he would be happier with younger children, it might be wise to move him back to the grade he skipped."

The former owner and his sister, Marilyn, just back from Winona, came in. They still didn't know if they would sell the pump, so Dee gave them an address where we planned to pick up mail later. "If you decide to sell it, let us know and we will stop by to pick it up early in October when we go back to Prescott to get our car."

Judee invited us to see their upstairs living quarters where Gary was packing to return to Minneapolis for the rest of the week. "The former owner will help me run the store while Gary's gone," she said, as we sipped a glass of white wine.

It was mid-afternoon when we left Fountain City for one of our shortest runs, eight miles to Winona, Minnesota. We were looking forward to shopping at the Winona Woolen Mills where we had been told we could get "real bargains" on sweaters.

At the Winona dock we spoke briefly with a couple that reminded us of Herbie and Irene, friends of our Clearlake neighbors. Dee asked "Irene" if she knew how to get to the woolen mills.

"Yes, up to the second street, then left. It's about six blocks, but it's closed now."

"We'll go tomorrow," Dee said, thanking her for the information.

We quickly unfolded our bikes and hauled them up a

long, steep stairway to the top of the levee that surrounded the marina. We had just enough time for a quick ride around town and dinner at the highly recommended Hot Fish Restaurant. It was almost dark when we returned to the boat and stored the bikes aboard. Tomorrow we would walk to the Woolen Mills.

Before we reached the mill we were wishing we had used the bikes, the six blocks became twelve and a-half. We searched through the bargain table, selecting two sets of matching sweaters. Our plan was to store the sweaters under our cuddy-bed for use at home next winter. Little did we know that a "norther" would strike that very afternoon, dropping the temperature into the forties and forcing us to don our new sweaters, along with gloves we had purchased at a factory store near the marina.

Our next overnight stop was La Crosse, where we learned that the name of the town was derived from an Indian game played with a ball and a wicker "glove" used to catch and throw the ball. A beautiful statue depicting the game stands in a small plot just above the new Radisson Hotel.

Dee, always wanting to go to the end of the road, urged me to go as far up Black River as I could. a desire which almost got us into trouble as **Sol Seaker's** propeller began to kick up sand a few hundred yards below the closing dam. Fortunately, we were able to tilt the outdrive and let the current drift us off the sandbar with nothing more than a well sanded prop.

FISHING COUPLE   FIGURINE

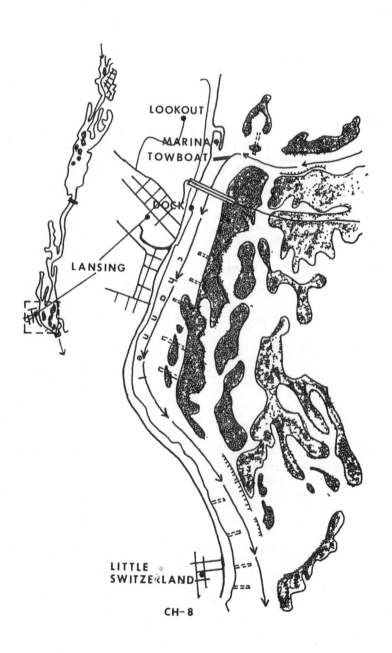

LOOKOUT

MARINA
TOWBOAT

DOCK

LANSING

LITTLE
SWITZERLAND

CH-8

8

KINDRED SOULS

Next day the weather was windy, but much warmer, as we stored our sweaters and began a leisurely thirty-four mile run to Lansing, Iowa. The view from the bridge was magnificent as we journeyed through wide expanses of river dotted with sand islands, stump fields, cattails and water lilies.

At 2:02 P.M. we left Minnesota behind, and picked up Iowa on the western bank with Wisconsin still on the eastern bank. At mile 672 we tried a short cut through one of the many channels that form an intricate circulatory system amid islands and marshes. Almost immediately **Sol Seaker** touched bottom forcing us to turn back into the main channel.

Reluctantly we passed the villages of Genoa, De Soto, Stoddard, and Victory, wondering what vistas and adventures we were missing. At mile 666 an osprey swooped down, snatched a fish from the river, and, with powerful wings, lifted his substantial cargo to disappear behind a tree-covered island to feast in privacy.

"Do you realize we haven't seen a towboat all day?" Dee said.

It was true. Except for the osprey, several turtles, some fishing boats, and dozens of monarch butterflies, we had had the river to ourselves for thirty-three miles. At mile 664 we caught up with a large towboat with fifteen loaded barges. The tow was standing still in the channel, blocking the entrance to the Lansing Marina. Stopping a hundred yards behind the tow, we waited for it to move around the bend so we could enter the marina.

It didn't move. We waited. Finally I moved around the tow to stop at a small dock below the Lansing bridge. As we passed, the tow began to back up. Having failed to negotiate the sharp turn above the Lansing bridge he had to move upriver a half mile to get a new heading. While we had been waiting for him to move, he was waiting for us to move. He had tried to call us on the radio, but our radio wasn't on. After this incident we vowed to always have the radio on when in the vicinity of a towboat just in case the captain needed to contact us.

At the small dock we met Vernon and Darlene, who live in a retirement community about two miles below Lansing. They had come to town by boat because a new concrete road that ran from town, past their home, and to the power plant had not yet "cured" sufficiently to allow traffic. They invited us to stop by for a visit before we went on downriver. An invitation we hoped to honor.

At the Lansing Marina we were greeted by manager Jan Griffith and Blackie. Jan, at age twenty, was in her third year as marina manager. Tall, slender, tanned, and attractive, the young lady was dressed in white shorts and a T-shirt emblazoned with the words, "It's What's Inside That Counts." Her long blond hair flowed in the gentle warm breeze. Blackie, the large family dog, wore a massive bandage on his right front leg.

"He's had two tumor operations," Jan said sadly. "My folks got Blackie when I was a little girl, and we grew up together. He almost didn't make it through the last operation. If the tumor comes back again, we'll have to put him to sleep. It's gonna be hard. My parents are farmers near Waterloo, and I come here for the season. Blackie and I stay in my parent's vacation home. He's my companion. I sure hope the tumor doesn't grow back."

I sat down on the steps to scratch Blackie's ears as I asked Jan how she became a marina manager.

"It's a long story," she replied. "The Army Corps of Engineers built the dikes that created the harbor, and a corporation of local businessmen built the docks and other facilities. The plan was for the marina to pay off the stockholders in a certain number of years, but income was not sufficient to accomplish this. I've been leasing the marina for three years. Part of the profits go to the stockholders, part to me, and part into maintenance. When the stockholders are paid, then the city may acquire the marina. I'm not sure what will happen next year. A lot of cities don't put enough money back into their marinas to keep them in good shape. I don't know if I want to manage a run-down marina. I don't know if I'll be back next year or not."

74

"You must have started managing the marina when you were seventeen," Dee said. "How did that happen?"

"Well, in high school I was good in math and physics. I was offered a college scholarship in engineering. But the more I thought, the more I realized I didn't really want to go into engineering. I found out about the marina job. I like it. I like working with people. Oh, I get some bad ones now and then but I just stand right up to them."

About that time a fishing boat with two men arrived for gas. Jan's quick response to their flirtatious suggestions gave evidence that she could handle herself in most any company. She used her charm, sense of humor, and good looks in a mature and lady-like manner that enhanced her skill in making the Lansing marina a pleasant place to be.

When the fishermen were on their way, Dee asked, "What will you do next year, if you don't run the marina?"

"I'm not sure. When the season's over, I'll go home to Waterloo for the winter. I think I'd like to buy a marina someplace where it's warm enough to be open all year. Do you know about marinas in California?"

"There are lots of year round marinas in the delta east of San Francisco Bay." I replied. "Some have trailer parks, repair shops and restaurants."

"When we get home, we'll send you a map of the area showing all of the marinas," Dee said. "We'll also send you a copy of the 'Bay and Delta Yachtsman.' It'll give you an idea of the San Francisco Bay boating scene."

"You know, Jan," I said. "Perhaps you ought to consider going to college now. If you want to work with people and perhaps own a marina, a degree in business or public relations could be very helpful."

Jan thought for a moment then said, "You're probably right. I should really think about that."

"The river is so big and relentless," Dee said, changing the subject, "with all the towboats, houseboats, wing dams and floods it seems that it could be dangerous, yet we haven't heard about any drownings."

"Oh, there are drownings, all right," Jan replied. Some of the drownings are caused by too much drinking, and some by a lack of understanding or fear of the power of the Ole' Mississippi. I don't know why some of the people on boating weekends drink so much."

Blackie had fallen into a restless sleep on the

steps and Jan was called to duty, so we unfolded our motorized bicycles for a riding tour of Lansing. Unlike the other river towns we'd visited, Lansing's principal thoroughfare does not parallel the river but starts at the river and runs due west. Its main street continues on west as Highway Nine to Waukon and Decorah. Also, Lansing is one of the few small towns which has a bridge spanning the river.

We stopped at Horsdahl Variety Store where Dee selected a straw hat from a sidewalk sale table. Inside, the store was piled high and deep with everything from hardware to clothing. "Do you have a 12 volt heater for heating water in a cup?" Dee asked a clerk, when he finished waiting on a charming young lady.

"I might have something like that." he replied leading us through the cluttered aisles to the back of the store. "If I have one it'll be here." He pawed through the assorted items on a gadget table. After a few minutes he said, "I guess we're all out. We usually keep one or two but sometimes things get sold and we forget to mark it down."

Just as I was wondering how he ever knew where anything was, he pulled an emersion heater from beneath a pile of twice pawed through gadgets. "Oh. these are for regular house current," he said. "I guess we don't have them for 12 volt."

Continuing up the street, we saw "Mississippi River Rat" T-shirts in the window of a well organized, but small, department store. "Let's get matching shirts " Dee said.

Inside, we noted that the cashier was the same young woman we had seen in the "piled higher and deeper" store. "I wonder if she works here and patronizes the other store," Dee whispered to me as we searched for matching sweatshirts and T-shirts.

"Maybe she has something going with the clerk at the other store." I whispered back.

When we couldn't find T-shirts that matched, Dee asked the young woman if she had any others. "No, but maybe the other store has some," she replied. "I'll call my husband."

The mystery was solved. She ran the "neat and tidy" store and her husband the "piled higher and deeper" store.

While we were waiting for the husband to bring shirts from the other store, the lady further clarified the situation. "We've been married a year. He owned that store and the man who owned this one had let it run down. When he decided to sell, my husband thought we'd better buy it. My husband is very relaxed about everything. He has the right personality for that store."

When we told her we wanted the T-shirts for our voyage downriver, she said. "I don't like the river. You'd never get me on a boat. I'm even scared to death to drive across the bridge."

Between the two stores we were able to find matching maroon sweatshirts, but had to settle for T-shirts of slightly different hues of blue.

Like other river towns, Lansing boasts of a bluff top park with "the best view of the river anywhere." For once, our tiny bike engines were not equal to the task as the road to the top was much steeper than at Alma or Red Wing. We settled for a pleasant ride through town, around the high school, and past picturesque homes. I had just taken a picture of a French-style house when Dee said, "Did you see the car that was parked in front of that house?"

"No, I was too intent on setting the camera for the picture."

"It was a Kaiser."

"I'm sure I got a picture of the car too," I said.

The next day we rode our bicycles along the river road south of town. Beyond a fish house, where carp (netted locally) are processed for market, and past a small marina with houseboats for rent, we came to a barrier which marked the beginning of the new concrete road. The road looked "cured" to us. Gravel had been piled up to provide access and it was obvious that several vehicles had driven on the road. Three men and a large dump truck were guarding the way.

"Is it okay to ride our bikes on the new road?" Dee asked.

The three men looked at each other, each waiting for the others to answer. Finally the oldest, a frail, weather-beaten skeleton with badly broken, discolored teeth and a three days growth of beard, spoke. "We really can't say you can. The road's dry enough, but we really don't have the authority to let you through. The foreman said, 'don't let nobody come down this road for two more days.'"

He turned to a younger, sturdily built man standing near the dump truck. "Why don't you call Jake on the radio to see if it's all right to let the bikes on the road." Then to us, "Jake's the foreman."

The younger man went to the truck, but couldn't seem to make the radio work. "Maybe it'll work if you start the engine," said the skeleton.

Although the loud engine covered his voice, we could see the young man working the microphone, apparently making contact. Turning the loud motor off, he told us it was okay, but we might not be able to make it all the way because there was a fence across farther down.

What a great road for a bike ride! New, smooth concrete, no cars, beautiful scenery, and we could ride side-by-side. Ahead of us another couple on bicycles were talking to a man beside a pickup where a second barrier marked the entry of a side road. Soon they were on the road ahead of us, walking their bicycles up a rather steep hill.

When we came to the side barrier, we learned that the guard was Jake, the foreman. We thanked him for allowing us on the road, then turned our motors on for the climb up the hill, soon overtaking the couple walking their bicycles.

We greeted each other and Dee said, "You need motors like ours."

The woman answered, "Right now that sounds great, but we really need the exercise."

"We usually use our pedals," Dee said. "We only use the motors on hills or on long rides. We're travelling downriver on a boat and these bikes are our only land transportation."

We "putted" by, crested the hill, turned off the engines and coasted slowly down a long incline. Houses and mobile homes began to appear on the right. We tried to remember what Darlene and Vernon had said about how to recognize their house. We remembered that there was a mobile home on each side and several flag poles along the main roadway. And, yes, something about two evergreens. Did they say at the corners of the house?

Ahead were the flag poles. Behind them were a number of houses and mobile homes. Two evergreens, about twelve feet high, marked the lower corners of a large, well-manicured lawn in front of a very charming home commanding an excellent view of the river. As we stopped to look at this tiny residential area, dubbed "Little Switzerland" by the residents, our fellow bikers caught up with us. "We're looking for the Leichtman's house." Dee said. "From their description, that must be it."

"Yes," answered the lady. "We're the Smiths. Bob and Jo."

"We're the Parkers," I said. "Dee and Weldon. We met the Leichtmans yesterday and they invited us to drop by for a visit."

"If you have time, come over to see us," said Bob. "We're in that mobile just down the road."

The Leichtmans weren't home, so we rode over to the Smiths. We immediately "hit it off" with Bob and Jo. Over a glass of wine and a spicy Mexican cheese dip, we were soon chatting like old friends. Since retirement, Bob, a railroad engineer, and Jo, an electronics worker, spend a great deal of time at this summer place in "Little Switzerland."

"Our country gets too involved in the economic problems of foreign countries," Bob said, as the subject turned to politics, "That's because of our large companies. They have too much influence on our government because of their economic interests abroad. Sometimes I think we're not governed by our elected representatives, but by the chairmen of the boards of large corporations."

"You're right," I replied. "And it's our young, innocent men and women that lose their lives to satisfy the needs of those corporations."

Bob said, "I've always thought, although I don't know how it could come about, if all of the young men and women of all of the countries of the world would just say 'no' when they were told to fight outside the boundaries of their own country, that would pretty much end economic wars."

Dee told them about our own son, John, who often seemed troubled during his last year of high school. "That was at the time of the draft lottery. Numbers were drawn according to birthdate. The low numbers got drafted. Although we knew he had strong anti-war convictions, it wasn't until after graduation that we realized how much he had been worrying that he might have to make a decision between the draft and Canada. What a mental relief we all felt when his lottery number was 309."

When I told Bob and Jo that we hoped to write a book about our cruise down the Mississippi, Bob's eyes lit up. He motioned for me to follow him into the house.

Dee and Jo continued to chatter like school girls as Bob and I went into the house. On the dining table was a small portable typewriter and boxes of typewritten pages. Bob, too, was working on a book.

"It's kind of an autobiography," he said. "It's about life on the railroad and things like that. You know, if it was just me, I could spend four or five hours every day writing. But Jo doesn't always share my enthusiasm. Sometimes these thoughts or inspirations just come to me and I know if I don't write them down right now I'll lose them."

"I know what you mean," I replied. "I sometimes have a whole poem just pop into my head. But if I don't write it down, I lose it. Dee will say 'you like to write poetry, why don't you write one for Kathy and Ted's anniversary.' She doesn't understand that it's difficult to write a poem on command. I've come to realize there are two kinds of poems. There's inspired poems, which come full-blown from who knows where; then, there's manufactured poems. For these, I sit down with a topic and start listing ideas and words that might apply. They are hard poems to write. I'm never quite satisfied with a manufactured poem."

Again a gleam came into Bob's eyes as he pulled out a folder, opened it, and handed me a poem. "This isn't the one I really want to share, but I thought you might like this one too."

I read the poem about life on the railroad depicting each crewman's daily tasks. It was good, at least to my untrained mind. Bob then shared a poem about a rose growing along a path - a rose that people would admire and pass by. The rose was beautiful, but, as is the habit of roses, hidden beneath the leaves were thorns. One day a young man came by, admired the rose, and reached down to pick it. In so doing, he learned that to possess the beauty of the blossom, he had to endure the sharpness of the hidden thorns.

Although he didn't say so, I suspected that this poem was the story of Bob's meeting and marrying his beautiful Jo, only to realize that along with the sweet and beautiful he had to endure an occasional "thorn."

As Bob returned the poems to the folder, he said, "There are some other poems, but they are maybe not so easily shared."

I didn't press him, but wondered if perhaps he, like me, had written some inspirational poetry and was reluctant to share them with a comparative stranger. Or perhaps he thought he might be imposing on me.

We talked more about our "artistic" endeavors, Bob confessing he wanted to try oil painting sometime. I said I had done a little and found it very satisfying.

Bob told me that two brothers and a sister are ministers. I got the feeling that he almost considered himself the "blacksheep" of the family.

I saw in Bob so much of myself, that it's hard to believe that our meeting on the new road was by chance. Perhaps there is a special time and place for events and people, if we aren,t afraid to share a little of our inner-sols.

Dee and Jo were still chatting when we returned to the screened porch. Dee will share their conversation.

DEE: As Jo and I sipped our wine on the shady deck of their small mobile home, I told her we preferred wine to other alcoholic drinks. She and Bob also preferred wine.

"This is Manichevitz Creme White Concord from New York, my favorite," Jo said.

"I haven't tried it before. It's very good. And the dip is spicy. I love spicy food."

"It's easy to make, and keeps a long time in the refrigerator. All you do is blend a can of tomato and chili with two pounds of processed cheese. I have an extra can of the chili you can take with you."

"Is this your home?" I asked Jo. "Are you here year round?"

"No, our home is in Waterloo. Our grandson is staying there now. Last winter we went to South Texas. Motels were expensive. One night cost fifty dollars. This year we plan to take our van. We can sleep in it if we can't find inexpensive lodging. We hope to rent an apartment and spend the winter there. We'll return here for spring and summer."

"Do you miss your family and personal things?" I wondered.

"No, I don't miss them. Our two daughters have lovely families and very good jobs. We keep in touch, but don't need to be in constant contact. I feel free of worldly possessions and responsibility. I would like to wander as you're doing, but Bob seems to like to stay home and read and write. We enjoy being together in retirement, so I read some too."

"It seems to me," I said, "some couples work at being together while others work at being apart. I'm glad Weldon and I like to do the same things."

"I'm up early and take my morning walk into town, have a cup of coffee then walk home. It's about five miles. I enjoy the exercise, and it gives Bob time to himself. Some retired husbands go into town to the bar and don't return 'til dinner time."

We were glad our husbands enjoyed being with us and didn't seem to need the bar environment to make their lives meaningful or enjoyable.

We sat looking out over the beautiful river, and the little boat houses along the shore. "I wish we had a houseboat to use on the river," Jo said, "but our daughter's boat is a fast ski boat for the grandsons to enjoy waterskiing. It's in our boat house. Our little fishing boat is the one tied up next to the boathouse."

I felt that she might have wanted to come along with us downriver if there had been a houseboat in the boat house, and if Bob could have brought along his writing and reading.

WELDON: When Bob and I returned to the screened porch, Dee told the Smiths about how our boat is equipped for the river voyage. Bob said a bit hesitantly, "I don't want to pry, but do you have a T.V. set?"

"No," I answered.

To Jo, Bob said, "I was just wondering. We aren't going to be using our portable T.V. anymore are we, since we got a new color set?" Then to us, "We have this little portable T.V. which is also an AM/FM radio. We've used it on camping trips. It's just a thought, but you might find something like that worthwhile. It's really small, just a five and a-half inch screen."

Dee and I looked at each other. We had discussed buying this type of T.V., but with so many last minute things to do before leaving home, we decided to forego the T.V. set.

Bob, still rather apologetic, said, "It's just a thought. I don't really know if we should sell it. I'll go get it and show you how it works."

The two La Crosse stations came in clearly on the short rod antenna built into the set. "It has a rechargeable battery pack inside," Bob said, "You can use it on the batteries, regular house current, or plug it into a cigarette lighter."

Bob and Jo went inside to discuss between themselves whether or not they really should sell it. While they were gone, Dee and I decided that we would buy the set, if the price seemed right. When they returned, an agreeable price was fixed and the set was ours. Then we realized that we couldn't possibly carry it with us on our bikes, already loaded with cameras, purse and the emergency "ranch."

Bob said, "We'll get the T.V. to you at the marina tomorrow. We'd like to see your boat anyway. And we'll take you to the bluff park for 'the best view' of the Mississippi River."

"Do you have room to carry some apples and tomatoes?" asked Jo.

"Sure we do," said Dee, who can never pass up a fruit stand.

With a bag of fruit strapped precariously to our bikes, we bade "so long" and rode back by Vernon and Darlene's. They were home. With them were the Kniefs. We had met Ed Knief briefly when we were at the Smiths. He had walked by, shirtless. in the warm humid weather. "I'd like to take a trip to California," Ed had said. "I could stop by Las Vegas on the way!"

"If you do that," I had replied, "you might lose your pants as well as your shirt."

As we sat down with the Leichtmans and Kniefs, Darlene said, "Ed is the mayor of 'Eagle Heights.'"

"Self appointed, of course," volunteered Ed.

As we sipped a glass of wine, Ed said to Darlene, "Why don't you play your new organ for us."

We accompanied Darlene into the next room where her newly purchased organ sat near the window. She was pleased to share some "mood" music with us, having once played professionally at churches, weddings, and with traveling combos. Vernon had been a farmer near New Hampton for forty years before they retired and moved to "Little Switzerland."

After meeting another neighbor, who came by to show-off his catch, a stripped bass and a sauger, we prepared to leave. "Wait, I have something for you," Vern said, heading into the garage. In an instant he returned with a tiny one-inch rectangular structure built like a bird house. "It's a mosquito house," he explained. "Just the thing for your boat."

As we rode back toward the marina, both Dee and I had a nice, warm feeling. Perhaps a bit of it was caused

83

by the wine, but mostly it was because we had spent a very enjoyable afternoon with some warm, friendly, "kindred souls."

The next day we rode to the bluff with Bob and Jo, where we watched two large towboats meet just above the bridge. In passing, the upriver tow apparently got it's front barges stuck on a sandbar. Although hidden behind some trees, we could see great columns of black smoke as the towboat used its powerful engines to back off the sandbar and continue its slow pace upstream. The captain of the downriver tow was either more skillful or luckier than the one we had followed into Lansing, for he negotiated the sharp bend and slid between the bridge supports without a moment's hesitation.

Back at the boat, Vern and Darlene were waiting with a box of onions, potatoes, carrots, and cucumbers from their garden. We thanked them and showed them the mosquito house hanging above our table.

When our guests left, we said good-bye to Jan and Blackie and headed downriver. As we passed "Little Switzerland" I tooted our horn, but all that came forth was a feeble stutter. We waved our arms, but were not sure if the Smiths and Leichtmans saw us.

JAN AND BLACKIE

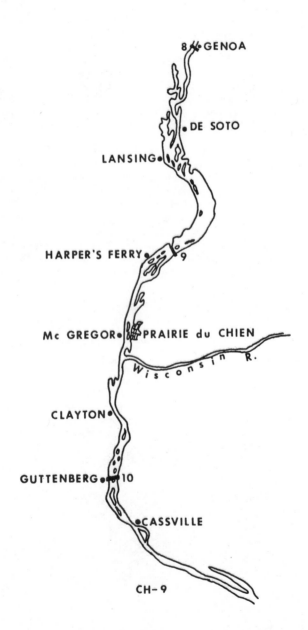

8 GENOA

DE SOTO

LANSING

HARPER'S FERRY 9

Mc GREGOR PRAIRIE du CHIEN

Wisconsin R.

CLAYTON

GUTTENBERG 10

CASSVILLE

CH-9

9

STERNWHEEL DON

As we motored slowly through Sunfish Lake on our way into the harbor at Prarie Du Chien, a large gull-like caspian tern folded its wings tightly against its body and plummeted thirty feet into the water, emerging a split second later with a fat fish flopping helplessly in it's strong orange beak.

"I wonder who's watching our terns back home?" asked Dee.

Did I detect a slight note of homesickness in her voice?

Inside the harbor we saw an elegant houseboat with the name **Islamorada** painted boldly across the stern, and wondered if the owners had brought it all the way from the Florida Keys. As we moved through the harbor we tried to imagine the significance of other boat names. A very old and slow-looking boat bore the obvious name – **Pokey.** Next to **Pokey** was **Ron-Dee-Voo**, surely meaning Ron and Dee together. **Missis Hippy** was easy. but we weren't sure whether **Sunnysideup** meant the owner always wanted sun on his deck, or described the way he liked his eggs. Our game ended as we found a vacant slip.

Paul and Naomi had vacationed in Islamorada and liked the area so much they had used the name for their houseboat. Paul told us this was their sixth, and largest, houseboat. On the wall, were color photographs of all their previous boats.

After our tour of the **Islamorada**, Paul asked what we were doing on the river. When we told him we had trailered **Sol Seaker** from California and were going to to write a book, he asked, "Are you familiar with the recent book by the Englishman."

"You mean OLD GLORY?" I replied.

"Yes, that's the one. I never did finish it. I didn't like the man's attitude or his approach to learning about the river. He never got acquainted with many real river people. He seemed to be looking for the past, so he ended up in old buildings which are mostly the sleeziest bars in town. I don't think his picture of the river is very accurate."

"We read a borrowed copy of OLD GLORY just before leaving home," I replied. "We've tried to buy a copy along the river to compare Raban's Mississippi with the one we are discovering, but all the bookstores are out."

"I have two copies at home," volunteered Paul, "I'd be happy to send one out to you if you can give me a place to send it. We're going home today, could send it out tomorrow."

We settled on the Eagle Point Marina at Dubuque. The harbormaster, Dan Nelson, was a friend of Paul's and would hold the book for us. "We'd like to pay you for the book," Dee said.

"No," replied Paul, "we collect books about the river, but we certainly don't need two OLD GLORY's."

"Do you have MISSISSIPPI ODYSSEY?" asked Dee.

"No, I never heard of that one."

"Come over for a tour of our boat and I'll give you our copy. We've finished it. 'Course you'll have to excuse our clutter, we don't have a vacuum so the carpet has a collection of river sand and other assorted debris."

"Would you like to borrow our vacuum?" asked Naomi.

We borrowed the vacuum and tidied **Sol Seaker** before Paul and Naomi came aboard. "We certainly envy you your trip," said Paul.

Naomi agreed, "We'd like to do that some day, but we still have two kids, fourteen and seventeen, to get through college."

"You have to wait until you have a little more gray hair," came Dee's stock answer as she fingered her "salt and pepper" locks.

After a hike around town, we left Prarie Du Chien at four in the afternoon for a short run, just three miles, across the river to McGregor. Bobby Myers, manager of the McGregor Marina asked if we were going to stay long.

"Just overnight," we replied.

"You've got to go up to Pike's Peak," he said. "There's a park up there that gives you the 'best view of the river anywhere.' That's my truck right there. Soon as you're ready come over. I'll give you the key and show you how to get there."

86

Not wanting to miss the local "best view of the river," we took Bobby up on his offer, marveling at the trust of the river people.

At Pike's Peak we were joined by a group of people on a weekend bus tour. One man, wearing a Guayabera shirt like the ones I buy in Mexico, said he and his wife often took trips to Mexico and he, like me, liked the loose fit and many pockets of these Mexican shirts.

Back at the marina, Bobby was waiting for us. He wanted to know all about our trip, and to share his experiences in bringing a gas powered boat upriver from New Orleans.

"Do you have an extra motor?" he asked.

"No," we replied.

"You sure ought to get one, especially for the lower river. It's a long way between gas stops, and there ain't hardly no marinas. You got a chart?"

"Yes."

"Let me show you the gas stops on the lower river." Bobby both reconfirmed and added to our chart notations.

Next morning, in a light rain, we glided slowly out of the harbor. The river was glassy smooth except for tiny pock marks and slowly expanding concentric circles left by the falling raindrops. The intersections of these expanding circles created a delicate pattern on grayish-green silk. Dior might fashion such fabric into an elegant garment.

Each time the rain stopped, the river changed to an expanse of smooth silvery silk, which was gently ruffled into tiny pleats by the slightest breeze. We moved very slowly, watching the ever-changing patterns as rain, calm and breezes sculptured and resculptured the river surface around us.

We stopped at Clayton. We wanted to visit as many "sleepy" river towns as possible. Clayton was more than sleepy, Clayton was taking a nap. In a half-hour walking tour, we saw no store, no post office, no people and only a few houses. We did see a beautiful old stone schoolhouse - the plaque on the door stated that it had been used for one hundred and three consecutive years before being abandoned. The town's few children, if there are any, probably are bussed to a consolidated school several miles away.

At the end of our walk we decided that the town was inhabited by a black cat, a gray cat and two barking dogs. Then we spotted a bar/short-order restaurant.

Inside were a grizzled old man at one end of the bar, a tired looking lady behind the counter, and a younger heavy-weight man sipping a beer. We ordered two hamburgers. The lady - who was cook, waitress, bartender and busperson - took our order without a word and headed for the kitchen.

As we ate, Dee, afraid to break the silence, whispered to me, "Shall I ask the waitress where all the people are?"

I thought for a moment, then whispered back, "No, this town's asleep, I think we'd better leave quietly or we might wake it up."

Without a word being spoken, we paid our check and walked out the door. Even **Sol Seaker's** engine seemed to whisper in fear of disturbing the peace, as we slowly and quietly took our leave. We were more than half a mile downstream before I pushed the throttle forward. Only the village of Lund had been quieter.

Again, the dark silky beauty of the placid river held our attention. The rain had stopped, and we were once again at our bridge helm. Although the current here is about two miles an hour, we couldn't tell that the water was moving except where it expanded into lazy V's behind the red and black buoys.

We slowed as we neared the Guttenberg Lock, undecided as to whether we should stop at the marina above the lock or go through, stop at Doug's dock for a quick tour of town, then continue to Cassville and STERNWHEEL DON.

As we discussed these options, the light flashed green and our decision was made for us. I headed into the lock, and Dee took her usual potty break. The lockmaster motioned to me to hurry. As I speeded up, Dee called from below, "Hey slow down. You're going too fast!"

When she returned to the bridge, I explained that the lockmaster had motioned me to hurry in. As soon as we were inside, the gates began to grind shut, and by the time we had grabbed the ropes, **Sol Seaker** was descending to the lower level where an eight-barge tow was waiting to lock up.

"I tried to call you on the radio, but you didn't answer," the lockmaster said as we descended.

"We were debating whether to lock down or not," Dee explained.

"I almost went down to get that waiting tow when I got no answer. I see you're from California, and you got motor bikes, and what's that thing?" He gestured toward the folded Porta-Bote.

"That's our dinghy," I said. "It folds for easy storage. We're going to the Gulf."

Just then a single blast from the lock's horn told us we were down and could leave the wall. As we pulled away the lockmaster said, "There's not too much room, but you can go by left of the barges."

I looked up and understood what he meant. The waiting tow was parked against the wall, his lead barges right up to the gates. There was a narrow opening through which we could easily maneuver, in smooth water. But the water was not smooth. The rapidly emptying lock chamber had the surface boiling in all directions.

In a turbulent situation, it is best to speed up so that cross currents do not have time to throw you sideways into the barge or into the opposing lock wall. Of course, if you **are** thrown against one or the other, the faster the speed the greater the chance of significant damage or injury. I sped up.

We felt the tug of the water as we kept near the center of the opening. The bow swung first toward the lock wall, then suddenly back toward the barges. Our speed was sufficient to propel us safely through. I turned the helm over to Dee and headed toward the head, marveling at how each encounter with a lock, wing dam, or towboat is a new adrenaline activating experience.

The sign above the rickety dock read, DOUG'S. We headed for the main street of Guttenberg (pronounced locally **Gut** tenberg).

A small brochure-map from the Chamber of Commerce proclaimed: "GUTTENBERG, IOWA - Loved by its residents, Remembered by its visitors."

We'll remember the well planned walking-tour that took us past the Albertus Building (built entirely by hand by Mr. and Mrs. Albertus in the early 1850's) and by numerous other well-restored stone and brick buildings from the 1850-1890 era.

The sign on a large stone building at 531 South River Street read, ENVIRONMENTAL OPTIONS INC., but the brochure indicated that the building, built in 1858, was originally used as a wheat warehouse by the Fleck Brothers. ". . .Farmers would come from miles around and wait in line for hours to discharge wheat to the warehouse. It was then steamboated downriver."

Our biggest surprise came as we entered KANN'S

IMPORT SHOP, 530 South River Street. Expecting a small shop with a few knick knacks, we found room after room of fine porcelain, metal, wood and glassware, imported from all over the world. Kann's could certainly rival any import shop we had seen in San Francisco.

"How can you carry such a vast inventory in such a small town?" I asked one of the neatly dressed clerks, noting that there were no customers except Dee and I.

"This is Monday," answered the clerk, "that's always our slowest day. Some weekends we have thousands of people go through the shop. Lots of people come here from Waterloo, Dubuque, Cedar Rapids and Davenport, Iowa. We also have regular customers from Madison, and La Crosse, Wisconsin. Many people come all the way from Chicago and Minneapolis. The import shop was started with one room and it has just kept on growing."

We were especially intrigued by the Christmas Room. Each year we buy John and Kathy a special Christmas tree ornament. Recently we have also purchased them for John's daughter, Amber, and for Kathy's husband, Ted. We selected wooden ones - a sailboat for John, an antique car for Ted, a giraffe for Amber and a girl on a swing for Kathy.

On our way to Doug's Restaurant for "take out" chicken, we passed the Press Building at 10 Schiller street. This three-story stone structure, built in 1863 by the Fleck Brothers as a flour warehouse, still bore red blotches caused by an 1894 fire which gutted the building and destroyed the fourth floor.

Before entering Doug's at number 7 Schiller, we noted the date, 1859, in metal numbers and the ornate cast iron cornices at the tops of the doors and windows. The brochure told us that Doug's was "...operated as a general merchandise store by the Fleck Brothers, tunnels were discovered leading from the cellar to the river when renovation took place."

Ten miles below Guttenberg, as we passed Cassville Slough, two young men in an old cabin cruiser hailed us. One stood on the deck giving what we now recognized as the universal distress signal - slowly raising and lowering outstretched arms. On our shakedown cruise, this signal, had we known it then, would have brought us help much sooner. I reduced speed and turned toward the boat in distress. "Are you having a problem?" I shouted.

"Our engine froze up," one of the young men replied. "It started knocking. I think we're low on oil."

"Can we call someone to help you?"

"Yes, call the little towboat over there, the **Tiny Flame**. That's my brother. Tell him our problem and ask when he can come to get us."

I stayed with the upper helm talking to the boys while Dee went below to call the **Tiny Flame**. When she came out she said to the boys, "He's busy now and can't come until shift change, about six o'clock. It's five fifteen now." Quietly, to me, she said, "I don't think he's very happy about having to come help them."

The boys thanked us and we continued the short distance to the entrance of Jack Oak Slough, just below Cassville. As we passed the **Tiny Flame**, we agreed that this was an appropriate name for the smallest towboat we had seen. Smaller than **Sol Seaker**, the **Tiny Flame** was a rectangular steel box topped by a square wooden tower holding the pilot house. Except for its white color, it might have been mistaken for an oversized channel marker, yet this diminutive towboat was busily pushing a loaded coal barge toward the Wisconsin Power Plant.

We finally realized that the black, granular material we had first seen transported by the **Sioux** in Prescott, was coal, and not asphalt. Every town seems to have a coal-fired power plant that consumes great quantities of this "black gold."

"If that little fellow was in a train yard it might be called a switch engine," Dee commented. Later we were to learn that these little towboats were, indeed, called "switching tows."

Just as each encounter with a lock or towboat is a unique experience, so is each landing at a new harbor. The harbor at Cassville is about a quarter of a mile down Jack Oak Slough. From experience, we knew these sloughs could be very shallow. A red buoy marked the entrance, but there were no standard markers to separate deep water from shallow water once inside the slough. The water surface, darkened by the shadows of a sinking sun, gave no clues.

Ahead, a strange configuration of sticks served as the first marker. It was red, meaning we should keep it to starboard - "red, right, returning." Closer inspection showed the marker to be a crudely shaped arrow pointing toward the right side of the slough.

If we were to heed the color we would keep the marker to our starboard. But if we were to heed the point of the arrow we would keep the marker to our port.

91

We kept the marker to port as we moved slowly by. Next, we were greeted by a series of slender sticks protruding from the water's surface in an arrangement that could mark a section of shallow water to our left. Ahead was another arrow, this one yellow, but also directing us to the right. Following these innovative channel markers, we arrived safely at Cassville, Wisconsin where we would meet Donald Fluetsch.

I had made contact with Don by writing the following letter of inquiry to the postmaster in Cassville.

Postmaster
Cassville, Wisconsin

Since I could find no listing for a Chamber of Commerce in your Community, I hope that you can help me by providing the information I am requesting, or by giving this letter to someone in your town who can provide this information.

I am interested in knowing about boating and fishing on the Mississippi River in your area.

1. What months are best for safe boating (weather, etc.)?

2. Are there marinas, launching facilities, berths, etc.?

3. Are there marine gas stations, boat repair shops. etc.?

4. Are there any special boating and/or fishing regulations for your area?

5. When is fishing best? What kinds of fish are caught?

I am also interested in any information about your town - historical, pageants, celebrations, etc.

Thanks for your help.

Our letter had been given to Don because of his interest in the history of boating. His reply contained a card proclaiming: STERNWHEEL DON, Collector of River Lore.

Dear Mr. Parker;
I will try to answer your questions first.

1. Starting late in May to September is the best for traveling the Mississippi. Earlier the river may be

running fresh from the snow melt up north. Sometimes we get a raise in June but not bad.

2. There are marinas all along the river just wanting to sell you fuel and supplies. Gas is more expensive on the river tho. Your boat is probably a deep hull, so make sure that you stay in the channel, between the buoys. With a deep hull you may not be able to land any place, but if you carry a dinghy, you can use it to come ashore. The marinas have deep water.

3. The Coast Guard has a list of regulations for the inland waters. You will need an out-of-state fishing license for each state that you want to fish in.

In the spring, walleye are caught below the wing dams, and there is any number of other places to fish for pan fish and pike. There are rough fish in the river also, but a carp cannot be beat if you know how to cook or smoke it. You could put in on the Upper, Upper Mississippi River, which is just below the I-694 bridge above Minneapolis. Then you would come thru the Upper St. Anthony Falls Lock, and then the Lower St. Anthony Falls Lock, then you are in the Upper Mississippi. The Upper starts at Cairo, Ill. and goes to the above length. I put a rubber raft in at this spot in Mpls, and I was going to go to St. Paul, but when I got to Lock 1, I was so hot that I had to quit. I hope someday to finish the trip to St. Paul.

Most of the cities along the river have museums, and one may run into a celebration any time along the river. The people are all friendly and happy to see some new faces.

Last year a group of Swiss floated from Hastings Minnesota to New Orleans.

If you pass Cassville, look me up, and I will steer you from New Orleans to New York to Lake Erie, then down the Welland Canal and up another canal to Georgian Bay, then back to Lake Michigan to Chicago, then down the Illinois river to the Mississippi. I have post cards of the trip. I have been illustrating the rivers with cards and pictures since 1970.

Sincerely,

As we approached the gas dock, a young woman called to us from the door of her house, "Can I help you?"

93

"We're looking for a place to dock overnight." I replied.

"I'm all filled up."

"We're from California," I said. "We really want to visit Cassville."

"Oh, you're the ones from California. Mr. Fluetsch has been down here every day. Said he's expecting you. Wanted us to keep a lookout for you. I guess you can tie up at the end of the gas dock."

We made **Sol Seaker** fast and ran a long extension cord to an outlet on a pole outside the marina store. The cord hung down into the muddy water, making Dee nervous as she cooked some of our gift vegetables on her fifth burner while I called Don to tell him we had arrived. I learned that Don was on the night shift and would sleep until noon the next day. I made arrangements for us to come by in the afternoon.

We had just settled down to our feast when it began to rain - again. Soon we were experiencing a thunderstorm similar to the one in Prescott, but unlike Prescott, here we were not protected by a covered berth.

We were trying to hear the announcer on the Monday Night Football game over the sound of rain, driven by forty-mile-an-hour winds, and intermittent claps of thunder when a new sound captured our attention. The sound of a stream of water splashing onto one of the dinette seats. The water was pouring through a hole I had drilled to mount a bracket for our depth sounder.

As Dee placed a pan under the flow, I fought my way through the wind and rain to the bridge. Lying on my stomach in a two-inch puddle, I located the hole beneath the helm and stuffed a rag into it. Unfortunately when making the hole, I hadn't anticipated rain that would form a lake on the bridge deep enough to breech the board that protected the storage area.

My makeshift seal seemed to work, but we left the pan under the hole as an extra precaution. No sooner had we plugged one leak, when another started. This time from under the windshield, directly onto the bed. The dishpan was used to catch this drip. We then noticed water seeping in around a small window over the sink. After we stuffed towels under the window to absorb the water, the rain let up, but thunder and lightning continued, and the wind grew stronger. I checked our dock lines frequently, concerned that they might come loose, or worse, that the small floating dock might break from its tenuous moorings. As the wind, lightning and thunder played havoc with our nerves, we had visions of **Sol Seaker**, dock and gas pump all drifting down the river and breaking apart on a wing dam. Sometime during the night, the storm abated.

The next morning we took a bike tour of Cassville, until renewed rain drove us back to the boat.

The card enclosed in Don's letter had given rise to a mental image of a man in his mid-sixties, retired, six feet two, neatly bearded, distinguished looking, smoking a pipe and wearing a captain's hat. In short, the stereotype of an old-time riverboat captain.

The real Don Fluetsch was about 59, rotund, five feet six, with a round jolly face. If you put a stocking cap on his balding head and gave him a red suit and beard, he would be the perfect Santa Claus. Evelyn was about his height and "pleasingly plump."

"I thought, perhaps, from your card you had an antique shop or something," said Dee after we had walked beneath our large umbrella to the Fluetsch's house on East Bluff Street.

"No, I work at Dairyland Power," replied Don. "Right now I'm on the 8:00 P.M. to 4:00 A.M. shift. I've always been interested in the river. I had a boat years ago, but now I just collect things. I go to antique shops and pick up things that have to do with boats, especially on the Mississippi River. Mostly I collect picture post cards and old newspaper clippings. I look at these cards and do research on the boats and feel like I'm really there."

While Don talked, my eyes searched every nook and cranny of the living room for some sign of his riverboat hobby. The only visible evidence was a beautiful night-picture of a sternwheeler churning upriver, floodlight blazing. "Would you like to see some of my collection?" asked Don, half reluctantly.

"Would we! We've been looking forward to learning about your 'river lore' ever since we received your letter last February."

"It's down in the basement. It's too messy to keep upstairs."

Evelyn seemed a bit embarrassed as we headed down the narrow steep stairway into Don's "messy" library, research lab, and photography studio.

"Here's my filing cabinet," Don stated, pointing to an old refrigerator standing against the back wall. The

95

opened door revealed stacks of large binders, each
filled to overflowing with picture postcards, news clippings and typewritten information about river boats on
the Mississippi, Hudson, Columbia, and even the California Delta where we had purchased **Sol Seaker**.

"What would you like to see? "You won't have time
to look at all of them."

"The Mississippi," we said in unison.

"We'll start with these," said Don, as he pulled
out four fat binders. "Let's take them upstairs to the
dining table."

As we looked through the volumes, Don told us
stories about each boat. "Often a single boat would be
used for several different purposes during its lifetime.
Usually it was renamed by each new owner." We smiled
remembering our experiences of naming **Sol Seaker**.

Don knew about all the tragedies - fires, sinkings,
boiler explosions - that had been so common in the
steamboat days.

Long before we could look through even these four
volumes, dinner time approached. "Would you like to
take a boat ride with us up to Guttenberg for dinner?"
we asked.

Don was eager, but Evelyn was less than thrilled.
"I've only been out in a small boat," she said. "I was
scared to death. I don't know how to swim."

When we assured her that riding inside the cabin
would be like riding in a car, she reluctantly agreed.

It was already getting late, and although facing
into a misty north wind, I put **Sol Seaker** up on a plane
at twenty-five miles an hour, flattening the slight chop
with our weight and speed. I glanced periodically at
Evelyn, noting that her hands were clinched knuckle-
white. I tried to keep the conversation in a light
vein.

About half way to Guttenberg we rounded a bend and
realized that the north wind wasn't the only thing meeting us head on. A half mile in front of us was a fully
loaded tow coming straight for us. As I slowed quickly,
Evelyn let out a small gasp. Pretending that I was as
"cool as a cucumber," I lifted the microphone and called
the captain on sixteen.

"Skipper, do you have six?" came the reply.

I switched to six. "I'm the cabin cruiser ahead of
you. Which side should I pass on?"

"Skipper, why don't you pass on my starboard.

That's the black can side. That's the two whistle side, Skipper."

"Understand," I replied, as I steered **Sol Seeker** farther over toward the left bank. "I'll stand by on sixteen."

In a few moments the voice of the tow captain came over the radio again. "Skipper of the **Sol Seeker**, or whatever your boat is, yall don't have to move over that far. Wouldn't want you to get tangled up in one of them rock dams."

Although, according to the Army Corps charts, I was not in an area of wing dams, I slowly moved closer to the passing tow. A glance at Evelyn told me that a large towboat was the last thing she wanted to meet.

"There's lots of room," I said, feigning confidence. My comment must have worked as there was a sigh of relief from Evelyn's direction and her clinched fists relaxed a little.

The landing at Doug's didn't help Evelyn's nerves any, or mine. I tried to come in at the same angle I had the day before, but the wind and current made this impossible. On the third try we docked safely, if not expertly.

We ate hurriedly. The rain had stopped when we headed back to Cassville. Our fast trip upriver and quick meal made it possible for us to travel back at a more leisurely pace.

Finally Evelyn relaxed and began to enjoy the beautiful Mississippi River scenery. "Tomorrow you must have dinner with us," she said. "I'll bet you're ready for a home cooked meal."

"I'll pick you up at 10:00," Don said. "Then you can look at more post cards."

In the dim light of approaching dawn, I was startled awake by the roar of an outboard motor bursting to sudden life nearby. In my half-asleep state, I heard the unseen boat go tearing off, full-bore, into the backwaters of Jack Oak Slough.

Dee was awake also. We kissed good morning, then both fell asleep again. In what must have been only a few moments, a second outboard came to life. As the motor was revved several times, gassy fumes began to enter through **Sol Seeker**'s open windows. I drew myself up on one elbow and watched as two people headed down the slough in a fourteen foot jon boat. There would be no more sleep this morning.

97

Dee turned on the radio, hoping for some "easy listening" music, instead she caught the tail end of the Community Calendar. One announcement amused us, "Tuesday evening the La Leche League will meet. ...The topic will be the advantages of breast feeding. To be followed by snacks and refreshments."

We switched stations.

"This is Reverend Raymond Brady of the Bible Brotherhood Church. Today I want you to meet Brother Billy Starr. Brother Billy is running for Sheriff, and I want to encourage everyone to git out and vote for the candidates of all the offices. Brother Billy is not going to campaign on the radio today, but he is going to talk to you about the Word of God. Brother Starr."

"Folks, my text for today is Moses on the Mountain talking to God and receiving the tablets. '...Then I cast it in the fire and out came that Golden Calf...' Now Aaron would not accept the responsibility for the golden calf, the idol that they were worshiping. Aaron didn't accept the responsibilty. **Responsibility**, that's the important word. Everyone must accept the responsibility. I urge you to accept your responsibility by getting out to vote on Tuesday. Accept your responsibility."

"Now they's lots of different kinds of irresponsible men. They's the ones that's late to work; them that put money in their own pockets or drive when drinking; or them that don't try to learn. Accept **your** responsibility."

"Thank you Brother Starr for your Word of God. And I urge each of you to git out and vote on Tuesday. And folks, remember that Billy Starr is running for sheriff of the county. And I just wanted him to share with you today his belief in God. He's a member of our church and I wanted you to get to know him better."

The only thing missing was the tag that said, "This has been an unpaid political announcement by the Bible Brotherhood for Starr Committee." We turned the radio off, preferring our own conversation and snuggling.

Don very kindly drove us to the post office and to a small local plant which manufactured plastic cones for radio speakers. We had happened by the plant on our bike ride the day before. Roger, the foreman, had given us one of the speaker cones and in our conversation the subject of old hand pumps had come up.

"I have a couple of them around the house," Roger
98

had said. "I might be willin' to sell one. I'll bring it in tomorrow. You can look at it and decide if you want it."

We looked at the pump in the back of Roger's pick-up. "I called the two antique stores to see what pumps was worth. One said fifty dollars and the other said probably fifteen. So I don't know what to ask."

"Would you take twenty-five?" I asked.

"That would be okay."

At Don and Evelyn's we eagerly poured through several more volumes of postcards, pictures and histori-cal articles. "What's that?" I asked pointing to an old photograph of a huge log raft with a large steamboat at the back and a smaller one fastened sideways to the front of the raft.

"Well, in them days," Don said, "when they rafted logs and lumber downriver, them big log rafts couldn't be tied together tight like today's steel barges can. So the towboat pushin' the raft of logs couldn't control them too good. They couldn't make them turn around bends without breakin' apart. So this 'bow boat' was tied to the front of the raft sideways. When they was goin' straight ahead the bow boat was pushed along in front. When they wanted to turn the raft, the bow boat would move forward to move the front of the raft in one direction and it would go in reverse to turn the raft in the other direction."

As he had promised in his letter, Don had cards and stories to show and tell us how a boat could leave New York, go up the Hudson River, through Lake Champlain, into the St. Lawrence River, to Lake Erie, then through the Trent-Severen canal system to Georgian Bay, then Lake Superior, Lake Michigan, the Illinois River and back to the Mississippi.

We were hooked and vowed that someday we would make the complete circuit, if God was willing.

The amount of historical information contained in Don's volumes and in Don's head was staggering. In all, we thumbed through only eight of the twenty-five or thirty volumes in the old refrigerator. Don's materials had been photocopied by several museums for display and publication.

"What do you plan to do with these?" I asked.

"Well, when I retire, I'd like to give talks about river boats. You know, at organizations and schools."

I attached my camera to Don's makeshift photocopy

stand and took pictures of the log rafts and bow boats. "Dinner's ready," called Evelyn.

We sat down to our first real home-cooked meal in several weeks. It's not easy to prepare a full dinner on our hot plate.

As I ate the roast beef and gravy, potatoes, cabbage, tiny carrots and homemade beet pickles, a twinge of sadness tore at my heart. This meal reminded me of the thousands of similar meals my mother had prepared with such loving hands when she was alive. When the homemade apple pie arrived, it was all I could do to hold back a tear.

After dinner Dee and Evelyn did the dishes while Don and I looked at one more binder. Evelyn then showed us the beautiful needlepoint that fills her time when Don is occupied with his boat hobby. "Of course you can see just by looking at us that I also love to cook," she said.

At 2:45 we reluctantly prepared to leave the warm hospitality of Don and Evelyn Fluetsch for a planned 3:30 departure. Evelyn loaded us down with homemade pickles and Don gave us some duplicate photographs and some brochures he had collected for us. One of the brochures was about the **Mississippi Queen** and **Delta Queen**.

"We saw the **Mississippi Queen** at Red Wing," Dee said.

"Did you get to tour her?" Don asked.

"No."

"If you ever get a chance, she's a beauty. And you know the **Delta Queen** is from where you live in California."

At the boat, we said our good-byes and promised to keep in touch. Our list of "keep in touch" people was growing daily.

As we prepared to cast off, the young man that had waved to us from his disabled boat, roared up in a small outboard. "Do you know who owns that old houseboat half sunk up there?" he asked Ron, the marina owner. "It's got a motor just like mine and I wondered if I could buy it for parts."

Ron said a name I didn't hear. The young man wished us a good trip and roared off in the direction of the derelict houseboat. Ron turned to us and said, "That engine's been under water several times, I don't think it'd be any good."

100

Another outboard came up to the dock with a man and woman. The woman wanted to show Ron her fish. "It's a northern," she said. "I caught him crappie fishin' with just a cane pole. Didn't think I was ever gonna land him." She held up a beautiful, ten pound Northern Pike.

I was wishing I could stay and do some fishing as we nosed **Sol Seaker** out into Jack Oak Slough, and headed toward the river.

When we drew even with the half-sunken houseboat, a tousled young head raised from the engine area. The young man waved, shouted more well wishes, then warned, "You know you need to be careful stopping to help strangers on the river. They could be pirates." His head sunk back into the engine compartment.

Ron, Don and Evelyn were still gazing after us as we rounded the bend and moved out of sight. In Don's eyes we had seen the same expression of envy and longing we had seen in the eyes of many of our new river friends, but Evelyn showed no such longing. She was obviously happy that it was us, and not her, aboard as **Sol Seaker** moved toward our next adventure on the Mighty Mississippi.

"What did he mean about pirates?" Dee asked.

STERNWHEEL DON

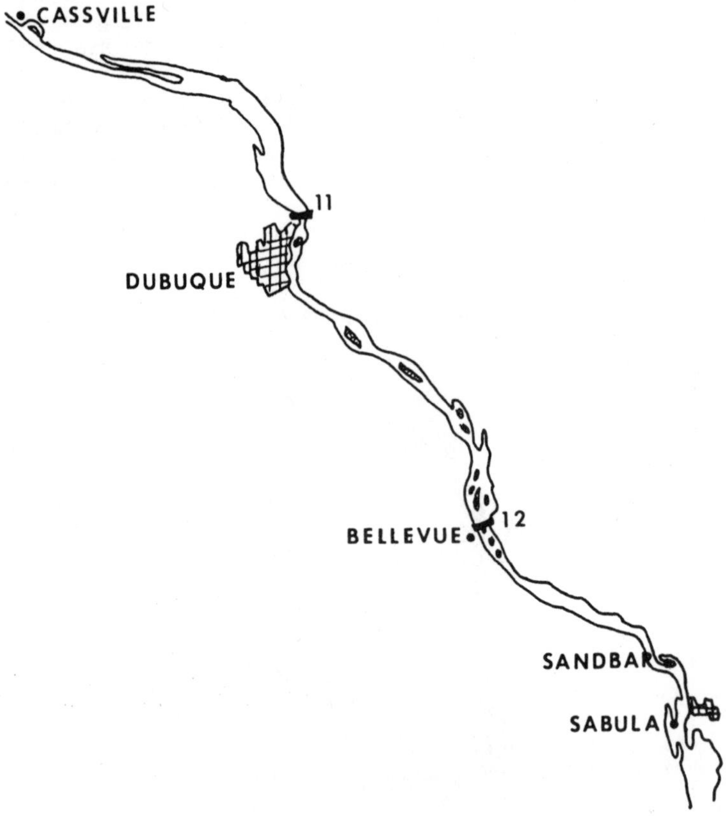

CASSVILLE

11

DUBUQUE

BELLEVUE • 12

SANDBAR

SABULA

CH–10·11

10

ROCKIN', RAKIN' & SCRAPIN'

It was September 15 when we left Cassville at mile marker 606. We had traveled just two hundred forty-one miles in fifteen days. At this rate it would take us more than four months to complete our voyage. To be home for Thanksgiving, we had to increase our downriver speed, but, not wanting to increase speed at the risk of missing out on the adventures the river had to offer, we tucked this information into the backs of our minds. Things have a way of working out!

In the first six miles below Cassville, the channel made four sweeping meanders past the lower end of Jack Oak Slough on the left and Bunker Chute on the right. At the tiny community of Waupeton, we began to hug the Iowa shore with the Chicago, Milwaukee, St. Paul and Pacific Railroad running so close that we could almost touch the passing freight trains.

At Mile 596, Finley's Landing was little more than a notation on our chart. At 592, Specht's Auto Ferry traveled between the Iowa and Wisconsin shores by way of the Potosi Canal, a small channel dredged through an extensive stump field. Though the river below Waupeton was wide, about two miles, treacherous wing dams constricted the navigable channel to a narrow ribbon which ran along the Iowa shore for ten miles, then meandered among the stump fields before moving back to the Iowa side at lock 11, at the city of Dubuque. A strong wind from astern pushed us into the lock, bouncing us off the wall.

At Eagle Point Marina we picked up the copy of OLD GLORY from Dan Nelson and spent a quiet, but very cold, evening reading. In the morning, we lost our bearings for a moment as we glided slowly along Hamm Island. Directly ahead was an arching highway bridge which did not show on our charts. I remembered that the upper river chart was published in 1978. This new bridge was near the Wisconsin/Illinois state boundary, and at 10:20

A.M., we left behind the second of the two states that had flanked the river at our starting point.

Barges and commercial docks lined the Iowa shore. Not since St. Paul had we seen such a busy waterfront.

Near the railroad bridge, we passed the Old Shot Tower that had been used to make lead shot for Civil War firearms until someone discovered that the same spherical shape could be obtained by dropping molten lead into a few inches of water instead of ninety-feet through the air.

We scanned the shoreline looking for the entrance to Ice Harbor, where we wanted to visit the Riverboat Museum and tour the **William M. Black**, one of the last of the giant Army Corps sidewheel steam dredges. Where Ice Harbor should have been, we saw nothing but levee and the high wall that protected the city when the river reached flood stage.

Thinking we had passed the entrance, we turned **Sol Seaker** and retraced our watery steps under the railroad bridge and past the Shot Tower, but all we found was a large and busy commercial harbor. We turned again. As we neared the old highway bridge Dee exclaimed, "There's an excursion boat! Where did it come from?"

It was as though the sternwheel, **Spirit of Dubuque**, had come through the impenetrable wall. By tracing her wheelwash, we spotted a large metalic gate set in the wall. The entrance to the harbor faced downriver and was thus obscured until we were beyond it. The entrance, similar to a lock gate, could be closed during periods of flood water, thus protecting Ice Harbor and the lower streets of the city. Today the gate was open.

There was the **William M. Black** on the right, and on the left, grain barges, and one of the Coast Guard buoy tenders which ply the river checking and maintaining the various navigational aids.

The museum was an arrangement of displays of various methods of river transportation from canoes, to keelboats and, of course, steamboats. The **Black** was a marvel of engineering whose giant vacuum cleaner heads could suck up great quantities of river mud and sand as easily as our Hoover can lift soil from a carpet. Although it was not now operational, we could imagine the noise and vibration that must constantly emanate from the great steam engine and the labyrinth of powerful suction mechanisms. Surely there was little peace and quiet for men working aboard this mechanical monster. ·

Downriver from Dubuque we saw great numbers of monarch butterflies, and took pictures of wing dams so near the surface they were clearly marked by logs and branches that had been captured by the underwater rocks. Opposite Wise Lake, we met the **L. J. Sullivan** headed upriver with fifteen empty barges.

At mile 557, we could see lock 12 and the small town of Bellevue, Iowa. Entering the lock, we faced into a gentle breeze - ideal for an easy locking, right? Wrong! The wind blew our bow against the wall, leaving both me, at the bridge helm, and Dee, at the stern, too far away to reach the waiting lines. I backed away and tried again, and failed again. The third time I finally made it, tending my line with head down in embarassment.

We stopped at a small dock below a tired looking building proclaiming itself "Wayne and Rita's". Two unkempt and unsavory looking characters, fishing from the rip-rap just upstream from the dock, seemed to be eying our bicycles and folding dinghy as we made our way up the steep concrete walkway into a dingy, ill-equipped combination cafe, fish market and bait store.

A chubby girl of twelve, almost as unkempt as the store, greeted us as we entered. Inside was a small eating counter, which didn't appear to have been used for that purpose recently, and at one end, a meat case contained smoked catfish, smoked carp and some catfish that had been fresh at one time. We bought cans of coke from the cooler, and headed toward town.

As we walked, we looked at each other, then turned back. "Let's go to the marina below town," Dee said. "I don't trust those two men down by our boat."

"Right," I said. "Let's go. It'll be farther to walk to town, but we need the exercise anyway." And thus it was that we came to spend a pleasant night at Point Pleasant. As we pulled into the dock, we were greeted by a young boy. It appeared that in Bellevue, Iowa, the riverside businesses were all operated by twelve year olds. Age of the person in charge was, however, the only similarity between Wayne and Rita's and Point Pleasant.

Point Pleasant was a small marina with gas dock and a few slips. About twenty flat-bottom rental boats lined the shore, some with tilted outboard motors in place. Several more motors were on a rack along the outside wall of the store. When we told the young man that we wanted to stay overnight, he took us into the

104

store where he phoned his father to see if there was
room for us.

Junior (as we later learned to call him) took an
obvious pride in being able to look after the family
business. While we waited for Junior's father, Cliff,
we looked around the well-kept bait and tackle store.
The wall hung heavy with different kinds of fishing
lures, lines and rods. There were bins of sinkers and
shelves of life vests, rope, anchors and other boating
and fishing supplies. At one end was a small gift shop.
Among the knick-knacks were several Mexican lamps of the
kind we had purchased in Tijuana twenty-five years ago.
Purportedly, these were made from old metal motor oil
cans that were cut and bent into scrolls.

Still waiting for Cliff, Dee asked Junior if there
was a good restaurant in town. "The best is right
there," he said, pointing to a building across the drive
and up the bank from the store. "That's why I spend so
much time up there after I come home from school."

I caught Dee's smile as she looked again at
Junior's chubby body. She was thinking that perhaps he
spent a bit too much time up in his mother's restaurant.

Cliff arrived and told us we could stay at the far
end of the gas dock. "I don't run no 'lectricity out on
the gas dock. It's too dangerous." Cliff's speech was
obviously not Iowan, but rather from someplace farther
south. "I collect about $2.00 for overnight. I got a
Army Corps boat comin' in early fer fuel, about 7:30 or
8:00 in the mornin', so you may have to move your boat
to make room. They's surveyin' the bottom of this pool
all the way between lock twelve and lock thirteen. They
go back an' forth across the channel with a recordin'
depth sounder. They git a picture of the bottom, then
they know where they have to dredge to keep the channel
open. They take about ninety gallon ever day. I shore
don't want to miss out on a ninety gallon sale. Some
folks won't take the government credit cards, but me,
hell, I'll take any credit card if I can sell ninety
gallon of gas."

We moved to the extreme end of the gas dock, where
we saw, at the next dock, a strange looking craft. A
simple open pontoon boat had been enclosed to make a
cabin. For stability, or because ·the additional weight
had made it too heavy, two large aircraft wing tanks had
been added as outriggers. The entire boat appeared to
have been made from scavenged materials.

105

We were still laughing about the strange craft as we walked toward town. A park ran along the river side of Water Street. On the left were well-cared-for homes giving way to small businesses - a convenience market, ice cream stand, clothing store, hardware, law office, several antique stores, and service stations.

First Street, parallel and a block away from Water Street, also contained small business establishments. The residential district was beyond First Street away from the river. Many of the streets were gravel. To our surprise, the business district streets were lined with parking meters. Two hours for ten cents, twelve minutes for a penny.

No bridge crosses the river at Bellevue. Residents who want to get to the Illinois side must go upriver twenty-two miles to Dubuque or downriver twenty-two miles to Sabula.

Although it was near dinner time, we purchased red raspberry soft ice cream cones on our way back to the boat. Who says dessert should always follow the meal?

Outside the Point Pleasant restaurant we met Elsie, Junior's mother. "Junior sure raved about your cooking," Dee said. "He really seems to take a lot of pride in helping run the store. He said he had eaten uptown a couple of times, but told us never to go there because the best restaurant's right here."

A look of pride lit up Elsie's face.

"We're from Arkansas," volunteered Elsie, "but we lived about twenty years in Chicago. All you can see in Chicago is brick walls here and brick walls here and brick walls here." She gestured in several directions. "Then you git here an' look out an' see all that." She pointed toward the river. "It's shore like heaven bein' here, after Chicago. Why, it's somethin' different ever' day. The river's always a changin'. I never noticed things like that 'til I got here an' had time to look. Yes, after Chicago, it's jist like Heaven."

"Why, we see all kinds of birds," she continued. "Purple martins nest in our little bird house. Last year they had a late hatch. We wondered how them babies would ever git big enough to go all the way south. One day the mama pushed them babies right out of the nest an' next day they jist flew away. This year they're already gone. That little house shore does look empty."

"Do any of the birds stay through the winter?" I asked.

"Yeah. We got cardinals 'n jays 'n goldfinches 'n orioles. No, I think the orioles leave too. I cain't remember. This is the first time I've really had a chance to watch the birds and I cain't remember all of them. Well I gotta' go in now," she continued, "Yall comin' in fer supper? I been feelin' poorly the last two days so I don't have nothin' special. When I'm feelin' good I always make somethin' special. Sometimes I stir up a meat loaf. We always got shrimp 'n chicken 'n catfish. But I ain't got nothin' special."

"Do you close in the winter?" I wondered.

"No. We close maybe two weeks. We don't git too much trade, but we git some town people and some ice fishermen. I'm most famous for my good breakfasts. Get town people out fer breakfast."

We followed Elsie into the restaurant and took an end table where we could observe the entire room. The atmosphere was the relaxed "down home" variety. The "folks" who came into Elsie's were true river folks who hunted and fished in season, who came in after work for a beer or two before going home, who kidded and joked with each other and were quick to let a stranger join in the joviality.

Three men came in together and ordered beer. They were talking about fishing and about a car that had transmission problems. One man was the mechanic who was working on the car. "Some of them gears has the teeth broke plumb off," he said. "Gonna' cost him about $450.00 to git it fixed."

"I guess the Corps'll pay for it," said one of the other men, "seein's how it's used by them three feller's that are doin' the bottom survey."

After a couple of beers the men began to kid each other about getting drunk before going home. Two of the men left, the mechanic stayed. Elsie asked him, "Is Linda commin' back?"

"I doan know."

"Well, she left that glass of coke. Hardly drunk any of it. That's such a waste. She's always a doin' that."

In a few minutes Linda came in and finished the coke. Linda is the mechanic's wife, and daughter of Carl, the former owner of the marina. Carl still owns an auto repair shop on Water Street just up from the restaurant.

Elsie brought our food and stood next to our table.

"This place was really run down when we bought it," Elsie said in a quiet voice so the others couldn't hear. Then more loudly, "We bought the marina, restaurant, fishing store and a mobile home a year and a half ago. We been a rakin' an' a scrapin' to git the place goin' good. We paid $75,000 fer the place. It should be paid for in eight and a half years more."

While we ate, two men and two boys (aged four and eight) came in and sat at the table near Cliff. Cliff began teasing the younger boy. The boy was teasing right back. It was a pleasant sight watching this easy give and take which lets children know they are loved, respected and important. Cliff grabbed the boy's shirt and pulled it over his head exposing his pink stomach. "Here's how an ol' crawdad pinches." He nipped the boys flesh between thumb and forefinger.

The boy pulled free, a red mark disappearing beneath the falling shirt. Both boys ran behind the counter, the older one had something in his hand. When they came back to the end of the counter, Cliff said in a serious but pleasant tone, "Let's don't play around behind the counter, all right? They's dangerous things there could hurt you. Them glass doors on the pop case an' things to trip over an' such."

The boys accepted the warning in good humor and returned to the table.

After a beer, the two men got up to leave. One of the men was looking for his hat. Finally, the older boy pulled it out from the end of the counter where he had hidden it. He walked up to the man and extended the cap in his hand. Just as the man reached for the cap, the boy dropped it on the floor and ran out the door, laughing. The younger boy followed.

"Shit," said Cliff, "Them boys shore is full of life ain't they?"

"Full of life," I thought, was certainly an apt phrase to describe the mood at Point Pleasant.

As we left, we told Elsie we'd be back in the morning for one of her famous breakfasts. Cliff said, "Yall don't worry none in the mornin'. If you feel yore boat a movin' it'll jist be me a movin' it to make room for the boat comin' in fer gas."

That night, the river too was "full of life" as a thunder storm and several passing towboats kept **Sol Seaker** bouncing up and down.

Early morning fishermen woke us long before the

survey boat came in for fuel. One group, a black family,
pulled in with a late model car and a beautiful boat
with a seventy-five horse Chrysler outboard motor. A
heavy, elderly, crippled woman seemed to be the matri-
arch. After extensive preparations, they backed the
trailer down the ramp. Before getting the boat completely into the water, the car stopped suddenly, the
boat rolling off the easy loading trailer at a steep
angle. I held my breath as the boat hit the water stern
first, expecting the motor to hit bottom and damaging
the lower unit. Fortunately, the water was deep enough.
The boat bounced a little water over the stern, then
floated upright alongside the dock.

As we headed for breakfast, we stopped to ask the
family about their planned fishing trip. Both men were
standing by the boat, hands on hips. The older woman
laboriously made her way to the front of the boat and
sat in the driver's seat. The younger woman pumped the
bulb on the fuel line to prime the carburetor. The two
women tried unsuccessfully to start the boat as the two
men continued to watch.

On our outboard at home, we have to choke the engine before it will start. I suspected the same was
true of this engine, but I'm always reluctant to make a
suggestion about another person's machinery. We wished
them "good fishing" and continued toward the restaurant.
I heard the old lady say, "Sometimes we has to wipe off
the plugs. I been tellin' him to put in new plugs."

Looking out the window later, we could see that
they had the cover off the engine and one of the men was
inspecting the spark plugs. Our food came, diverting our
attention from the would be fisherpeople. It wasn't
until we were finishing breakfast that the younger black
man entered the restaurant and said quietly to Cliff, "I
think we need yore hep."

Cliff left to go down to the dock and I decided to
follow along. I still had it in my mind that they were
not choking the engine as they should. Cliff took one
look at the engine with the cover off, then held down
the choke lever with his hand and told the old woman to
"try it." The engine sputtered to life, then died.
Cliff went to the controls and pulled out a button to
disengage the gears. He then turned the key and pushed
in. The engine coughed a few times then began to purr.
Cliff said, "Here, let me show you somethin' about this
engine. Yall have to pull this out, then when you start

it give it a little gas with the lever and push in on the key to choke it. It won't start 'til you choke it."

They thanked Cliff for his help. As we turned to go back to the restaurant I heard the old woman saying half under her breath, "I forgot to choke it. That's what I done. I forgot to choke it."

Back at the restaurant, I found Dee and Elsie in conversation. "We got four boys," Elsie was saying. "Three are grown. Junior was a surprise. An' like a lot of surprises, we've enjoyed him more'n the others. He really works hard around here."

"He certainly is proud of this place," Dee said.

Later, as we headed on downriver, we talked about the subtle and gradual changes we had been experiencing as we moved south, changes in speech, and in the people themselves. We seemed to be moving from a formal and conservative environment to one that is more open, informal and relaxed.

We marveled at how similar this transition is to the one we experienced several years ago as we traveled by VW camper south from Scotland and England to France, Italy and Greece. We wondered if it was the colder climate that influenced people toward formality. It certainly seemed that everywhere we traveled, warm climate and informality went together; Spain, Italy, Greece, Mexico, The Caroline Islands, Guam and Saipan.

As happened more frequently than we liked, a misty rain was falling when we left Bellevue. Once again we reluctantly drove from our "T.V. screen" cabin. Dee took the helm and as luck would have it, around the first bend we came face to face with a tow of fifteen empty barges. Since we were not anxious to meet this tow in the narrow wing dam infested area along Bowman Island, we looked at the chart for a safe spot to pull outside the channel and wait for the tow to pass. We selected a spot several hundred yards above the first charted wing dam.

Even though it was still raining, I went up to the flying bridge to take control where I could make use of the depth sounder mounted there. I moved slowly toward the right bank. The sounder showed a very safe depth of twenty feet. Dee came up to the bridge. It began to rain harder. I had my eye on the sounder, when a strange premonition inside said, "look up!"

I did, just in time to spot the tell-tale ripples that marked an uncharted wing dam just a few feet down-

stream from the drifting **Sol Seaker**. I quickly headed
upstream away from the treacherous rock pile. At a safe
distance, I pushed the shift to neutral. The rain came
down harder. Dee scurried below to turn on the inside
key and take over the helm in the dry cabin. I waited a
few moments, then turned off the topside key. The engine stopped. I had turned off the key too soon.

Hurring below, I tried to restart the engine, but
was greeted by a strange whirring sound - the engine
refused to start. I tried again, and again. We were
drifting back toward the wing dam. I tried again. No
luck. **Sol Seaker** and the wing dam were definitely on a
collision course and there was no doubt which would be
the winner if the two should tangle.

I initiated plan B. I slipped and slid my way
along the four inch walkway to the bow and quickly cast
the anchor over, holding tightly to the line and praying
that the anchor would hold in the sandy bottom. The rope
suddenly snapped taut almost pulling my arms from their
sockets as **Sol Seaker's** stern swung sharply around in
the current. We stopped about fifteen feet short of the
underwater hazard.

I sat like a drowned rat on the foredeck while Dee
tried to restart the engine. On the second try I heard
her gleeful shout as it started. Directing her to ease
the boat forward, I began to haul in the anchor line.
As the boat passed directly over the anchor, it came
free. As I started to stand, to get better leverage on
the line, Dee shouted, "Hang on!"

At that moment, the first of a series of violent
waves hit us broadside. The sternwash from the forgotten towboat! I fell face down onto the deck, skid-
ding forward up to, and almost under, the bow railing,
anchor line firmly in hand. As I wedged my right
shoulder against a railing support, a vision of the
cookie fortune, **Leave Your Boat and Travel on Firm
Ground**, flashed through my mind. Slowly I inched my
body side-ways as wave after wave pounded into us.

Dee was finally able to get the bow turned into the
waves and little by little I made progress in getting
the anchor on board. Once the anchor was secure, I
motioned for her to continue downriver. The rain came
harder, but I stayed on the bow clinging to the railing.

In the far recesses of our minds we had known that
someday we would face a real danger to body or boat. We
had imagined being adrift in front of a monstrous tow or

111

being capsized by storm or sternwash. Now that we had actually experienced our first real danger, I felt an exhilarating relief. I actually enjoyed my wet roller-coaster ride until mind, body and smoother water made possible my return to **Sol Seaker's** snug cabin. I changed to dry clothes and sneezed a couple of times as we continued through the rain toward our next port-of-call, Sabula, Iowa.

Along with the subtle changes in people, we also began to notice changes in the landscape. The inevitable cliffs were giving way to a more gradual rise from the river to the farmland beyond. Sometimes the fields ran almost to the water's edge. The woods became sparser, providing longer and more extensive glimpses of the fields and houses beyond. Where Alma, Fountain City and Pepin had been constricted between river and bluff; Lansing, Cassville and Bellevue were spread more leisurely away from the riverbank.

Somewhere beyond the rain clouds the sun must have been setting as we rounded the tip of Big Soupbone Island and wondered how it got it's name. It was still six miles to Sabula and daylight was rapidly giving way to what would be a dark and rainy night. As we glided past Little Soupbone we met our second tow of the day, the **Margie Logan**, hugging close to the red nuns on the inside of a sweeping bend in the river. Along with the fifteen empties in front of the towboat, the **Margie Logan** had a sixteenth barge attached along her port side.

Since the tow's proximity to the red markers prevented us from meeting her on the inside of the curve, we once again found ourselves searching for a place to hide. There was none. Our only choice was to meet her on the outside of the bend and endure the inevitable sternwash. I began to look for the widest point in the river. The widest spot was just below the tip of Indian Island. We headed toward the Iowa shore. Going only fast enough to maintain control in the modest current, we prayed that there were no unmarked wing dams in this stretch of the river.

Slowly, the lead barges came alongside. We felt the line of small waves set up by the bow of the first barges. As each succeeding set of three barges passed, a new set of waves rocked us. But the bow waves were like the ripples from a dropped pebble in comparison to the water mountains that erupted from deep beneath the surface, where the giant propellers clawed through the muddy river. Each mountain moved slowly downriver as a new eruption occurred. In the darkening distance we could see that in undiminished strength the line of mountains had reached the Iowa shore, creating a crashing surf against the rock revetment and breaking over two wing dams. These mountains of water completely cut off our downriver path.

Should we turn and run upriver beyond the **Margie Logan** and look for a place to pass on the other side? No. The bend above Big Soupbone curved the other way. By the time we would get past the long string of barges, there would be a similar sternwash pounding the Illinois shore. Dee quickly put all loose and breakable items on the bed, as we braced ourselves for the rough water.

Our boating experience in the Pacific Ocean had taught us that you never get sideways to sharp waves, nor do you take them head on. Sideways, these waves could roll **Sol Seaker** in a minute. Head on might break her in two, or at the least send water crashing over the stern, perhaps killing the engine.

I angled toward the first wave, carefully maintaining enough speed for helm control. As we reached the crest, I throttled back to avoid gaining too much momentum on the downward slide.

It was immediately apparent that the waves of a sternwash are much closer together than ocean waves. **Sol Seaker's** stern was still moving down the first wave when her bow was making a frantic effort to climb wave number two. As there was no giant hinge in the middle of the rigid boat, the broader stern won out and the bow sliced through the wave, sending a wall of muddy Mississippi water against the windshield, temporarily cutting off all vision.

Moments after this water passed, the next wall hit. Between the watery walls, I could see just enough to keep **Sol Seaker** quartering against the waves. After what seemed like hours, but was only minutes, we broke through the last of the water mountains. Violent rocking and shaking continued for about a mile as the river was alive with millions of irregular waves and eddies created by the deflection of the sternwash from the rock revetments, wing dams and river bottom.

As we rounded Keller's Island, the rocking stopped and we slid through the inky waters toward Sabula, still five miles away.

11

SANDBAR PARTY

As we passed beneath the Savanna Highway Bridge,
lights began to come on along the water front. Three
miles below the bridge we pulled into Island City Harbor
at the south end of the town of Sabula, the only river
town built entirely on an island. We would remember
Friday, September 17th as one of the most tiring days on
the river. We had travelled only twenty-one miles, but
it seemed like a thousand.

Two men waited on the dock to help us with our
lines, and, for the moment at least, the rain had stopped. When the boat was secure, Al and Ray introduced
themselves and told us they were here for a weekend of
houseboating. It started to rain again so our new
acquaintances scurried to cover in their houseboats a
few slips down the dock.

As Dee and I sat recording the day's events, we
were thinking that, so far, we had been more successful
in finding **souls** than in finding the **sol**. After an hour
of writing, we decided that we had to get off the boat
and walk around, rain or not. As I opened the large
golfing umbrella we had purchased to keep off the blazing river sun (so far it had been used only for keeping
off the rain), Al and Ray with their wives, Edith and
Elaine, tapped on our door.

"We're going to Luke's to eat," said Al. "It's rib
night. Would you like to go with us?"

"Sure!" Dee replied.

On our way to Al's car, I was thinking, "If we have
to give up something, I guess its better to give up the
sol than the **souls**."

The food and company were both excellent, and
we emerged from the restaurant to a burst of starlight
and a rapidly receding line of clouds.

On the way back to the marina, Al stopped next to a
fixer-upper pontoon boat. "We're buying that boat. It's
not much to look at now, but we'll make it real nice,"

114

l said, with an enthusiasm that indicated he was eager to get started on the remodeling job. "All we have to do is sell our Gibson Houseboat. We'll build a new kitchen, add a bath and re-finish the exterior."

In contrast to Al's enthusiasm, Edith sat quietly in the back seat with Dee. In confidence she whispered to Dee that she wasn't very happy about selling their beautiful houseboat to work on this old derelict. When Al had finished talking about his plans, Edith asked, "Where did you stay last night?"

"At Point Pleasant," Dee answered.

"Oh, we know it well! Aren't Cliff and Elsie nice?" We agreed.

"Did you happen to see a rather strange looking pontoon boat when you were there?" asked Al.

I described the outrigger pontoon boat that had been on a dock near us.

"That's it," shouted Al and Edith together. "That's **The Scrounger**."

"That was our first boat," said Al with obvious pride. We made it entirely from things we scrounged, so we called it **The Scrounger**. We had a lot of fun in that old boat."

The truth was out. As is often the case, especially with men, Al was remembering all the fun and attention he had gotten while working on **The Scrounger**. He saw this latest fixer-upper as a chance to recapture some pleasant moments from the past. Unfortunately, trying to repeat the past is seldom successful. One usually has forgotten the aches, pains and frustrations that were a part of those "pleasant" experiences. Dee and I feared that an older Al might find that, this time, the difficulties would outweigh the fun. We hoped we were wrong.

Back at the marina, Ray and Elaine invited us a-board **The Lucky Duck** for wine. Like several other families who keep boats at Sabula, Ray and Elaine are from a boat club in Aurora, Illinois, about a hundred twenty miles away. They come to Sabula on weekends and holidays for their favorite pastime, "sandbarring."

Now that Ray was retired from the telephone company and Elaine from nursing, they had a lot of time for boating. Like Dee and I, they seemed to be thoroughly enjoying each other in retirement. Many of the men we've known have said, "When I retire I'm just going to putter around the garden, relax and enjoy life." Often in a few weeks they become bored with puttering and their wives become nervous wrecks from having them "under-foot." The most successful retirements seem to be those in which the retirees look to the future as a series of new challenges, activities and occupations, rather than as the end of an active work life.

"We're going sandbarring tomorrow," Ray said. "There'll be Elaine and me, Al and Betty, Jim and Roberta, their son Scott, and his new wif , Cindy. We'd like to have you join us."

"We'd love to!" We both said, almost too enthusiastically.

"Aren't Al and Edith going?" Dee asked.

"No, Al wants to get their houseboat all cleaned up and ready to sell," Elaine interjected. "I think he's making a big mistake buying that pontoon boat."

"What do we do about food?" Dee asked. "Is it potluck or everyone do his own?"

"It's everyone for himself this time," Ray answered. "Sometimes we have potluck."

That night the warmth of our new friendships, a bright starry sky, and the gentle rocking of **Sol Seaker** held us in a deep and peaceful sleep.

We woke to the promise of a day filled with both **sol** and **soul**, even though it was laundry day. We went by boat to the dock at Luke's Restaurant, where it was a short walk to the laundromat. I tended the washing machines while Dee walked to the grocery store for food and wine for the sandbar party She returned with the food, but no wine. The only wine in the store is Mogan David in tiny bottles," she said.

A young man overheard our conversation and said, "You can't buy wine in Iowa except at state operated stores, and there ain't any here in Sabula. I'm goin' across the bridge to Savanna in Illinois. I'll be glad to take you to the liquor store there, then drop you back here."

When I returned with a gallon of Colony Gold Chablis, the wash was done and we headed for the sandbar. Ray and Elaine were there and helped us set our anchors against the current and the breezes.

Dee and Elaine donned bathing suits, set up folding chairs on the sandy beach, and settled back to enjoy the warm early autumn sunshine, while Ray and I set out worm baited fishing rods. To the end of my rod I attached a small bell Dee had bought for me. This bell would summon me in the event a fish found the worm to be a tasty morsel

Jim, Roberta, Scott and Cindy arrived in a large houseboat and, soon after, Al and Betty nudged their tiny houseboat, **Guppi**, up to the sand. Betty got off the **Guppi**, and all of the men, me included, climbed aboard for a run back to the marina to get Ray's outboard, which we would use to collect limbs and logs for the evening's bonfire.

In his speedy runabout, Ray was like a kid with a toy. He sped over the wake of a passing towboat throwing spray in all directions. Once he hit a wave that was larger than he had anticipated and a wall of water came over the bow and crashed against the windshield.

Once past the towboat, Ray challenged Al to a race. For a while the two boats were side by side, then little by little, the **Guppi** pulled ahead. That's the fastest little houseboat around," said Ray. "He could leave me in his wake if he really wanted to."

Before beaching the boat, Ray made a speedy turn near the sandbar trying to throw spray on our sunbathing wives.

When we were on shore, I noticed that my fishing pole was in a different place on the stern of **Sol Seaker**. "Did my bell ring?" I asked.

Dee had a smug look on her face as Elaine and Betty giggled. "Did Dee catch a fish?" I insisted.

More giggles. "Did Dee catch more than one fish?" I demanded.

Dee went to the boat and lifted the fish basket, proudly displaying two plump sheepsheads.

We men then took the runabout across the river to an area of thick woods, where we found several dead logs and limbs. The limbs we lay across the bow. The logs, each about twenty feet long and six to eight inches in diameter, were tied behind with a long rope to be towed across the river.

As we started back, an upstream towboat with fifteen empties was rounding the bend just above the bridge, heading our way. "I can beat him across," Ray shouted, as he gave more gas to the outboard engine. Under the weight of four men plus the drag of the three logs, the little boat refused to go fast.

Ray gave it more gas, The speed increased a little, but Al yelled, The logs are diving! Better slow down! If they hit the bottom they could pull the boat apart."

117

Ray throttled back and the logs began to re-surface. When they were flat on the surface, Al shortened the rope causing the logs to roll over so that the near ends were curved slightly upward. "Now they'll ride okay," said Al, "Give her the gas."

Ray pushed the little boat to the maximum. My heart was in my throat as we moved into the "blind spot" about fifty yards in front of the towboat, and remained there until we had reached the other side of the channel and were making a safe approach to the beach.

When we had unloaded the boat, the ladies began to giggle again. I walked over to the fish basket. A third and larger sheepshead had joined the previous two.

As we all sat down to enjoy nibbles and drinks, the bell on my fishing rod began to ring. I clambered up on the bow and tracked sand all along the walkway to the stern deck. I grabbed the pole and came up with an empty hook. After rebaiting, I had just returned to the beach when the bell rang again. Once more I was greeted by an empty hook. This ritual was repeated several times. Each time it was accompanied by giggles, as I added more sand to the boat, but no fish to the basket. Finally I gave up, suspecting that Dee had made some kind of deal with the fish.

After dinner, Jim used a quart of lighter fluid to start the damp wood When it started he nursed the flames along until they began to dry the wood and produce a bright, warm fire.

As we formed a circle around the now dancing flames, Ray looked at the fire appraisingly. In a tone of exaggerated pride he said, "This is one of our more average fires."

No, I think this fire is a little above average," said Jim, who had done most of the work to get it going.

Later, with more wood added, the fire became so hot we had to expand our circle. As he moved his chair away from the inferno, Al said with great pride, "This is one of the best fires we've ever had. I wish we had some hot dogs."

"Not me," said Ray.

"You remember the last time you had hot dogs," Elaine said, "you and Ray both got sick."

"Yeah, but remember we had hot dogs, cheese cake and lots of beer," Al replied.

My stomach began to feel a little queasy at the thought of adding hot dogs, cheese cake and beer to the peanuts, caramel corn, hamburgers, soft drinks, wine and screwdrivers we had already consumed.

How about marshmallows," exclaimed Cindy as she and Scott headed arm in arm toward the boat.

They probably won't be back," smiled Jim with a wink. But they soon returned with marshmallows and sticks to roast them on.

As the evening wore on, conversation touched upon several subjects. It was soon apparent that Jim was an expert on almost everything. As he continued to consume glass after glass of burgundy, he became even more expert. "The Datsun 610 pickup has the best engine of any small pickup, foreign or American," he said. "The Japs build everything better. They learned it from the Germans. K-cars have less maintenance problems than any other American car on the road today..."

Finally. Ray and Al got around to swapping the latest jokes. "This guy was in an automobile accident," Al began the joke session. "He lost his nose and one of his big toes. They rushed him to emergency where the doctor quickly sewed back the severed appendages. Unfortunately, he made a little mistake and put the toe where the nose should be and the nose where the toe should be. Now when the man sneezes he blows his shoe off."

The jokes got raunchier as each man tried to out-do the previous one. "I have a gorilla joke," said Ray. "A man and wife go to the zoo where they stop in front of the gorilla's cage. The gorilla eyes the lady. 'I think he likes you,' says the husband. 'Don't be silly,' answered the wife. 'Just take off your blouse and see what he does,' says the husband. Reluctantly the lady removes her blouse and the gorilla goes wild, shaking the bars and emitting loud grunts. Item by item, the husband gets his wife to remove her clothing. As each garment is removed, the gorilla becomes more excited. Finally, when the wife is completely naked, the man opens the cage and pushes her in with the half crazed gorilla, and says, 'Now tell him you have a headache!'"

"I've got a gorilla story that tops that one." chimes in Al. "These two women are standing in front of the gorilla's cage when the gorilla grabs one and drags her inside. The friend starts screaming for help as the gorilla begins to rape the woman. The zoo keeper rushes up with a gun, but each time he tries to shoot, the gorilla puts the woman between himself and the gun. He continues to rape her. This goes on for about twenty-four hours, finally the gorilla tires and is shot and killed. The woman is rushed to the hospital where she is treated and sedated."

"The next day her best friend comes in to see her. 'How do you feel?' says the friend. 'I'm okay,' says the lady. 'How do you **really** feel?' insists the friend."

"'Well, he never calls - he never writes...'"

At this point Elaine changed the rapidly deteriorating subject by saying to Dee and I, "You know there's a rule about the campfire. No one is supposed to go to bed until a towboat passes with all of its lights on."

It seems that even among these people who are accustomed to seeing Mississippi River towboats, the sight of one of these behemoths ablaze with lights is almost a reverent experience.

We waited, and waited and waited, then, one by one, the tired revellers began to give up and head toward their beds.

Ray, Elaine, Dee and I continued the vigil. We searched the horizon, upriver and down, for a tell-tale glow that would herald the approach of a towboat. No glow appeared, and finally at 1:30 we, too, reluctantly gave up. I re-baited my hook and cast it out before falling exhausted into bed.

The sun was already climbing above the tree tops when a faint tinkling sound roused me from a dreamless sleep. I lay there trying to identify the sound when Dee suddenly sat upright next to me. "Are you going to bring in that fish, or do I have to do it for you?"

"The bell," I exclaimed as I bolted, pajama clad, out the cabin door. I reeled in a nice sheepshead, my first "keeper" since starting our Mississippi River trip.

After breakfast we demonstrated **Sol Seaker, Jr.,** our folding Porta-Bote. Several people took rides in the strange looking plastic craft, then we sat on the beach to share more stories and fellowship.

Everyone was fascinated by a large caspian tern that was diving in the water, and by a great blue heron that stalked its prey among the weeds along the water's edge. "Why don't you share your stories about the heron and tern you wrote at Anderson Marsh?" asked Dee.

Reluctantly, I shared these bits of writing along with "Do You Remember", a sentimental poem about our early courtship. When I finished, Dee whispered to me,

120

"You know if you want to really get to know people, you
have to share some of yourself with them. Those poems
and stories gave them a glimpse inside you."

We shared a few more jokes and stories. I even
persuaded Dee to tell her favorite joke.

"Do you know where the Artisians live?" She asked.

"No." answered the group in unison.

"In lady's bras," Dee answered. "You can tell
because when it's cold their little noses stick out."

I must admit her joke got more laughs than most of
the ones told the night before.

Beneath a warm noontime **sol**, we reluctantly said
our good-byes, and once again turned toward the Gulf of
Mexico, now only fifteen hundred miles away.

SOL SEAKER JR.

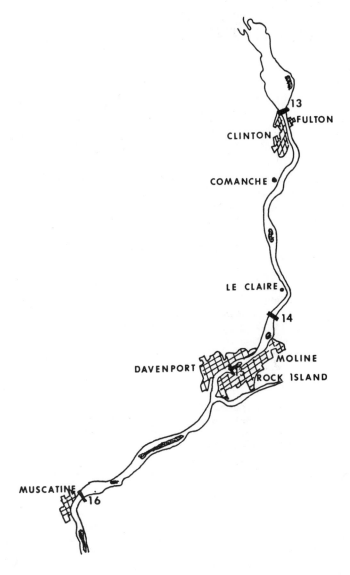

13

FULTON

CLINTON

COMANCHE •

LE CLAIRE •

14

MOLINE

DAVENPORT

ROCK ISLAND

MUSCATINE

16

CH-12

12

HOG CHAINS AND 'POSSUM TAILS

Pool thirteen, also known as the Clinton Pool, is more than three miles wide for a distance of ten miles above the dam. Below the dam the river is constricted to less than a half-mile between the cities of Clinton, Iowa (population 33,000) and Fulton, Illinois (population 4,000).

It was Sunday afternoon. A crowd of thirty or forty people stood on the observation platform watching a towboat complete its upstream locking. We waited. The green light flashed almost before the tow's stern had cleared the gates. As we headed in, the sternwash of the departing tow bounced us vigorously and flung us from side to side. We looked along the rusty wall for the lines that are always hanging down, ready to be grabbed. There were no lines.

Dee rushed below to inform the lock master that there were no lines. While she was on the radio, I spied the lines coiled on top of the wall. With boat hook in hand, I guided **Sol Seaker** through the turbulent water trying to get close enough to reach one of the coiled lines. Just as I caught the line on the tip of the long boat hook, we were bounced hard against the wall.

I shouted, "Dee, come get this rope while I get another one!" There was no answer. I clung to the line trying to fend off the wall with the boat pole. Dee emerged from below just as the dockmaster handed me a second line and apologized for forgetting to lower the lines. By the time we had the boat secure and stable we were almost down to the lower level.

Dee said, "I got an answer on the radio I thought was the lockmaster. He asked me if it was rough in the lock. I told him it was a little rough, but our main problem was we couldn't find any ropes. We needed him to give us some ropes. Finally, the man on the radio said, 'This is the **Brewmaster**, not the lockmaster!'"

Later, I would laugh at this humorous situation, but right now I was trying to hide my embarrassment at an inept locking operation in front of our largest audience. Half-heartedly, I returned the many wave's and hello's from the spectators, wishing inwardly that the gate would hurry and open. When it did we were thankfully swept quickly out of sight in the swift current.

At the sandbar Al had asked if we ever listened to towboat conversations. We hadn't. Now we went below to drive from the inside helm where we could listen to our V H F radio. Just as I turned on the radio, one of the Minnesota Towing Company boats was receiving a radio-telephone call from the home office. "Drop one empty at Dubuque," a male voice stated. "Pick up two at Cass-ville, numbers D-6102 and D-7208. Drop two at Prarie Du Chien. Pick up one at La Crosse, 7801. Six outa' St. Paul."

"Seven empties. We can make that a single."

"You must be a single now."

"No sir, we still got these three."

"Oh, yeah, I forgot that. Then you won't be a single 'til you get outa Prarie Du Chien. Business shore went into the doldrums last week. Nobody movin' and nobody shippin'! I sent the **Hawkeye** up the Ohio to try to drum up some business. It's about time for you to get off isn't it?"

"Yes sir, it shore is!" came the enthusiastic reply. "Next Tuesday it will have been thirty days. I shore get anxious to see my wife and boys after 'bout two weeks out. But when I'm home I get a longin' to be back on the river."

"Have a good trip up. I'm clear."

Rounding the sharp bend at Beaver Island we met the **Agamemnon**, whose stern wash sent a refreshing spray of cool brown water over **Sol Seaker's** bow.

We passed Albany, Illinois before pulling into tiny Kime's Dock at Princeton, Iowa (population 900). It was after 4:30 and we were ready to stop for the day, but there appeared to be no room, as a large houseboat and two small outboards filled the transient spaces behind the gas dock. A man from the houseboat motioned for us to come on up to the gas dock. When we were close enough, he said, "We're leaving in a few minutes. You can have our space."

"Thanks!" Dee answered, then asked, "Where's a good place to eat?"

"The smorgas restaurant up there's good and inexpensive," said the man as the houseboat pulled away from the dock. We saw the name **Brewmaster** on the stern.

Dee ran to the radio. "We didn't realize you were **Brewmaster**," she said. "We're the boat you talked to in the lock. Over."

"We planned to go up to Sabula," a man's voice replied, "but we were afraid the water might be too rough in the Clinton Pool. Sorry we confused you when you were looking for the ropes. Over."

"There's a little chop up there," Dee answered, "but you shouldn't have any problems. Over."

"Thanks. I think we'll stay in Clinton tonight then go on up tomorrow. Have a nice voyage. Over and clear."

"Thanks. **Sol Seaker** clear on 68."

Two young men, who had been eying our boat, helped us walk **Sol Seaker** around behind the dock. Noting their curiosity, Dee invited them aboard for a tour. As they stepped back outside, a third young man came up and said, "You guys are dreaming again."

"Keep right on dreaming," Dee commented, "In a few years and with a few gray hairs your dreams will come true."

At the restaurant we ate heartily, then tumbled into bed.

The next morning was cold, but sunny. We had traveled only five miles, to Le Claire, Iowa (population 1,124), when we spotted three loaded tows parked side-by-side on the bend in the river. The **Washington**, **Yazoo City** and **Beldon** were waiting for lock 14, located about three miles downriver. Closer to the lock we could see two more waiting tows. "There's quite a line up," Dee commented as she called for locking instructions.

"Skipper, there's a double just commin' into the lock. It'll be about an hour and a half."

We went back past the three waiting tows, stopped at The Le Claire Municipal Dock, and got off the boat to stretch our legs. Our first, and last, stop in Le Claire was the Buffalo Bill Museum. "I'm Harold Kennedy," said a wirey, bewhiskered gentleman as we entered the museum. "If yall have time I'd like to show you around. We got things here from Buffalo Bill and we've got lots of interestin' things from the steamboat days."

In appearance, Harold Kennedy was everything Stern-wheel Don should·have been, but both men knew and loved

The River. Don's knowledge was broad and related to all
the boats that had plied the Mighty Mississippi. Harold
had an intimate knowledge of the art and artifacts of
river boating and of the history of Le Claire, a typical, yet unique, river town.

I started to say that we really didn't have much
time, but something about this man with the brusque
confidence of a riverboat captain, and the smoothness of
a riverboat gambler, made me hold my tongue. Quick to
seize on the opportunity of Harold's expertise, Dee
said, "We'd love to have you show us around. We really
don't know much about how steamboats were run."

"Well, to tell you all about everything would take
more'n a day, but I'll show you some of the things I
think are most interesting. 'Course you know that
Buffalo Bill lived here-abouts as a boy."

"No, we didn't know that. In fact, we wondered why
a museum in Le Claire would be called The Buffalo Bill
Museum. We always associated Bill Cody with the wild
west of Montana and Wyoming," I answered.

"That's what most folks know about. And I bet you
didn't know that Weyerhauser started in the lumber business right here, not in Oregon and Washington where all
the lumber comes from today. Fact is, Weyerhauser is
buried just down the river in Rock Island, Illinois.
But even though Buffalo Bill lived here and Weyerhauser
started his lumber business here, Le Claire was most
important because it had a special place in the history
of riverboating. Here, let me show you some of the
interesting things we have here in the museum. Now I
usually take school children on tours, so I might begin
to talk to you like you was fifth graders."

"We are fifth graders when it comes to knowing
about riverboats," Dee said.

"See that metal thing hanging there? What does
that look like?"

We studied the object for a few moments, then I
said, "It looks like an acorn."

"You're right. But to a river man that was the
same as a rabbit's foot. That's a riverboat good luck
charm. Almost every riverboat had a good luck acorn,
sometimes they had lots of them. 'Course they didn't
always work, 'cause lots of boats sunk from boiler explosions, fires, or runnin' aground. See that? Know
what that is?"

"No."

125

"That's a boat whistle. Run by steam. Look at the end of it."

"It's shaped like an acorn!" Dee exclaimed.

"Yep. Look around."

As we looked at the metal artifacts from steamboat days, we saw that many of them had the acorn emblem cast into the metal.

"You've come down from Minneapolis, so you've gone through several locks. Now I guess you've got some plastic or rubber fenders you use against the lock walls. Well there weren't no locks in the early steamboat days, but them big wooden boats still needed fenders. They made them from pieces of old rope. It was a real skill to 'knit' that rope into a large pendant. They always made a loop from one strand to hang it by. There's one hangin' there. What does it look like to you?"

"Maybe a monkey hanging by it's tail," Dee said.

"That's almost right. A 'possum. The riverboat men called them 'possums 'cause they looked like 'possums hanging by them rope tails. Ain't no monkies 'round here, so they called them 'possums. Still do today. One thing you gotta learn about true river men. They don't ever change the name of something, even if the name no longer fits the circumstances. Take a 'towboat' fer instance. On your trip down the river did you ever see a boat towing a barge?"

"No."

"'Course not. They push them. But at first barges was towed. Then they learned they could control them better by pushing, but they still call the boat a towboat. 'Hogchains' is another name that stuck even after they quit usin' chains. Now boats are made of steel and hogchains ain't used. But when they started making bigger and bigger wood boats, they found they would warp and buckle in the middle if they hit an underwater obstruction, which they was doin' all the time. Well, a bracing was invented to keep this from happinin'. Heavy chains were run from the bow up over an iron bar to the stern. They looked a little like a suspension bridge. Like the Golden Gate Bridge in California. These chains were pulled tight and they prevented the boat from warpin' up in the middle. Folks called them hogchains. Well, they finally learned that solid iron bars worked better. But they still called them hogchains."

"We've visited lots of river towns since we left

Minneapolis, but we haven't had the opportunity to talk to anyone with your knowledge of and interest in history," I said. "Le Claire looks like a typical river town. Is it?"

"Well, yes and no. In many ways Le Claire has a unique place in the history of riverboating. In this part of the river are the Rock Island Rapids. The Indians called it 'Pau-pesha-tuk' which means 'agitated water.' A narrow twisting channel lined and dotted with high rocks made this one of the most dangerous stretches to navigate on the entire river. Specially trained pilots were needed to take steamboats safely through the rapids. Ever hear of the 'Green Tree Hotel?'"

"No." Dee and I replied in unison, waiting eagerly for the story to unfold.

"Well, great rafts of logs used to be floated from the woods up north to sawmills all along the river. By 1870 there were nearly a hundred sawmills. Some were above Le Claire and some below. Clinton, Iowa was called "the sawdust city" and had seventeen millionaires who got their wealth from the lumber business. The main problem was getting large quantities of logs downriver quickly and safely. It often took days for floatin' rafts of logs to get through Lake Pepin up in Wisconsin, because of the slow currents and frequent high winds. Several people experimented unsuccessfully with using steamboats to help move the log rafts. Then, after the civil war Thomas Doughty, a local man, built a small sternwheeler, **Le Claire**, which he tried to use to move log rafts, but the boat was too light and too small."

"A young boat builder named Sam Van Sant had watched Thomas Doughty's experiment with great interest and, although the experiment failed, young Sam believed that the idea was sound. With the aid of Henry Whitmore, an engineer, he designed a boat similar to the **Le Claire**, but much larger and more powerful. The boat, **J. W. Van Sant**, was finished in the spring of 1870 and headed upriver in May for its first tow of logs. Aboard, on that maiden voyage, was Frederick Weyerhauser, a young lumberman from Rock Island, Illinois. The boat was a great success. Weyerhauser memorized the basic design of the boat and ordered 'rafters' for himself. Unfortunately for Sam Van Sant, Weyerhauser had them built cheaper at a larger boat yard. Of course you know Weyerhauser became one of the world's largest lumber barons. He started right here."

"Well, to get to the 'Green Tree Hotel,' when the use of steamboats to push log rafts became widespread, many old time floating raftsmen found themselves competing for jobs on the ever fewer floating rafts. While they were waiting for their next job, they often ran out of money for hotel rooms. Over near the waters edge was a huge, umbrella shaped elm tree. Stranded raftsmen would bed down under the tree. When they finally boarded a steamer to go back up to the north woods, they would tell everyone they had slept at the 'Green Tree Hotel.'"

"The tree became one of the most famous in the United States, and in 1912 was elected to the National Hall of Fame for Trees at Washington D.C. It stood as a living symbol of the great log-raft days on the Mississippi until 1964, when it died of Dutch Elm disease."

He paused for a moment, eying us intently. "I could go on and tell you stories all day, but I can see you're getting anxious to get back to your boat on the river. There's a magic to that ole river you know. Better be careful or you'll become hopelessly trapped by it's magic spell."

We thanked our host profusely for a very pleasant and enlightening tour. Before we headed back to **Sol Seaker** we purchased a copy of LE CLAIRE, IOWA; A MISSISSIPPI RIVER TOWN, by Dorothy Lage, a small book which chronicles the history of Le Claire from Indian times to the present.

As we left the museum, we could almost feel a magnetic force pulling us toward the river. Was this the "magic spell" that Harold Kennedy had warned us about?

Back aboard **Sol Seaker**, we learned that we had missed several opportunities to lock through. "I been wonderin' what happened to you," said the lockmaster when we called him on the radio. "I got a small asphalt tow, two barges, ready to lock down. If you want, I'll call them and see if it's okay for you to lock down with them."

"Sure," we said, in nervous anticipation of our first opportunity to share a lock with a towboat.

We heard the captain of the **Gilda Shurden** agree to letting us lock down with him. "**Sol Seaker**," said the lockmaster, "this is how we'll do it. Them two big asphalt barges will fill one side of the lock from end to end. The captain will push them barges in on the starboard side and when we git them tied off I'll signal

you to come on in on the port side, you come all the
way up and git your lines. Then the towboat will unhook
from the barges and come up behind you. When we git
down you can go on out first, then he can hook up again.
That way you'll be in calm water."

"I understand," I replied. "This is **Sol Seaker**,
Whisky, Romeo, Whisky 2683 clear and standing by on
fourteen."

As we moved into the lock beside the two asphalt
barges, we had to laugh at ourselves for having mistaken
the open coal barges we had first seen in Prescott for
these huge closed 'tankers' which were topped by a net-
work of pipes through which the liquid asphalt was
pumped in and out of the barge. As we looked at the
pipework, we suddenly realized that we had also seen
barges like these at Prescott. They were the "Midnight
Monster" that had sent such fear and trembling through
us that first night aboard **Sol Seaker** in the marina
parking lot.

We made an exceptionally smooth stop along the left
wall and watched as deck hands quickly and skillfully
undid the huge cables which had bound the **Gilda Shurden**
and her two barges into a single unit. The large towboat eased backward, careful not to create any turbu-
lance that might cause us to bounce against the wall,
then turned to clear the back of the barge and moved
slowly toward us. We stood, mouths agape as we looked
up at the towering pilot house and the massive pusher
"knees" coming closer and closer. Several yards behind
us, the **Gilda Shurden** came to a gentle stop and was
quickly made fast to the side of her own barges.

After leaving the lock, Dee called to thank the
captain for letting us lock through with him. "We'll see
you in New Orleans for Christmas," she said.

"No, I don't think so," came the reply, "I'll be a
lot farther west. We're takin' these barges to Galveston, Texas. Yall have a good trip."

As we moved downriver, the weather became cold,
cloudy and windy. Dee went below and brought up our
Winona sweaters and gloves.

We slid past Hampton (population 1800). At mile
marker 491 we came to Campbell's Island, where the
braves of Chief Blackhawk had once done battle with U.
S. forces under the command of Lt. John Campbell. We
continued past a large metropolitan area which included
East Moline, Moline and Rock Island, Illinois and Bet-

129

tendorf and Davenport, Iowa. Combined population of these cities is more than 240,000. Each time we passed a community, large or small, we knew we were missing something important, but it wasn't possible to stop everywhere.

Just before we entered Lock 15, we passed the historic site where, in 1856, the first bridge was built across the Mississippi River. At mile 417, Enchanted Island slid by on our right.

Two mallards flew overhead as we glided along Smith's Island. On our right a red nun floated horizontally between two submerged wing dams, far on the black can side of the river. We had heard that sometimes a towboat would dislodge a marker which would then float "wild" until stopped by some obstruction. We were looking at our first "wild nun."

We drifted leisurely between the twin villages of Buffalo, Iowa (population 1441) and Andalusia, Illinois (population 1235), then glided along Andalusia Island, which separates Andalusia Slough from the main channel. We met a Gladders towboat pushing six coal barges, then slid past the tiny fish hatchery village of Fairport, Iowa. In the shallows on both sides of the channel were duck blinds. Most were mere wooden skeletons whose willow branch flesh had been blown or washed away since the last duck season. A few were dressed in fresh green in preparation for the fall hunting season which would begin in a few days.

At Muscatine, Iowa we pulled into a pleasant marina within easy walking distance of the downtown area. As we started across the ever present railroad tracks, Dee slipped, falling to her hands and knees and sustaining several scrapes and bruises. These injuries, plus a rapidly falling thermometer. caused us to cut our walking tour short.

That evening we fried the fish we had caught at Sabula, remembering our sandbar party. Immediately after dinner, Dee sought the warmth of our bed under an extra sleeping bag, while I sat close to the five inch television screen watching Monday Night Football. That night the temperature dropped to thirty-nine degrees. Not cold by mid-west standards, but freezing to two thin-blooded Californians.

HOG CHAINS

13

THE TWO NAUVOOS

In the long, wide, straight stretch below Muscatine, the curvature of the earth gave the illusion that
we were cruising up an incline, and would eventually
reach the crest and descend the other side; an illusion
that was broken only when we rounded Bass Island and
swung toward the Illinois shore. Like hundreds of
others we had passed on our downriver trek, Bass Island
had a beautiful tree-fringed beach, ideal for sandbar
parties.

We were intrigued by the names of islands, towns,
sloughs and chutes that appeared on our river charts.
Ahead, we would pass Bogus Island. We wondered if it
would actually be there, or if the name "Bogus" meant
that it didn't really exist. It really existed. In fact
it stretched more than two miles, separating the main
channel from Bogus Chute, which also really existed. We
passed Turkey Chute, Otter Island, Otter Tail Island
(separated from Otter Island by lock and dam 17), Keg
Island and Brass Island.

As we glided past the village of New Boston, we
noted on our chart, . . ."Original Survey and Layout by
Abraham Lincoln - 1834." How we wanted to stop, but we
saw no dock for **Sol Seaker** and our goal for the day was
to make a stop at Oquawka some eighteen miles downstream, to meet Bob Reader, then travel another thirteen
miles to Burlington before nightfall.

At mile 429 a flock of large, white Egrets stood on
the marshy end of Blackhawk Island. As we passed
Keithsburg, Dee noted that the major streets of the town
were Washington, Jefferson, Jackson, Madison and Main.
"It seems that every town has these same streets," she
commented.

During the next several minutes she thumbed through
the chart, confirming her suspicions. "There are also a
lot of Chestnut, Walnut, Oak and Cedar Streets. Even
Clay, Pierce, Polk and Buchanan have their share in the

larger towns. Water, Front and First seem to be the most popular names for the street that runs closest to the river."

"Comanche, Iowa, has the simplest street system," Dee stated. "The streets run parallel to the river and are numbered consecutively one through nine. Numbered avenues run the other way, starting with Second Avenue on the upriver edge of town and ending at 17th Avenue on the downriver edge."

As she was completing her street game, Oquawka's Front Street became visible along the left bank. Slowly, we glided past Fulton, Clay, Hancock, Calhoun and Lincoln streets on our way to Devore's Marina, about a mile below town.

"Let's walk," I said, not knowing that by road the distance was more like two miles. At the post office we received the directions to the Reader's home, just a few blocks away.

Vi Reader met us at the door. At first she was puzzled as we explained who we were, then her face lit up. "Yes, I remember your letter," she said. "Bob's doing some work over at the church. I'll call him."

Before Vi could call, Bob appeared. He, too, greeted us with warmth. "I was hoping you'd stop and look us up."

Over cookies and tea we talked about our trip and heard about how they had fixed up this, their vacation house, as a retirement home on the bank of the river where they could sit and watch the activity. "The river's always changing," Bob said. "Sometimes it's peaceful like today, but sometimes it rages. You wouldn't want to make your trip during the high water in the spring."

"One of the things we like most about the river is the birds," commented Vi. "Thousands of them go by on their way south. Our favorites are the wood ducks. Maybe you've seen some wooden houses like that one." She pointed to a bird house nailed to a pine tree in the yard. "That's our wood duck house. Every year a pair nests in there."

We looked at the house, a vertical wooden box about ten inches wide. Near the top was a hole about three or four inches in diameter. There was nothing near the hole for the bird to stand on while entering and exiting the house. I asked about the lack of a perch.

"Don't need one," Bob replied. "The duck flies
132

full speed straight into the hole. It's amazing how they zip right in without the slightest hesitation. Then just a few days after the young'uns hatch they climb up the inside edge of the house and fall right to the ground. Doesn't seem to hurt them a bit. They just get up and follow the mama duck down to the river."

"I wish they were here, but they left the nest a long time ago," Vi added. "Probably gone south already."

As we started to leave, after our short but pleasant visit, Dee spotted a row of clam shells lining a flower bed. Each shell had several round holes in it. "Are those the famous button clams?" She asked.

"Yes, would you like one?" asked Vi.

"We'd love one. We've read about how there are thousands of them along the river. We've looked and looked, but haven't seen any."

"You don't see them much anymore, but I have several."

She picked out two shells for us, then she and Bob drove us back to the marina. We learned later that the next day they had driven downriver all the way to Keokuk hoping to see us to apologize for not asking us to stay overnight with them. It seems that no one is a stranger along the Mississippi.

It was well after dark when we cautiously rounded the buoy at the end of a long wing dam separating the main channel from the O'Connell slough entrance to the ETCO Marina at Burlington. We were grateful we had carefully read Quimby's Harbor Guide which stated, "Dock is visible from channel, but do not cross direct to it because of submerged wing dam. Enter from downstream only, coming up along shore from black buoy..." Had we not read this guide we probably would not have seen the black buoy in the darkness and might have turned too soon, ending up as one more wing dam statistic.

The harbor was very shallow. We touched bottom and had to raise the outdrive to pull **Sol Seaker** along the gas dock to a safe moorage. I quickly heated some canned beans and tomales as Dee, who wasn't feeling very well, sat quietly at the table. We guessed that she had caught "rakin and scrapin" Elsie's "feelin' poorly" bug.

Dawn was changing the riverscape from the gray-black monochrome of night to the soft fuzzy hues of first color as we awoke. We eased away from the shallow marina just as the sun began to show above the trees on the east bank. The air was warmer than the day before but there was still enough crispness to cause columns of mist to rise like giant stalagmites near the eastern shore. As the columns reached a few hundred feet they bumped into an invisible ceiling of denser air and spread out, creating a giant, misty, columned temple reminding us of temples we had seen in Athens and Delphi. As we glided effortlessly through this ancient scene, the rays of the sun quickly dispersed the veil of mist and we were once again moving over a clear smooth surface on our magical river.

Below Burlington, the channel held to the right bank where the forest hugged the shore line. "I see one. Over there!" Dee exclaimed, as she pointed toward the wooded shore.

I peered intently but could see nothing.

"A wood duck house. See, there."

Then I saw a familiar elongated bird house which was identical to the one Vi and Bob had shown us. We marveled at the variety and specialized behaviors of the earth's creatures.

The light winds and wide channel made it possible for us to relax and enjoy the magnificent scenery as we glided past sand islands, forested shores and backwater sloughs. Occasionally a monarch butterfly would be attracted by **Sol Seaker**'s bright orange flying bridge and hesitate as though to alight, then thinking better of it would continue downriver.

At mile marker 384 we glided beneath the long, two level bridge which is purported to be the world's largest double track, double deck swing span. Below the bridge we stopped at the River View Marina. Dee was vary cautious as we crossed the tracks to stand by Chimney Monument near the site of an army fort that was built here in 1808. From our vantage point, the city of Fort Madison looked beautiful and prosperous.

We were delighted by the restored Victorian business district, where we purchased film and a canvass suitcase from two elderly clerks who looked and behaved as though they had clerked in this same store in 1880. In a building displaying and selling a variety of handicrafts made by senior citizens, Sister Dorothy told us that she had attended summer school in Santa Clara, California some years before. Her most vivid memory was how every afternoon, about three o'clock, a cool breeze would begin to blow and at night she always needed to sleep under a blanket.

Soon, we were on the river again. Below Fort Madison we entered pool nineteen, famous for its forty foot high dam located downstream at Keokuk, Iowa. The broad river reminded us of Lake Pepin, but here were only gentle breezes to transform the river's surface into a random patchwork of crinkly satin and textured corduroy instead of the violent foam capped waves that had chased us, panic stricken, into Wabasha.

As we approached a sweeping bend, the chart indicated the town of Nauvoo, on the Illinois bank, with the following notation, ". . .Ordered from Missouri in 1838, Mormons settled in Nauvoo in 1839. Forced to migrate in 1846. Led to Utah by Brigham Young."

Almost twenty years before, while traveling near Palmyra, New York we had seen reference to Joseph Smith and the Mormons. Only a few days after that we had again encountered reference to the Mormons near Cleveland, Ohio. Some years later, we had visited the great edifices in Salt Lake City, now we again intersected the westward trail of the Mormon faith, here on the banks of the Mississippi.

"Let's stop!" Dee exclaimed, "Perhaps we can find out what the Mormons were doing here."

"I don't see any place to tie up," I answered as I eased toward shore. "We'll have to anchor and row in."

A few yards offshore we made two anchors fast and, with some effort, unfolded our dinghy and rowed to a spot near Young Street. We noted that there were very few buildings in this lower section of town as we walked toward an impressive structure a few blocks ahead and to the left.

Soon, we were inside the Mormon Visitor's Center as part of a group being led by an attractive and bright young lady in her early twenties. Denise led us past a series of displays depicting the life and revelations of Joseph Smith Jr., founder of Mormonism. In complete faith and confidence she explained how, in 1827, on the Hill Cumorah near Palmyra, New York, the Angel Moroni delivered to Joseph Smith a set of gold plates which contained the writings of the prophet Mormon. Now known as the Book of Mormon, these writings tell of God's dealings with ancient America just as the Bible relates the sacred history of Old World Christianity.

She explained how, with the help of Oliver Cowdery, Joseph Smith translated the gold plates. Later, Cowdery and Smith were baptized by a resurrected John the

135

Baptist, who said to them, "Upon you my fellow servants, in the name of Messiah I confer the Priesthood of Aaron, which holds the keys of the ministering of angels, and of the gospel of repentance and of baptism by immersion for the remission of sins."

When word got out that a book had been published purporting to be equal to the Holy Bible, it was bitterly denounced by all but a handful of believers. Joseph Smith was arrested and then harassed until he and his followers began a "holy migration" which led to Ohio, Missouri and then Commerce, Illinois which Smith called Nauvoo, derived from the Hebrew and meaning "The beautiful location."

In 1842 Joseph Smith and Orrin Porter Rockwell were arrested and charged with the painful, but not fatal, shooting of Lilburn W. Boggs. Boggs, former Governor of Missouri, had taken a prominent part in the expulsion of the Mormons from Missouri. About this time Joseph Smith uttered a prophecy ". . .the Saints will continue to suffer much affliction and will be driven to the Rocky Mountains, many will apostatize, others will be put to death by our persecutors or lose their lives in consequence of exposure or disease, and some of you will live to go and assist in making settlements and build cities and see the Saints become a mighty people in the midst of the Rocky Mountains."

Although Smith and Rockwell were freed on a writ of **Habeas Corpus**, Smith was arrested in 1844 on a charge of treason. On June 27, 1844 Joseph Smith, Jr. and his brother Hyrum were shot and killed at the Carthage jail by an angry mob. The prophet was dead.

On February 4, 1846, in the dead of winter, the first company of Mormons, under the newly accepted leader, Brigham Young, was ferried across a frigid Mississippi River. A few days later, the river froze over. It remained frozen for three days making possible the crossing of several thousand pioneers and teams of wagons to support the pilgrims who called themselves the "Camp of Israel." Our guide went on to describe the arrival in Utah and the establishment there of a powerful and worldwide religious body.

At the end of the tour she invited questions, which she answered with charm and skill. None of us asked about polygamy. Denise concluded the tour by pointing to a beautiful, two acre garden containing monuments to women and by inviting us to visit the homes and businesses that had been purchased and restored by the Mormon Church.

The statuary, Monument to Women, was impressive, but carried a clear message that, . . ."a woman's place is in the home."

As we strolled along Main Street, we marvelled at the amount of money and effort the Mormons were investing in this monument to their history. We were guided through the restored bakery and print shop by a very erudite and oft spoken older man, then we turned right on Kimball Street, past the Brigham Young House and blacksmith shop. As we turned onto Hyde Street, we saw ahead what appeared to be another visitor's center.

We soon found ourselves inside the Joseph Smith Historic Center of the Reorganized Church of Jesus Christ of Latter Day Saints. Our heads were spinning with confusion and curiosity. We listened eagerly as an extremely nervous and fast talking guide related a story somewhat different from the one we had just heard. All but one of the basic facts were the same until the death of the founder of the church, Joseph Smith Jr. But that one difference was a blockbuster.

Whereas, the Salt Lake City group based their claim to being the "real" church on Joseph Smith's Rocky Mountain prophecy, the Reformed group based their claim on a prayer of blessing given by Joseph Smith Jr. on January 17, 1844 in which he designated his eleven-year-old son, Joseph III, to be his presidential successor. The story goes like this:

"Rival claimants to leadership of the church arose after the loss of Joseph and Hyrum Smith. Some were drawn toward Sidney Rigdon, some to James J. Strang, and others to the Council of Twelve Apostles. Many remembered that Joseph Smith had designated his son Joseph III to be the presidential successor, by a prayer of blessing on January 17, 1844. Joseph III was only eleven years old in 1844, however, and could not lead the church.

"Conditions in Nauvoo became increasingly unsettled in 1845 and early 1846. Persecution was renewed, and the church members began to disperse in many directions, settling in Iowa, Wisconsin, Pennsylvania and Illinois, with a large contingent making the historic trek to Utah. The temple, though unfinished, was hurriedly dedicated on May 1, 1846, and in 1848 was fired by an arsonist. By then, Nauvoo was hardly more than a ghost town.

137

"In the spring of 1849, a small party of Frenchmen who called themselves, 'The Pioneers of Humanity,' came to Nauvoo. With the exception of family, everything was in common among them. They flourished for a few years but internal strife soon took its toll. The Icarians, as they were called, disappeared from Nauvoo in 1858. With the disbanding of the Icarian commune, others, mainly German and Swiss, came to take up residence in Nauvoo.

"Against this background, young Joseph grew to manhood. He farmed and studied law. On several occasions he was invited to cast his lot with various factions of the church which his father had established. It was not until 1860 that Joseph III presented himself before a remnant of the church to which he believed he had been guided by the Holy Spirit. He was ordained president of the church in 1860.

We stopped at Nauvoo to hear about its place in the history of the Mormon Church, but had found not one but two Nauvoos. A conflict that began in 1844 continued to exist on this beautiful spot beside the Mighty Mississippi. If the conflict over the "true" church is to be won by numbers, wealth and worldwide influence, then the Salt Lake City Church with its 5,000,000 members, magnificent choir, impressive temples and Donnie and Marie will be the clear victors over the 200,000 Reorganized Latter Day Saints members with headquarters at Independence, Missouri.

Both groups believe that one of the tribes of Israel sailed to the United States about six hundred years before Christ and were God's people in America. They both believe that the golden tablets were written by the Prophet Mormon and hidden by his son Moroni about four hundred A.D., and that the tablets had lain hidden on the Hill Cumorah until 1827 when God and Jesus appeared to Joseph Smith and directed him to their hiding place.

"Except for the question of leadership, are there other differences between the two groups?" I asked our guide, after the tour was over.

"Yes there are. I don't talk about them unless someone asks me. The question of polygamy arose before the exodus to Utah. Joseph Smith was always against it. Brigham Young was a kind of upstart. Some of his critics thought that he advocated polygamy to get more men to back him and as an excuse to have multiple wives.

138

Some say he was really a cruel man. He threatened to burn Emma Smith's house if she did not accompany them to the west. An attempt to carry out his threat failed."

"We also differ in our views of the Negro race, men of the Negro race were ordained in Joseph Smith's time and we never changed this procedure. However, the Mormons had a rule against Negro ordination until 1978 when their President Spencer Kimball announced '. . . the long promised day has come when every faithful, worthy man in the church may receive the priesthood. . . without regard to race or color.'"

"We don,t practice baptism for the dead," he added.

"What's that?" Dee asked.

"It's a procedure where a living person can be proxy for a dead person who had not received forgiveness for his sins before he died. The living person is baptized, thus assuring the dead person's salvation."

"You know," Dee said when we were out of earshot, "The two groups really have a lot in common. Why can't they see that and re-unite?"

"I get a little upset," I replied. "The Reorganized Latter Day Saints stayed here and have had a visitor's center since 1918. Then in the past few years the rich Mormons have moved in to buy up most of the land. It looks to me like they are here primarily to flaunt their wealth and power."

"You're always for the underdog," she chided.

"Maybe."

Dee continued, "It seems to me that God isn't going to concentrate his power and favors on 200,000 or even 5,000,000 'chosen souls' in a world of billions of people. I just can't buy this exclusive club concept of religion. I believe the power of God resides in every person. Too often churches, sects and cults usurp this power for their own selfish purposes, creating ore problems than they solve."

"Well, it has been an education," I said. "At least the start of an education. When we get home, I'm going to do a little more research. There are still some questions I'd like to have answered."

"What questions?"

"For one, why didn't Denise mention polygamy? Did polygamy really start with Brigham Young instead of Joseph Smith? And, what was the theological justification for polygamy?"

"Sounds like you're too interested in polygamy,".

Dee answered. "Don't get any ideas!" We turned right on Young Street.

"There's a cheese shop!" Dee exclaimed. "I bet this is where that Nauvoo Blue Cheese comes from." Inside we found Blue Cheese, a variety of flavored cheeses, crackers and local wine. With our arms loaded, we headed back toward **Sol Seaker**.

As she climbed into our dinghy, Dee said, "We stopped to see Nauvoo, but we really found two Nauvoos, the Mormon Nauvoo and the Reorganized Latter Day Saints Nauvoo."

"I guess you'd have to say there are really three Nauvoo's," I said as I handed her the crackers, wine and cheese. "And I'm looking forward to sampling these products of the third Nauvoo."

MONARCH BUTTERFLY

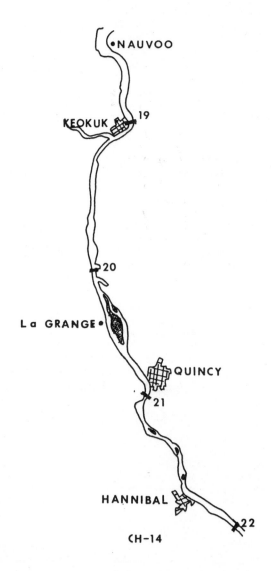

•NAUVOO

KEOKUK 19

20

La GRANGE•

QUINCY

21

HANNIBAL 22

CH-14

14

DOUGH BAIT

As we approached the Keokuk lock, the **Renee G**, with nine barges of grain, was already inside. "Hurry on down and you can lock through with her," answered the lockmaster to our radio query.

The Keokuk lock differed from all previous locks. Its lift was much higher, forty feet, compared to ten at most other locks. Instead of grabbing attached lines, we looped our own lines over bollards on barrels recessed in the lock wall, and which floated up and down with the changing water level.

When we were secure, the lock gate rose like a giant phoenix from the water behind us instead of closing double-door fashion. The chamber was twelve hundred feet long by six hundred feet wide, about twice the size of the upstream lock chambers.

As the **Renee G** left in front of us, we were tossed violently by her wheel wash. "Wheel wash" is one of those terms held over from steamboat days, but the diesel driven propellers of today's powerful towboats create a much more turbulent wash than their paddlewheel predecessors.

Below the Keokuk lock, boils and eddies, created by the forty foot drop, superimposed their unique character on the satin and corduroy river.

We also shared the next lock with the **Renee G**, where her captain told the lockmaster that her nine barges carried 12,600 tons of grain.

At 4:40 P.M. we passed the mouth of the Des Moines River, marking the boundary between Iowa and Missouri. Our first flock of migrating birds, Canada geese, flew overhead and before long, we were tied to Pete's Dock at Le Grange, Missouri.

As soon as we walked across the tracks toward Main Street, our hearts were saddened by the sight of a giant spreading elm with withering, curling, yellow leaves. The tree was obviously diseased. We were reminded of the "Green Tree Hotel" which had succumbed to Dutch Elm Disease and wondered if this beautiful tree was about to experience the same fate.

We were further depressed when we reached Main Street. One glance told us that Le Grange, like the giant elm, was diseased and dying. Once sturdy stone and brick buildings were falling apart. A boarded up antique store still contained pieces of furniture and knick-knacks which had been left to mold and decay. A former gas station now held sacks of animal feed, and many buildings were empty. A brick house with tattered lace curtains and eroded mortar seemed ready to drop a brick on us as we hurried past.

Next to a vacant brick store, a frame house was being dismantled, perhaps to salvage the lumber. It appeared this endeavor had been abandoned like the carcass of some fallen animal, only half devoured by a satiated vulture.

Here and there broken sidewalks exposed clam shells discarded from a once flourishing button industry. We collected several shells and continued along Main Street, looking up toward the large homes on the bluff as we walked. In the dimming light we could see that many of these once magnificent homes were also suffering from whatever economic or social disease had attacked downtown Le Grange. Here and there among the decay were tidy, well maintained homes, one with a lovely garden of bright red salvia. These islands of beauty served only to magnify the extent of the decay.

Ahead stood a large, modern, manufacturing plant, hardly what we had expected to see. We questioned how a town with a prosperous looking plant could be in such a state of disrepair.

Pete, owner of the Boat House Restaurant, answered our question. "That's H. G. Industries," he said. "They manufacture components for large industrial air compressors. That plant used to employ three hundred people full-time. Le Grange was doin' well then. But now the plant operates only one four-day week out of ever' three weeks. Even then it employs only about eighty people.

The warm, friendly atmosphere of Pete's riverside restaurant was the one pleasant note in the otherwise depressing and discordant Le Grange waterfront. We lingered over our steak and potatoes until closing time, then wrote the day's events in our log and settled down to what proved to be a restless night.

142

Pete's floating dock is located on the outside of a slight bend in the river and is unprotected from the wakes and washes of passing boats. The flotation consists of a series of metal barrels loosely fitted beneath a wooden walkway. The slightest wave causes the barrels to roll back and forth, banging against each other in a rhythmic pattern which sounds like rolling thunder. The more severe the wave action, the louder and more prolonged is the "thunder."

During the night several tows passed. As they rounded the bend, their wheelwash was pushed directly into the dock providing the sound and motion of a severe thunderstorm on a raging sea. Each time we awoke to a new onslaught we thought again about Main Street and the homes we could see on the bluff. "Tomorrow let's walk to the top of the bluff and look at the rest of the town," Dee said, during one of our waking periods. "I don't think it would be fair to Le Grange to look only at the waterfront."

The next day was September 23rd. Normally this date has no significance in our lives, but today we were going to celebrate Dee's fifty-second birthday. Her birthday is really August 23rd, but on that day we were towing **Sol Seaker** across the plains of North Dakota and I had totally forgotten the date. Several days later, when Dee reminded me, I felt terrible, but decided to wait until an appropriate time and surprise her. "Happy Birthday," I said as I awakened her with a big kiss.

We started the day with a birthday breakfast at Pete's. Dee had her favorite omelet with lots of bell pepper, onion and ham.

After breakfast, we bundled against the wind and mist and walked up Washington Street to the top of the bluff. As we moved away from the river, we began to see well-manicured lawns, neatly painted houses and tidy gardens. It was as though the people had turned their backs on the waterfront and hidden themselves up here out of sight of the river. But, perhaps it was the other way around. Perhaps the Mississippi, which had once been the life blood of this thriving community, had forsaken Le Grange. Whatever the reason, we found that the nearest grocery store was a full mile away from the river.

Back at Pete's we bought broasted chicken to have later, then headed slowly down an angry river toward Quincy, Illinois, where I hoped to find an appropriate

143

birthday present. As we passed a beautiful sand beach on Hogback Island, I thought about how the people in every community upriver had told us that their stretch of the river was the most beautiful. "You won't see much when you get more than fifty miles downstream," we had heard in Prescott, in Winona and in Lansing. Here, more than five hundred miles from Minneapolis, the river was still beautiful. "Look at that sandbar," I said to Dee. "I thought all the good sandbars were upstream."

"Well, one man's upstream is another man's downstream," she replied with a twinkle in her voice.

It was cool and rainy when we docked at a long, wooden retaining wall at Quincy. We speculated that the wall was probably used as a tie-up for barges. A man and woman were fishing from the end of the wall.

"How's the fishing?" I asked, after we made **Sol Seaker** secure.

"It's okay," Tony replied as he sat down his can of beer and pulled in a stringer with a carp and a sheepshead attached. "I use 'dough bait' for them carp," he went on. "I make it with flour, water, cornmeal and vanilla. Vanilla smells a little bit like bananas. Them fish really likes bananas, them carp do. If you get a old, too ripe banana or a rotten banana and mix it with the dough, them carp really like it. We also use worms," he continued. "Worms 'n dough bait."

Tony was tall and gaunt with a full beard, his hair disheveled by wind and rain. A substantial paunch, which he called his "beer-bellie," was evident beneath an ill-fitting, fishing sweater. His face and hands were well tanned.

"Do you fish here often?" Dee asked looking first at Tony then at the quiet woman beside him.

"Most ever chance we git," Tony replied, his eyes looking past Dee toward our boat.

"Do you fish too?" Dee asked the woman.

"Sometimes. I'm JoAnn. We're married."

JoAnn was also tall, thin and gaunt. Her face looked tired, sad and sallow behind her large round glasses. She, too, was dressed in ill-fitting clothing.

"Where do you get your worms?" I asked. "I'd like to get some."

"We digs 'em mostly," Tony answered. "But you can buy them at a bait shop." He told us how to get to the bait store.

"Should I walk with them?" asked JoAnn, who looked

older than her thirty-seven years. "Wouldn't take more'n a hour."

"First we want to go uptown to do some shopping," Dee said. "How do we get there?"

"You go right up that street about three or four blocks then turn that-a-way. You cain't miss it. if you want to eat, go to the Park View Cafe. It's got the best food and it's cheap. Them other places is just dives. Don't want to eat at them places, but the Park View's real good and cheap too."

"Are you going to be fishing long?" I asked.

"I got me one more beer," Tony replied. "I'll be fishin' for a while yet."

"Can we bring you back something from town?" Dee asked. "A beer or something?"

"A beer'd be real nice," Tony said.

"What kind?"

"Ah, oh, Falstaff'd be good."

"If you'll keep an eye on our boat while we're gone, we'll bring you back a beer," I said.

Tony's eyes lit up. "Shore will."

Our walk around Quincy led us past a cardboard box factory, into an antique store where we priced old pumps, and finally into Dame and Hurdle Jewelers. While Dee was inquiring about small crystal turtles, I spied some glasses and goblets, hand painted in the Franciscan Desert Rose pattern. I quickly selected a large wine glass and carried it to the rear counter without her knowledge. This would be the perfect birthday gift!

By the time Dee got to the back of the store, the glass was gift wrapped. "Did you find a turtle?" I asked.

"Yeah, but it's not like the one I saw on the cruise last June," Dee replied. "I wish I had bought that one. Mr. Nickelson is going to call their other store. They have a different one there. Someone will bring it over in a few minutes."

While we waited, Andy Nickelson gave us a map of the Great River Road and told us about places to visit and good restaurants in and around Quincy. He also gave us his home phone number and said, "Feel free to call me if you have any problems or questions while you are here or even after you leave Quincy."

The turtle arrived, but was not what Dee was looking for. As we left the store, it began to rain very hard. We hurried down the street to Walgreens to get out of the rain and buy some recording tapes so we could make tapes to send to my father in California. When the rain had let up we headed back toward the river, stopping for a few minutes at the office of the Wildlife Refuge to pick up a list of migratory birds and information about the extensive refuge along the Upper Mississippi.

We bought two beers and two Mountain Dews at a bar where we were surprised to see onions and roasted peanuts for sale. We bought some of each.

Tony and JoAnn were still fishing, despite the earlier rainstorm. "I caught another carp and a perch," Tony informed us as we approached. "My cat'll like them. After I scales 'em he eats 'em starting from the head. Eats ever thing, don't even leave an eyeball."

As I handed Tony the two beers, JoAnn said, "I wisht I'd ast you to bring me a Pepsi or sumthin."

"We brought you two Mountain Dews. Do you like them?" Dee asked.

"Yeah, they's fine! I like them fine!"

"Would you like to see in our boat before we leave?"

"Shore."

"See I told you they could drive from inside," Tony said to JoAnn, as they entered **Sol Seaker**.

"Them bikes has motors on them don't they," JoAnn said, more as a statement than a question.

While Tony and JoAnn were in the boat, I called the next lock, which was about two miles downriver. "We've got a tow in now locking down then we're comin' up for a government tow with two barges. We can put you in with them. Be about forty minutes."

"We always call the locks," Dee said, "so we know when we can lock through."

"It'll take you 'bout twenty minutes to get down there," said Tony.

We were glad that we still had a little time to visit with Tony and JoAnn.

"I was raised in Quincy," said Tony. "My mother was the Belle of three cities - Quincy, Hannibal and Keokuk. JoAnn's my second wife. She's younger than me, I'm fifty-three, will be in December. My first wife died. My second woman had a child but she wasn't any good, so I wouldn't marry her. She'd run around an' one time I told her to just keep going. She had a son. I'm the father. I see him ever once-in-a-while."

146

"I got three children," said JoAnn, as a cloud of despair crossed her face and brought tears near the surface. One's fifteen, one eleven and the other eight. I haven't seen them for eight or twelve years though. They took them away an' I cain't see them no more."

The tears came closer.

"It was real bad what they done," said Tony. "She cain't have no more children. I think she could have raised them kids okay, but they said she wasn't a fit mother 'an her dad had a stroke an' was in a rest home."

"I git real sad when I think about my children. I wisht I could jist see them at least."

"I guess we'd better go." I said, "if we want to make that lock on time."

"Yall send us a card or sumpin' to let us know if you made it," said JoAnn. "We'd like to git a card. We like to git cards 'n things."

"We will," answered Dee, "but it won't be for a long time, about Christmas time."

"Will you give me a hug?" JoAnn asked Dee.

As Dee hugged her, JoAnn kissed her on the cheek, tears streaming down her face. As we pulled away I could see tears in Dee's eyes and feel them very close to the surface in my own. We rode silently for several minutes.

I knew Dee was thinking about our own Kathy, who like JoAnn, is retarded and unable to have or care for children.

After a while she said in an anguished voice, "Oh why can't people realize that it's much better if the JoAnns of the world do not have children instead of having their lives ruined by taking children away from them. I'm just glad Kathy didn't have to endure what JoAnn has gone through."

"You tie off on the riverside wall," said the lock-master, as we followed the Corps of Engineers' tow, **Clinton**, into lock 21. We searched in vain for the dangling ropes, but all we saw were metal pins along the lock wall. Quickly Dee grabbed two of our mooring lines and brought one up to me. I hurriedly flipped it toward one of the pins - and missed. The strong wind didn't give me a second chance. I eased ahead hoping to catch the next pin. On the third try I managed to get my rope over a pin. It took all of my strength to hold the wind-driven boat until Dee could also secure a line. By the time **Sol Seaker** was in place, we were half way down

147

to the next level, bumping and scraping along the rough
and oily lock wall.

Between Quincy and Hannibal, we noticed that there
were fewer trees along the banks. In one area a number
of houses stood on stilts, and near the bank two fishermen in a jon boat pulled in a trammel net.

A few minutes after we pulled into the Hannibal
Harbor we watched a drama unfold unlike any we had seen
before. A towboat, pushing fourteen loaded grain barges,
was moving slowly downstream. One of the two lead
barges had apparently come loose at one end and was
beginning to swing outward away from the tow. Men
worked frantically at the cables attached to the other
end of the barge. The tow stopped. The current caught
the loose barge causing it to swing out in front of its
companion barge. The tow began to back up slowly. The
loose barge continued to swing around the front of the
tow. Just as the angle of the loose barge passed the
center of its companion, the towboat suddenly began to
move forward again. This action caused the loose barge
to come around on the other side of its companion. All
the time, the deck hands continued to work with the
restraining cables.

"They're moving it to the other side!" I exclaimed.
"It's not loose, they're moving it to the other side."

In a few moments we had observed an amazing feat of
skillful towboaters, as they loosened a barge holding
thousands of tons of grain, and slowly swung it around
the end of a raft of thirteen other barges to be re-
attached on the opposite side.

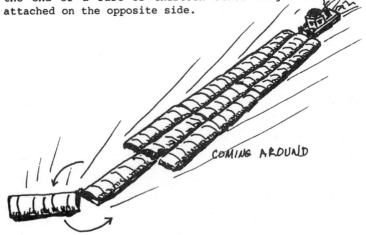

COMING AROUND

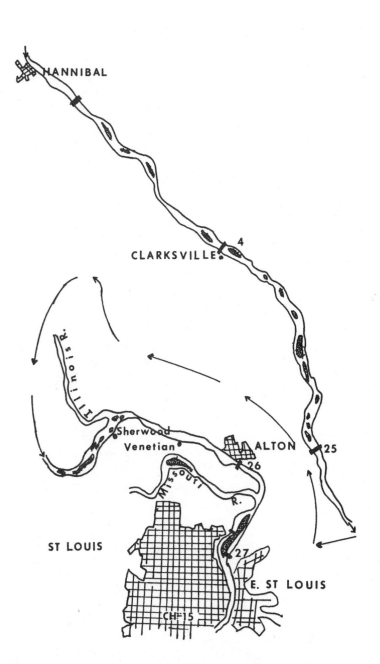

HANNIBAL

CLARKSVILLE 4

Illinois R.

Sherwood
Venetian

ALTON 25

26

Missouri R.

ST LOUIS

27

E. ST LOUIS

CH-15

15

RAINTREE ARTS COUNCIL

To say we liked Hannibal is an understatement. Even in a dreary drizzle, who could dislike the "St. Petersburg" of Tom Sawyer and Huck Finn.

Some may sneer at the crass commercialism evidenced by the Tom and Huck Motel, Huck Finn Shopping Center, Mark Twain Motor Inn, Injun Joe Campground and Becky Thatcher Restaurant. But we look upon these as a continuing tribute to the man and his writing.

Samuel Clemens' Hannibal centers around his restored home, the Becky Thatcher (Laura Hawkins) house, Cardiff Hill, and the Mark Twain Cave. Each year Hannibal hosts National Tom Sawyer Days for a week preceding the Fourth of July. The event is culminated by the finals of the National Fence Painting Contest.

But Hannibal is more than its memorials to Mark Twain. Hannibal was the home of other well known people, and even with the bombardment of Twainian lore, she hasn't forgotten her other claims to fame.

There was Molly Brown, famous for "spending her husband's money like water," and immortalized in the musical, "The Unsinkable Molly Brown."

Hannibal remembers Admiral Robert Coontz, Commander of the U.S. Naval Forces; William Henry Hatch, a U.S. legislator who sponsored bills that created the U.S. Department of Agriculture and the U.S. Weather Bureau; and Margaret Smith, the first woman doctor in the state of Missouri.

Hannibal also remembers "Hannibal's Cannibals" a professional baseball team, and she remembers that once there were fourteen cigar factories in town. She has not forgotten that at one time fifty-four daily passenger trains stopped at Hannibal, and that the first cement plant west of the Mississippi was located here. She also remembers the old ice house.

"A hundred thousand tons of ice was cut from the river each year and stored in a big ol' ice house for summer use," an elderly gentleman at the tourist bureau informed us. "They'd cut blocks, hook chains on them an' teams of horses drug them up the steep hill to the ice house. Story goes, one day a feller' was showin' off an' started ridin' one of them blocks up that hill. 'Bout half way up the block broke loose and came sliding back down at full speed. 'Hang on' yelled his fellow workers. 'I am hangin' on fer my life!' he yelled back. Well that block hit the frozen surface of the river and skidded clean across to Illinois with this feller still hangin' on fer his life!"

As was true in most river towns, we found the people of Hannibal to be friendly and helpful. When a letter we were expecting hadn't arrived at the Post Office on Friday, the clerk said, "We'll be open tomorrow, if it isn't here by then, come back on Sunday. The Post Office is closed, but there'll be people in here sorting mail. You just ring that bell by the door and they'll be happy to see if your letter's here."

Our jaws dropped. Never before, or since have we been invited to pick up mail on a Sunday. We were further impressed by the Post Office because it had made available a large unused space near the mail boxes for a display of beautiful water colors by a local artist.

Looking at a painting of the Old Federal Building, a magnificent pre-1900 Empire style structure, located just down the street, Dee stated, "His painting looks better than the real building."

By a slight exaggeration of perspective the artist had, in an almost cartoon statement, captured the qualities of age, mass, purpose and life which were slowly being lost in the real building, due to disuse and damage.

We also liked Hannibal because of several delicious mangoes I found in a back street grocery for thirty-nine cents each; albeit, in my excitement over the mangoes I forgot the instant coffee I had been sent to purchase.

We liked Hannibal because it was alive, yet quietly so. There was a balance between yesterday and today, between fact and fiction, between art and practicality.

On Saturday we were standing in the long line at the Post Office when the clerk from the day before spotted us. "It's here," he said, as he picked up a large envelope and motioned for us to come up and get it. How surprised we were that he would remember us among the hundreds of faces he must see daily.

150

We liked Hannibal - but even in Hannibal there were things that troubled us. Although many of the buildings in the historical section of town had been restored, there were still wonderful old buildings that were vacant and decaying, including the Mark Twain Hotel.

It was a rainy Saturday afternoon when we left Hannibal. After passing beneath the beautiful cliff at "Lovers Leap" we met the Phyllis pushing sixteen empty grain barges upriver.

Below lock 22, we met three small runabouts on a weekend outing. In one stretch of river we noted that several navigational aids did not coincide with our chart. A lighted daymark was two hundred yards from its charted location. There were two lighted daymarks which did not show on our chart at all, and a third that was on an island rather than at the charted mainland location. Assuming that these discrepancies represented changes in placement since the last update of our chart book, we agreed that we would need to be a bit skeptical of all chart entries.

Happily, we were able to stop at a small private dock at Clarksville where we sought refuge from the cool dampness at Rosie's Cafe. The waitress, Sue, wanted to take our picture. "We don't have a picture of anyone from California," she said as she showed us a large stack of polaroid shots of people from "lots of places" including Alaska, Hawaii and Lebanon.

I asked if she thought it would be okay for us to stay overnight at the small dock where we had tied Sol Seaker.

"I was Clarksville's Fourth of July Queen," she said, "and you can tell them I said it's okay for you to stay there."

While Dee and I dined on pork loin and catfish Sue told us about the Old Apple Shed. "Now it's used as a craft workshop and a theater, run by the Raintree Arts Council. Last summer a group from St. Louis did three performances of "The Beggar's Opera." She showed us pictures of the cast. "The place was packed every night. You ought to see the Apple Shed before you leave town."

As we left, Sue gave us two brochures. One was entitled "Beautiful Clarksville, Missouri - Home of the Famous Sky Ride," the other "Your Guide to a Walking Tour of Clarksville, Missouri." That evening we looked over the brochures and decided to take time to see more of Clarksville before heading downstream.

151

Next morning we were greeted at the Apple Shed by Jamie McIlroy and several ladies who were working on craft projects for an upcoming bazaar. "The Beggar's Opera was the biggest event of the year," volunteered Jamie. "Everyone in town got behind it and supported it. Would you like a tour of the Apple Shed?"

"Yes," we answered in unison.

"This is the cold storage room." she said, as she led us into an interior room. "In the winter time we do plays in here because it's well insulated and easy to heat. We also have craft shows and bazaars in the big packing shed. That big bar is solid oak. It came from an old hotel in St. Louis."

As we prepared to leave for the walking tour, Dee said, "Perhaps you could tell us where to start."

"Certainly," Jamie answered. "I designed and print-ed the brochure. My mother-in-law owns one of the old houses and my parents own the one that my husband and I live in."

After Jamie autographed our brochure, we started out. Our tour took us past restored homes, historical churches, the library and up the skyride to Lookout Point for the "best view" of the river, back country, the town, and lock and dam 24. The brochure noted that, ". . . 30,000,000 tons of freight pass through this lock every year."

Far below we could see an orange dot through the trees. "There's **Sol Seaker**!" exclaimed Dee. "I'm ready to go."

The magical river called again.

We shared lock 25 with the three small pleasure craft we had seen the day before. The lockmaster allow-ing us to float freely in the center of the chamber rather than hold to lines along the wall. How easy it was. We wondered why free floating wasn't allowed in all locks, especially when there was little wind and no towboats. As we were slowly lowered, we talked to the other boaters. "We've been to Hannibal," one man said. "We came up from St. Louis and are on our way back home. Where are you folks going?"

"New Orleans," we explained, noting that familiar look of envy.

As the gates opened and the three boats sped away downriver, Dee commented, "I guess if you only have weekends you have to hurry everywhere. I'm glad we can go slowly and don't have a schedule to keep."

At Kinder's Restaurant, we stopped for a late lunch. As we ate bowls of Chili we watched the diesel driven, paddlewheel **Golden Eagle Ferry** carry a full load of sixteen cars from the Illinois side to the Missouri shore. Twenty minutes later she returned for another load of waiting autos.

"There sure are a lot of cars crossing the river," Dee said to our waitress.

"It's Sunday afternoon," the waitress replied, "and the nearest bridge is more than twenty-five miles down at Alton. This is the shortest way to St. Charles and West St. Louis. Them cars are lined up two or three miles waitin' for the ferry."

After eating a piece of apple pie, we bought a bag of apples and headed downriver. The sun was about to set when we met the **Jessie Flowers,** at mile 219. We had seen the **Jessie Flowers** several weeks before, heading downriver with loaded grain barges, now she was on her way back up with empties.

Below mile 218, we swung around a junction buoy and headed up the Illinois River, moving slowly along the Grafton waterfront looking for a small boat harbor that was indicated on our chart.

"I don't think there's a harbor here." I said.

"It,s not listed in Quimby's Guide," Dee replied as she searched the pages. "It's five miles downriver to the next marina, it'll be dark before we get there, but I think we passed one about a mile upstream. Let's see, '. . . mile 219, Sherwood Harbor, Joe Krebec.' It says here, '. . . Enter cut and go straight to gas dock. Harbormaster lives in mobile near dock - transients welcome.'"

"Sherwood Harbor it is," I said, as I turned **Sol Seaker** back up the Mississippi and toward the Missouri shore.

The entrance to Sherwood Harbor was very narrow. In the drizzle and rapidly fading light, we could see many floating limbs in the cut. Picking our way carefully through the debris we entered the very, very muddy harbor. As we stepped onto the gas dock we could see the hulls of a row of burned boats lining one side of the harbor. Obviously there had been a massive fire at this marina.

We found Joe just finishing dinner in his mobile. "The fire hit about 1:30 A.M. on July 20th. I rushed out and cut loose all the boats that the fire hadn't

153

reached, and pushed them out in the middle of the harbor. All of a sudden I was trapped out on the end of a burning dock. I just managed to get aboard a pontoon boat that floated close by, and push my way out to safety. All together I lost sixteen berths and fifteen boats. I'm still trying to get all the debris out of the water. I didn't have no insurance. I was gonna retire at the end of this season. Now I don't guess I'll ever be able to retire."

Joe was a defeated man. In addition to his misfortune, he was crippled in one leg, making it difficult for him to walk over the rough ground and climb around the docks.

"How sad," Dee said, as, later, we guided **Sol Seaker** through floating debris to the covered berth Joe had assigned us. "He really looks like he needs to retire."

"It makes me feel a little guilty," I said, "retiring at fifty-two when older and disabled people like Joe can't."

We saw fish jumping in the harbor; so, as soon as we were docked, I baited a hook. We sat watching the final red glow fade from the western sky, as we ate another of our mangoes and sipped a glass of Boones Farm.

Inside the covered berth, it was almost pitch dark when I noticed two shadowy figures hunched down and moving slowly along a walkway at the end of the berths. "Look," I whispered to Dee, "what are they doing?"

As the mysterious pair came closer, we could see that the taller figure was holding a long stick, raised menacingly over his head. Both figures seemed to be staring into the narrow channel of water that separated the walkway from the bank. Both stopped. The tall one raised the stick higher, then suddenly thrust it forward and downward into the muddy water. As he slowly raised the stick we could see something wiggling at the end. At that instant the shorter figure snapped on a flashlight, and, in the beam, a large bullfrog kicked helplessly in an attempt to free himself from the barbed "gig." When the tall figure reached out to grasp the frog, he turned slightly, revealing a larger frog dangling from a stringer that hung down his back.

As he clipped the new frog onto the stringer, he noticed the light in our boat. "Did we wake you?" the tall figure asked. "We were so busy looking for frogs we didn't see that there was someone on the boat."

"No," I said, as I stepped out of the cabin, still not sure of these dark figures.

"Sorry we disturbed you. This is my wife Ruth. We thought there'd be more frogs than this here. We usually find more. We come here a lot for frogs."

The man apologized again for disturbing us, but before we could ask any more questions they extinguished their light and melted into the darkness, just as quickly and mysteriously as they had appeared.

"Yuck." Dee said as I returned to the cabin. "How could anyone gig frogs like that?"

At that instant, the bell on my fishing rod began to ring and I reeled in a catfish. "I guess there really isn't much difference between hooking a fish and gigging a frog," I said, as I released the catfish back into the water, and stowed my pole.

Our restless night in this depressing marina was rewarded by a glorious sunrise. 'Spirits rose with the sun and we hurriedly prepared to continue downriver.

During a short stop at beautiful Venetian Harbor, we encountered **My Brother's Boat** and **Shazam**, the first of numerous Florida bound yachts we would encounter in the next several weeks.

Dick and his wife Dorothy were transporting **My Brother's Boat**, a fifty foot Hatteras, from Illinois to Fort Lauderdale for a wealthy man from Chicago. "He plans to sell this boat and replace it with a ninety-foot, 2.2 million dollar boat, now under construction," Dick told us.

Dick had retired at age thirty-five and since has ferried thirteen yachts down the Mississippi. He was having lots of trouble with **My Brother's Boat**. One of the engines was smoking badly from faulty fuel jets which had been replaced in Chicago, but now, only thirty hours later, were again in need of replacement.

The **Shazam** was even bigger and fancier than **My Brother's Boat**. We learned from Dick that it was owned and operated by William R. Smyth (pronounced Smith), also headed for Florida.

At the Alton Lock we had one of our longest waits. Several tows were lined up, as a tiny switching tow moved barges in and out of the lock as quickly as possible. While we waited, the **Shazam** joined us as did another yacht, **Palace of the Cee**. After two and a-half hours, the three of us locked through together.

Seven miles 'below Alton we came to the confluence

of the Mississippi and Missouri Rivers.   We recalled having read, in R. Raven-Hart's, DOWN THE MISSISSIPPI, about the meeting of these two great waters, "...the river...if renamed 'Missouri' would become the longest in the world instead of the insignificant twelfth it is at present."

There would, indeed, be great justification for either changing the name of the "Mississippi" to the "Missouri" or the "Missouri" to the "Mississippi" for then it would in fact be the longest river in the world with it's headwaters in Montana and its mouth some 4,300 miles away in the Gulf of Mexico, below New Orleans.   The great Mississippi / Missouri and their tributaries drain roughly one-third of the continental United States.

The meeting of these two celebrated rivers poses a new problem for navigation. During high water the force of the collision, as the Missouri slams into the Mississippi at a thirty degree angle, creates great swirling boils and eddies that can tear apart the most securely fastened line of barges. This same collision slows the flow of both rivers causing tremendous quantities of sand and silt to be dropped to the bottom. During low water ever changing sandbars make navigation virtually impossible.

To solve these navigation problems, eight-mile "Chain of Rocks Canal" was built to bypass this treacherous section of the river. A large sign on the upper end of Chouteau Island directs all traffic into the canal. At the lower end of The Chain of Rocks Canal, we shared lock twenty-seven with **Shazam** and **Palace of the Cee.**"

Emerging from this final lock on the Mississippi, we could feel a new freedom in the mighty river. The flow was faster, and there were more boils, eddies and rips as the "old man" charged out of this last fetter and voiced his displeasure with man's attempts at control.

Bouncing and twisting on this increased energy, we were reminded that an awesome power had been only partially contained by man's interference. No matter how many dams and locks man might build, ultimately the billions of gallons of water, sand and silt are going to reach the Gulf of Mexico.

Only in the Gulf will this mighty off-spring of the sea and the sun be controlled as he, like all cyclical phenomena, returns to his source.

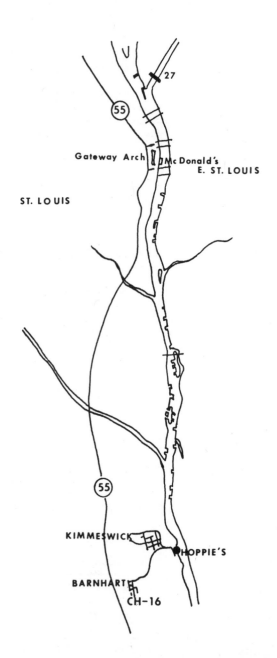

27

55

Gateway Arch McDonald's
E. ST. LOUIS

ST. LOUIS

55

KIMMESWICK
HOPPIE'S

BARNHART
CH-16

16

PA PA JOE

As we passed under the Merchant's Railroad Bridge, the third of nine bridges crossing the river near St. Louis, we began to have misgivings about the remainder of our journey, for here to the new unfettered current was added a variety of prop-bending, hull-thumping limbs and logs brought down by a rising Missouri River.

The noise and congestion of the St. Louis-East St. Louis Metropolis, of over a million people, pressed against the river on both sides, diminishing the size of **Sol Seaker** until we felt like a small leaf floating helplessly between great canyon walls.

Below the ancient Ead's Bridge and above the Poplar Street Bridge, the buildings were pushed back to make a place for the gleaming and graceful Gateway Arch, which vied for its place in the sun with the golden arches of a McDonald's Restaurant, floating in the form of a side-wheeler, a few hundred yards from the base of the silver monolith.

The arch and the congestion slid rapidly behind us as the relentless river bounced and joggled us south-ward. "We'll soon be at Hoppie's " I said, as a new excitement began to stir inside.

The excitement was prompted by my recollection of a reply to my letter of inquiry. The reply had come from Joseph W. Wonsewitz of Barnhart, Missouri. Joe, like Sternwheel Don and Bob Reader had been given my letter by the local postmaster.

As Dee drove the boat I took out Joe's letter and re-read it aloud:

Mr. Parker,

The postmaster at Barnhart Mo. gave me your letter requesting river information of the mighty Mississippi River. Mr. McCoy (postmaster) asked if I might be able to help you.

To start I will tell you I am Jos. W. Wonsewitz. I

have only an 8th grade education and as you can see am not very good at letter writing. I am an electrical contractor. I live on a 48 foot (sea going) houseboat. At present I live alone as I am separated from wife and two fine little girls.

My boat is documented and the name of this 1971 houseboat is **Cloud Nine**. **Cloud Nine** and I are docked at Hoppie's Marina. At this time we are the only ones at the dock proper. Normally this time of year all boats are in dry dock due to icing difficulties of the river.

Hoppie's Marina is located at Waters Point on the Mississippi River. Some maps and documents call this Windsor Harbor. At this location a gun boat of the Civil War was sunk. The name of the gunboat was the **Windsor**. Charles Hopkins (Hoppie) is the owner and operator of the marina. He has very good docking facilities. Most of the main dock is actually anchored to the sunken Windsor. I would recommend you contact Mr. Charles Hopkins for information of docking etc. I will enclose a letter head with his address. He (Hoppie) is the best authority I know of, on the subject of Mississippi river – Oh by the way, I am known as Pa Pa Joe here at the marina. Hoppie's oldest daughter gave me that name about four or five summers ago.

Now, I will try to answer your questions as best I can.

1. The best months for safe boating in this area are from April (a little chilly) to about the middle or last of November.

2. In this area there's only one marina, Hoppie's. He has all the services anyone could need. By the way, I may not have mentioned, Hoppie and his wife are the nicest people you will ever meet. Consider the third question as answered beings Hoppie's has all the services required.

4. The only special regulations are a fishing license and a boat inspection by the Coast Guard. The inspection is free.

5. There are about three regular commercial fishermen who fish these waters all year long. Fishing generally is always great. River Sturgeon, Blue Catfish, Mud Catfish, Drum, Carp, just about anything you

can want. I have hooked bass from this river. There
are a lot of wing dikes that form very nice coves in
back of them. In the cove you are protected from tow
boat backwash and are able to get out of the current.

        I tried to call you on the phone. The operator
said there was (no listing)
        As I have received company and am being disturbed,
I will close this letter and wait your reply and any
other questions I might be able to answer -
                                I remain,
                                Pa Pa Joe
                                of **Cloud Nine**

        I apologize for the paper and for not knowing where
to put all the marks. I will put the marks here and you
can distribute them where needed in this letter.
,,,,,,...??????"""""!!!!!;;;;;,,,,,,:::::'''''!!??????

        In my answer to Joe, I had thanked him for a most
informative letter and explained that our real purpose
was to travel downriver to the Gulf, and that we would
appreciate any information or suggestions he might have.
I re-read his reply:

        Hello Again,
        I received your letter today with very warm
feeling's.
        I sure hope you and yours get your trip down the
Mighty Mississippi. You will find the old guy (the
river) will treat you very kindly. Actually, the river
will treat you kindly only if you watch him very, very
close. If you turn your back he will get you!
        By the way, I'm looking forward to your stop at
Hoppie's. When you get to this neck of the river, I
will show you the Mississippi Triangle. I'm sure you
have heard of the Bermuda Triangle. Well, the Mississippi Triangle is much worse.
        I don't know how much experience you may have on
navigating the Mighty Miss. So, I will give you this one
bit of very important info. What ever you do, try to
give all commercial·towboats as wide a birth as you can.
Some towboat captains hate pleasure boaters and will try
to throw side wash along with the forward and stern wash
you will have to encounter. If you don't have a V.H.F.
transmitter I would say, "Don't travel the river." With
159

the radio you can talk to the towboat captains and you will find most of them are friendly and helpful. Like I say, give them all the room you can - Also, with the radio you have communications with Coast Guard, other boaters, and the marinas you will be staying at. The one part I forgot - "You will have weather info at all times."

Now, to get to your questions.

1. There are no marina's between Alton Lake and Hoppie's. St. Louis has not had a marina for fifteen years due to the commercial towboats and restaurants. Unless things have changed, you can't even tie to the waterfront restaurants you may want to visit.

2. I believe the next marina from Hoppie's to be 159 miles South. I have not taken the time to check this out, so don't quote me. I will make a point to find out, long before your trip.

3. The only books I would recommend would be the river charts.

I will save the telephone call to you for later - I have not written a letter to any one since I was in Algoa State Reformatory for boys (I was 17). You have received the only hand written correspondence from me, since then. Really, I should not be proud of the fact, but I really don't know why your letter would cause me to start writing again,

Its starting to snow again! Lord, I haven't seen this much snow in this area in my 44 years.

Later

Sorry about interruption in my letter, but I closed up shop and left to fight the snowy roads.

This morning, when I was leaving my boat to come to work I had a small accident. About $3,000 damage to the side of my suburban. It's a long story so I'll save it.

So far this year I have been iced in twice. I've been lucky because around my boat it only got to be a couple of inches thick. The towboat traffic on the river helps keep it broke up.

I have five electric heaters on my boat; they are doing the job. If my houseboat didn't have insulation in the walls I guess I would have been froze out by now.

Not much information in this letter but it should keep the communication going - I'll try to make the next one a little more interesting.

Joe

Our twenty-two mile trip from St. Louis to Hoppie's was uneventful except for the need to be on a constant vigil for floating logs, and the meeting of three tows; **The Creole Belle** out of Houma, Louisiana, **The R. H. Hoffman** with three cement barges, and **The Gloria G** an Apex Oil tow.

We had become somewhat complacent about the added speed of the river until making our turn toward Hoppie's Marina. As we came broadside to the strong current, it swept us right past the docks and a hundred yards downstream before we completed our turn.

We made our way slowly back upriver to the inside of the long dock (a series of flat metal barges connected end to end), where a man stepped off the cabin cruiser **Dixie Dee** and said, "Kinda fools you don't it," as he helped us secure our lines. "Don't matter too much how we tie them," he stated, "Hoppie'll be down to check the boat as soon as he finishes with them two big yachts. He'll probably re-tie your lines anyway."

Only then did we realize that both **Shazam** and **Palace of the Cee** had also stopped at Hoppie's. In a few minutes a man of medium build with brown hair and a ruddy outdoor complexion welcomed us as he methodically inspected each line. He loosened one here and tightened one there, then climbed aboard and turned the wheel hard to port causing **Sol Seaker's** stern to ride in gently against the well fendered dock.

"That makes it a lot easier to board, and keeps the boat from swinging back and forth in the current," he explained, then hurried back down the dock to take care of another in-coming boat.

Dee and I walked down the long dock searching for **Cloud Nine.** As we passed a covered and carpeted area known as the Living Room, a stumpy, rugged-looking man in his mid-forties with a round ruddy face and slightly bulging watery eyes, clad only in jeans, emerged from a houseboat. Several prominent scars were visible across his shoulder and down his ample stomach. His movements were quick and somewhat erratic like those of a hyperactive child.

161

"You must be Pa Pa Joe!" Dee exclaimed. "We're the Parkers from California."

"I've been wonderin' if you were really gonna get here. Come on in and I'll call Cindy. We'll go to the Southern Kitchen for dinner. You like fried chicken?"

We learned that Cindy was Joe's twenty-five year old girlfriend.

When Cindy arrived with her two girls we greeted a very pretty and well endowed young lady with shoulder length light auburn hair and a ready smile. One of Joe's daughters, Valerie, accompanied us to the small simple cafe.

Joe was obviously well known to the twin teenage waitresses. He ordered his "usual," which turned out to be a whole fried chicken and a double order of fries, without vegetables or bread. Along with his order, the waitress brought a damp towel instead of a napkin. I was so fascinated by Joe's eating that I could hardly attend to my own food.

Joe ate with the same hyperactivity I had noted earlier. He ate ravenously, but only the easy to get meat, stopping periodically to wipe his hands and to relate segments of a boating accident that had taken place at Hoppie's a few years before.

"One day," he began, "I was in a small boat about a mile and a half above the marina. The boat hit a rough wave and I fell overboard with a rope tangled around my body and the boat still going and pulling me under the water."

Joe ate some chicken.

"I was finally able to get loose, but I had a severe cut on my foot and some broken ribs. The boat was now going away from me and I can't swim much. I looked around for a log to grab but there wasn't any. I just managed to keep myself afloat by rolling on my back and keeping my feet pointed downstream. I could hardly breathe because of the pain. I began taking short, quick breaths, then realized I was getting dizzy from hyperventilation."

Joe ate some more chicken.

"I started blowing out air, but it hurt like hell. Every wave ducked me under again. All of a sudden I heard myself say out loud 'I'm gonna die, I'm gonna drown in this river.' I looked over and saw that I was even with Hoppie's."

Joe ate some fries.

162

"I started yellin' 'help' as loud as the pain would allow. Fern (Hoppie's wife) heard me. The young man who works for them dove in the water and swam to me while Fern comandeered a boat and came roarin' out."

Joe ate some chicken and wiped his hands.

"I had to pull myself onto the swim platform because I hurt so much I couldn't stand to let anyone touch me. When I got on the ambulance stretcher, I never moved. When they wheeled me into the emergency, I yelled for the nurse to get me some pain killer and a muscle re-laxer. Later, when my doctor came, I said, 'John give me some pain killer and muscle relaxer.' After he did, he learned I had already had some. He was furious. He said, 'Don't you know that if you go into respiratory arrest with that much stuff in you there's no way I can save you!' I said, 'I'm not gonna go into respiratory arrest, the pain hasn't even stopped yet.'"

Joe ate some chicken and fries.

"He wheeled me into surgery and started sewing up my foot. I was layin' where I couldn't see what he was doin'. Pretty soon I said, 'John, when are you gonna finish sewin' up my foot?' 'How'd you know I was sewing up your foot?' he asked. 'Can you feel that?'"

"'You damn right I can,'" I said.

"'Then I'll give you a local,' he said. So he stuck needles all around my foot. After a while he started sewin' again. I waited for a while then I said, 'John, aren't you ever gonna finish sewin' that foot?'"

"'You mean you can still feel that?' he asked. 'Damn right!' I said."

"'What does it feel like?' he asked. 'It feels like your sewin' up my foot.' I said."

Joe ate some chicken and fries and wiped his hands.

"I've taken so much pain killer from all my acci-dents that I've built up an immunity - no - a tolerance for it. Anyone else with half as much in them would be sound asleep! For three days I couldn't move myself. You saw them scars all over. I guess I'm just accident prone."

When planning our voyage, we had decided to leave **Sol Seaker** at Hoppie's while we flew back to Minneapolis to pick up our car and trailer. "Fern's goin' to the airport tomorrow," Joe said. "She'll be happy to take you."

"We're going to drive up to Lake Superior to look at the fall colors, and visit a few places along the

163

way. We won't be back for about a week," we told Joe and Cindy.

The next morning we were awakened by the sound of a towboat's diesel engine. A sound that seemed much closer than it should have been. Dee raised up on one elbow and turned to look out the sliding door at the rear of the cabin. "My God!" she exclaimed. "He's right behind us!"

I turned to see the pilothouse of a towboat towering above our stern, the "knees" only a few yards behind us and moving closer. In large black letters the name **Helen Capps** was written across the front. Slowly the towboat moved sideways across the current. It passed the lower end of Hoppie's long floating dock and continued out into the river. We watched as she gained speed and moved off toward a line of barges.

"You'll have to get used to the **Helen Capps** as long as you stay here," explained Fern on our way to the airport. "She's a busy boat. A new crew comes aboard every eight hours. She'll be going in and out lots of times. She has to come close to the end of our dock 'cause the best water is there, but you don't need to worry. She's got a good crew."

The fall colors were at their best. We toured the "House on the Rocks" in Wisconsin and spent a day in New Glarus, where we had fondue. We also stopped at Kampsville, Illinois, which has been "taken over" by a group of archeologists who run a year round school and research center.

Above St. Louis we crossed the **Golden Eagle Ferry** (at Kinder's Restaurant where we had eaten several days earlier). The combination of our Jeep Cherokee and trailer were too long for the small ferry. After five of us muscled the heavy trailer sideways to make it fit, one of the men exclaimed, "That's one hell of a trailer! I'd like to see the boat she carries."

We reached Hoppie's about 5:30 in the evening and decided to stay aboard **Sol Seaker** for the night before driving on to Memphis where we would leave the car and trailer. Joe met us at the end of the dock. "I'll call Cindy and have her prepare a home cooked meal for you!"

We protested, but Joe doesn't hear protests very well. While he was making the call, I was thinking, "Dee would kill me if I pulled something like that."

I'm sure Cindy wasn't very pleased with the sudden imposition, but she covered it well and was a charming

and gracious hostess.   During the meal Joe was very
gruff with the children and demanding with Cindy.   Dee
and I began to wonder if this was the same Pa Pa Joe
Wonsewitz who had written those two sensitive and informative letters.

As we prepared to leave, Cindy put her arms around
Joe and said, as if to excuse his behavior, "He's just
gruff on the outside.   Inside he's really a pussy cat."

A softness came over Joe's face and for the first
time since our arrival, I sensed that he might be ready
to lower his defenses and let us see the real Pa Pa Joe.

The next day it was after dark when we returned
from Memphis by bus.   We went quietly to bed where, as
we enjoyed the gentle rocking of **Sol Seaker**, Dee
sighed," It's nice to be home again."

After our return, Joe seemed much more gentle.   One
day when he and I were alone he told me the story of his
wife, children and Cindy.   "I just went through a divorce.   I'd give anything to have my wife and daughters
back.   It was all my own fault. There was another woman.
I wish I could say that woman threw her beautiful body
at me, but it didn't happen like that.   It was all my
fault.   It's strange how a man can screw up his whole
life.   Yes, I'd give anything to have my wife and
daughters back.   I really want them back, but now I have
Cindy too.   I really screwed up.   I can't ever marry
Cindy; with the age difference it just wouldn't work
out.   I really don't know what to do."

Joe's normally moist eyes were now on the verge of
real tears.   He believed God was punishing him for
"screwing up" the lives of those he loved.

To me it seemed that Joe had two viable choices.
He could break off with Cindy and try to re-establish a
relationship with his ex-wife, or he could ask Cindy to
marry him.   The decision would not be an easy one.

Joe felt a responsibility for Cindy's marital
break-up which created a strong guilt, while his love
for her drove the wedge between him and his ex-wife
deeper and deeper.   Indecision kept the wounds open so
that healing could never really start. Our sympathies
and prayers went out to everyone involved.

One day, as we were sitting in the Living Room, Joe
was starting to tell us another story about happenings
at the marina when suddenly he interrupted himself by
shouting, "Weldon, go get your camera, there's a cold
front coming in."   He pointed skyward.

We looked up to see a spectacular line of clouds moving in from the northwest. In front of the clouds the sun shown brightly from a clear blue sky. Behind was dark gray. The air which had been balmy-warm and still, suddenly stirred restlessly with a coolness that caused Dee to shiver.

After I took the picture, Joe invited us inside, where we sat cozily, as the sky darkened and rain began to fall. Joe poured himself another cup of coffee and continued his story. "There was a woman used to keep her boat here. A fast outboard runabout. She always gunned the engine when she left the dock. Took off like a 'bat outa hell.' This one time she and her man companion had too much to drink. As usual she jammed the throttle forward and burst away from the ramp at full bore. Only thing is, she didn't realize the wheel was turned hard to the right. The boat whirled around and headed straight for the mooring barge."

Joe held his two hands out palms down, fingers pointing toward each other, and moved them together in a demonstrated collision. "Only thing saved her was she hit the edge of a floating log, which made the boat veer so she caught the barge only a glancing blow. The impact threw her out face against the barge, then right back into the boat - out cold. The boat, still under full power, ran off across the river with her companion trying desperately to get to the controls."

"Fern saw the accident and yelled to her daughter to call the paramedics, while she jumped into another boat and headed after the runaway. Well, the man in the boat finally got it under control and brought it back in. 'Bout three minutes after it was back, the paramedics was there. Fern's quick thinkin' probably saved the woman's life. Fern and Hoppie have personally been responsible for saving fifteen or sixteen lives right here in the river - including mine. Hoppie and Fern just can't do enough for people. They go out of their way for everybody. Anything you need, they'll help you."

One of the major activities at Hoppie's is the care of transient boats - both power and sail. Because of the limited space, this often means rafting resident boats along side each other, sometimes three deep. One evening as we sat in the Living Room seven transient boats arrived. They included sailboats, power boats and the **Rufus B.**

The **Rufus B** was the first in. She's a miniature

sternwheel packet, powered by a diesel, but propelled by a real paddlewheel. What a thrill it was to watch the skill of the ancient skipper, as he edged her slowly into the dock by maneuvering two large rudders and alternating the paddlewheel between forward and reverse, back and forth until the boat snuggled gently against the dock in the swift Mississippi River current. Just before she touched, lines were tossed to Fern, Hoppie and son Mark who expertly snubbed them around huge iron cleats.

After taking on two hundred gallons of diesel, the **Rufus B** was moved to the forward end of the dock, where she would rest easy for the night. Dr. and Mrs. Rufus were greeted as old friends by Hoppie and Fern. "They've been coming here twice a year for many years on their way up and downriver," explained Fern as she hurried down the dock to guide another boat in while Mark and Hoppie relocated several resident boats, to make way for three more transients that were approaching from upriver.

Soon there was only one space remaining, and a large sailboat with stepped mast extending eight or ten feet beyond the bow was making her turn out in midchannel. It was obvious that the skipper was not familiar with docking against a strong current. Despite shouts of warning from the experts, he headed the boat almost straight in toward the dock instead of coming up against the flow.

By the time the skipper realized his error, it was too late. The current first swung the bow in toward one of the moored boats, then as he turned the wheel hard, the stern came in toward another boat. Only the quick thinking and brute force of Mark and Hoppie and several volunteers prevented a collision which could have seriously damaged the boats. As the bow turned, the mast narrowly missed giving one of the volunteers a blow that would have knocked him into the swirling waters.

Fern, Hoppie and Mark had been on a dead run for an hour and a half pushing, pulling, guiding and tying boats. When the last transient was secure, they collapsed on the Living Room couch for a few minutes before going off to help the last arrival get rid of garbage, take on water, a little fuel, and connect power cords for lights, refrigerators and T.V. sets.

Later Joe said, "We'd better turn in early tonight. Tomorrow's the big marina party. It'll begin about noon

167

and go 'til we carry Benjamin down to his boat and put him to bed. He won't stay in bed though 'cause he likes to take off in his boat and run across the river. Never has an accident. He seems to drive better when he's drunk."

We had planned to leave the next day, but it didn't take much to persuade us to stay for the big event of the year. Dee woke early to watch the exodus of the seven transients. The tow **Helen Capps** was leaving as Dee stepped onto our deck. She waved to the captain - a gesture that had become ritual since that first morning. I was never sure whether it was just a friendly greeting or Dee's subtle reminder to the captain that we were right in front of him.

By 6:30 the two sailboats were gone and Fern and Hoppie came down to see the **Rufus B** off. Dr. Rufus pulled away from the dock as a large tow was approaching from upstream. Fern seemed worried as the old stern-wheeler struggled to gain control over the rushing current of a rising river. She cleared the upper end of the dock and moved slowly upriver.

I was awake when Dee left **Sol Seaker**, but fell a-sleep again. When I awoke the second time, the outer dock was vacant and Dee was at the door telling me that Joe, Cindy, the four girls, and some of their friends were going to the Southern Kitchen for breakfast. "We're invited," she said.

After breakfast Dee and Cindy went shopping for food for the marina party, while Joe and I helped with the preparations by repairing and setting up picnic tables and moving benches and chairs to a central loca-tion. Several long tables were placed inside a large storage building to hold the "covered dishes" of potato salad, green salad, hot beans, lasagna, fruit and vegies, that began to arrive about noon.

The sight of these festive tables and the delicious odors emanating from the chicken, pork and hot dogs that were sizzling on the barbecue, brought appetites to the ravenous level by the time the dinner bell sounded.

Even on such a special occasion, the work of the marina had to continue. There were boats to fuel, leaky gas hoses to repair, dead batteries to replace and small boats to launch and retrieve. And, as evening approach-ed, there were the inevitable transients to dock, ser-vice and secure for the night.

Benjamin had started his first beer about 10:00

A.M. and still had a can in his hand at 10:00 P.M., when Dee and I said our good-nights and walked down the long dock toward **Sol Seaker**. On our way, we paused to talk for a few minutes to a couple aboard a transient sail- boat called the **Sundancer**. We learned that they were from Georgian Bay in Canada. The husband was on a sab- batical leave from his university, studying urban plan- ning practices of cities on or along bodies of water. Very conveniently this would include cities along the shores of the Great Lakes, the Illinois River, the Mis- sissippi River, the Gulf Coast states, Florida, the East Coast states, the Hudson River, Lake Champlain and the St. Lawrence Seaway. In one year he, his wife and their three children would make a complete circuit back to their home on Georgian Bay.

Now it was our turn to be envious of someone's trip. A trip we also hoped to make, but by stages, and at a slower pace.

"Perhaps we'll see you downriver." Dee said, as we continued toward our boat and bed.

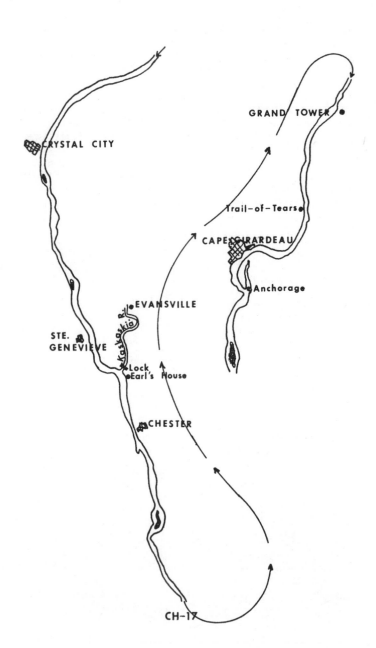

GRAND TOWER

Trail-of-Tears

CAPE GIRARDEAU

Anchorage

CRYSTAL CITY

EVANSVILLE

Kaskaskia R.

STE.
GENEVIEVE

Lock
Earl's House

CHESTER

CH-17

17

FLOTSAM AND JETSAM

"Parting is such sweet sorrow. . ." Old Shakespear had that right. With throat lumps and eye mist we waved farewell to Fern, Hoppie, Mark, Cindy and Joe. "Look out for them logs," Joe yelled. "The rivers risin. . ." His voice trailed off in the opposing breeze as the current quickly swept us downstream.

"What will happen to them?" Dee wondered, concern in her face. Her parents had divorced when she was a baby, and her mother had given her to her grandparents to raise. Divorce held a special meaning of abandonment which she would never completely overcome. She was especially concerned for the children.

But there was sweetness, too, in our departure. After two weeks we were back on our magical river - the unfettered Mississippi. Ahead of us were new vistas, new towns, new people.

"Do you realize it's a hundred miles to the next marina, at Trail-of-Tears State Park?" Dee asked as she thumbed through the chart. "Between here and there. nothing but dikes, levees and a few commercial barge landings. It looks like a lonely stretch of river."

It was a lonely stretch of river. but it wasn't, as we had been told, a monotonous and boring stretch of river.

After passing the **Creole Belle** we traveled an hour before seeing our first humans. In that hour we observed birds, bluffs, sandbars, islands and wooded shores. We enjoyed the peace and quiet of the river. And we dodged and maneuvered to avoid scores of floating limbs and logs.

Then, in rapid succession, we met the **R. H. Huffman** with three chemical barges, passed a local sailboat. and met the **Gopher State** with twelve coal barges. Just as we were riding out the last of the waves from the **Gopher State**. we spotted a castle-like structure on the Missouri shore. A look at the chart indicated that a dirt road approached the river at this point with the name "Selma" appearing at the location of the "castle". We took a picture.

"This chart names a lot of islands where there aren't any islands," Dee commented. "Calico Island, Harlow Island, Lee Island, Establishment Island - all just names on the bank of the river. And, it shows James Landing more than half-a-mile away from the waters edge."

"Remember, the water level is very low now," I replied. "Maybe when the spring melt comes these places become islands again. Or, perhaps, these once were Islands that have silted in."

A half hour beyond Selma we were throttled back letting the flow of the current provide most of our forward motion, when two sharp blasts split the air behind us. We turned to see the **Cooperative Vangard**, with one barge, approaching under a full head of steam (diesel). Her rapid approach, plus the relatively strong upriver breeze, had prevented the sound of her engines from reaching us before we heard her whistle.

As she drew alongside, the captain slowed his engines, as if suddenly realizing that his sternwash could bounce us unmercifully. His momentum took him swiftly past, where he immediately speeded up and went churning on down the river. "Wow, he must be going to a fire!" Dee exclaimed. "We've passed a lot of tows, but that's the first time one ever whizzed by us."

An hour passed. We spotted and photographed an old five story building at a spot named "Brickeys." Another hour passed. The chart said we should be even with Ste. Genevieve but our only indication was a ferry landing. The town was now separated from the river by more than a mile of sedimentation known as Baumstark Towhead.

We had hoped to stop at Ste. Genevieve for the night. The chart showed a commercial dock and a small inlet - the remnants of an old channel - at the lower end of Baumstark Towhead. We looked closely, but couldn't find a suitable place to stop.

"It's still early," Dee said. "Why don't we go on. The Kaskaskia River is only five miles farther. Mark said you can tie up behind the lock wall, away from the river traffic and floating logs."

"The Kaskaskia it is," I replied, as I dodged another log and nosed **Sol Seaker** back out toward center channel.

171

"Look! There's a sailboat!" exclaimed Dee. "It's the **Sundancer**. See if we can catch them before we get to the Kaskaskia!"

I pushed the throttle forward. **Sol Seaker**'s bow rose as the heavily laden boat slowly gathered speed. Inch by inch the bow began to drop as the hull lifted onto a plane.

"What am I doing?" I asked aloud as I eased back on the throttle and swerved to starboard to miss a floating log. "We can't go fast. There's too much debris."

With sanity regained I proceeded at a safe pace, only to see **Sundancer** rounding a downstream bend as we swung our bow into the narrow, gently flowing Kaskaskia River.

About half-a-mile upstream we entered the Kaskaskia Lock, where I let **Sol Seaker** drift freely in mid-chamber. When the lock was full, and the gates were starting to open, the lockmaster came over and said icily, "You're supposed to tie up to the floating drum."

"I'm sorry," I apologized. "The last two lock-masters told us to float free. It was so much easier, I decided to do it here."

"They're not supposed to tell you that. When you come back down, be sure you tie off."

"Yes sir!"

The Kaskaskia was very muddy, but was blessed with very little current. We enjoyed a quiet journey between low, willow covered banks. Cabins were scattered here and there, and an occasional pontoon boat was pulled up to the shore. At the town of Evansville, ten miles upriver, we spotted a gas pump near the water's edge, but no dock, only a pontoon boat moored against the bank.

Anchoring next to the pontoon boat we scrambled across her deck to shore, where we soon learned that most business establishments were closed including the shore-side gas pump and adjoining restaurant. "It's Columbus Day you know," said the elderly, razor thin, toothless, grocery clerk. "I don't know where the gas people live. I don't git much business no more." His voice made a kind of whistling sound between his tooth-less gums. "Most everybody drives out to the new Kroeger's store. They think they's gettin' a bargain 'cause they run them specials. But ever thin' else they buy is gotta be higher so's they don't save no money. They has to have ever'thin' else higher 'cause I heered their utility bill fer one month was $10,000. Them people that go there cain't save no money less'un they buy's only them specials."

"I heered one young girl cashier gets a hundred dollars fer jest workin' one Sunday. It ain't worth a hundred dollars to run a cash register jest one day. It's them kinda' things that makes the economy real bad. If sumpin' ain't done they's gonna git even worse."

We purchased soft drinks and peanuts, then headed back toward the boat. "Are you folks lookin' for gas for your boat?" The voice came from a young man in a pickup that slowed beside us.

"Yes," we replied.

"Well, I'm the owner. We're closed today. We close every Monday, but since I'm in town I'll open up and get you some gas."

"Thanks! Do you take credit cards?"

"No, but I'll be glad to take a check."

"You know the check is out of state," Dee replied.

"Sure, but anyone who owns a boat like that wouldn't be passin' no bad checks."

Dee and I looked at each. Here on the Kaskaskia **Sol Seaker** had status again. In the San Francisco Delta she had been just an average cruiser. At Clearlake she had been the **Queen Mary**. Across North Dakota she had been a source of amazement. And on the Mississippi she was "kinda small". Large or small, we didn't tell the man that about eighty percent of her still belonged to the bank.

We filled the tank and three five gallon cans we had purchased in St. Louis, relieved that we now had enough fuel to make it all the way to Hickman, Kentucky, in case we couldn't get gas at Cape Girardeau.

The sun was sinking low when we returned to the Kaskaskia Lock. With the breeze blowing from the south, I decided to pull up even with a floating drum on the north side and let the wind push us to the wall. I stopped a few feet out and waited, but the boat drifted away from, rather than toward, the wall. I eased forward and pulled up even with the next drum. Again we floated away.

By the time I realized that the wind was hitting the uncommonly high wall and bouncing back against **Sol Seaker,** the gates were closed and the water level starting to drop.

As I quickly moved across the chamber to a drum on
173

the south side, I was sure the lockmaster must be pulling his hair, after telling us, in no uncertain terms, to "tie off" when we came back. As soon as we were secured to the bollard, the loudest lock horn we ever heard signaled us to leave.

"I think he did that on purpose," Dee said.

We tied up behind the lower riverside wall and relaxed on the back deck, enjoying an approaching sunset that gave promise of being spectacular. Suddenly a small outboard roared by, heading toward the far shore. A lone man climbed out on a rock with a line in hand. Quickly he attached the line to the rock, then slowly backed the boat away from shore playing out line, then net, as he did so. About twenty-five feet out he lifted a large weight attached to the end of the net, stretched it tightly, then dropped it into the water. He roared off to a new location about twenty yards upstream, where he repeated the ritual. After five nets were set, he sped over to **Sol Seaker**. "Hello," he said.

"Hello! What are you fishing for?" we asked.

"Catfish, Buffalo and Carp."

"Are you a commercial fisherman?"

"Yes, part time. I did work on the tows - engineer and captain. I got thirty years into it and retired. Now I work part time for the sheriff's department and fish on my days off."

"When will you pull the nets?"

"Tomorrow. About nine o'clock."

"Maybe we'll still be here. We'd like to see what you catch."

"Maybe I'll see you tomorrow. I've gotta go. Gotta get home before dark. Don't want to run into any logs out in the river." He set one more net before heading out into the Mississippi and turning downstream.

I baited a hook with a worm, and almost immediately caught a small silvery-green catfish with black tipped fins. "What a beautiful fish," I exclaimed as I showed it to Dee then dropped it back into the river. "What a beautiful sunset," Dee replied. We sat watching as the familiar Mississippi mauve spread across sky, water and landscape, then slowly faded into the gray-black of night.

The air was crisp next morning, as our commercial fisherman, dressed in wool plaid shirt, heavy rain gear and rubber boots, began to methodically pull and stow his nets. Occasionally we saw him drop a fish into a

174

box at the bow of the boat. He had trouble with his fourth net, which seemed to be hung on something.

"Maybe he has a big fish," I guessed.

As he gave a heave, the dark end of a large limb became visible. After some minutes he freed the limb, finished pulling his nets, and came alongside. "Only got eleven fish," he said, holding up a carp. "A very poor catch."

"What you need is a cup of hot coffee," Dee said.

As Earl sipped his coffee, he told us about some of his experiences as a prison guard. "We have one man, a big strong man named Gomez, who did thirteen years in San Quentin - a murderer. You may have heard about him. He's from California. After he was paroled he came here and bought a farm. He has to take lots of medication' has a steel plate in his head and has seizures. It's real hard sometimes to get that thing into his mouth when he has a seizure. One time he was under the edge of his bed. It took three men to get him out. Most people think he's dangerous, but we get along good. I don't think he'd try to hurt me.

"Anyway, he's in jail being blamed for having sex with a fourteen year old girl. He claims he's innocent and has proof. The case hasn't come to court yet. Meanwhile his bail is set at $25,000, so he stays in jail. I don't know whether he's guilty or not, but even if he is, everyone knows that girl fools around with anyone. I don't think $25,000 is a fair bail. And the county gets stuck buying his medicine and food and handling all his seizures."

"Now, the other day I was in on a million dollar marijuana bust. This father, son and daughter-in-law had this big long building just full of eight foot plants - beautiful plants. They had a trash compactor they used to bale the plants. Had several bales they said were worth fifty thousand each."

"Now, they aren't in jail. Set their bail at only $2,500. It don't seem right to me that someone who is caught red handed with a million dollars worth of illegal drugs should get out on $2,500 and this man, who is accused of having sex with a girl everyone who wants to can have sex with, should get $25,000 bail. I guess it's just because they were first offenders and he's been convicted before."

Then Earl said, "I didn't get to bed last night, worked the night shift, then came right over here. I'm getting a little tired. I almost flipped my boat over on the way up. I hit a log in the river. It jerked the motor handle out of my hand and caused me to get into the wake of a passing tow that kept me rockin' so much I didn't think I was ever gonna' get hold of the handle again. Took on quite a bit of water. That, and fighting that log that got tangled in the net, really tuckered me. The coffee sure helped."

As Earl climbed back into his boat, he continued, "When you come downriver, if you look to your left about a mile down you'll see my house on the bluff. It's the brick house that isn't finished yet. You can't miss it."

After Earl left we, too, headed downriver. The Mississippi was full of logs and limbs - even more than before. We kept zigging and zagging to avoid collisions with large logs, but there was a constant thump, thump as smaller limbs and assorted junk bounced against the hull.

"There it is," said Dee, pointing toward the eastern shore. I glanced up just long enough to see Earl's unfinished brick house, as another log bounced off **Sol Seaker**.

Five miles below the Kaskaskia we met our first big Mississippi River tow. Up until now we had seen towboats with a maximum of sixteen barges. As we entered a straight stretch two miles above the Chester Highway Bridge we saw a monster moving toward us. "My God, that tow is five barges wide," I exclaimed and moved as far over to the side of the channel as I dared.

As we drew even with the front of the lead barges we could see that the tow contained seven sets of barges. "There's thirty-five empties," Dee said.

I was too concerned with other problems to worry about counting barges at the moment. The broad swath cut by this giant tow, in addition to creating a series of severe side rips that kept swinging **Sol Seaker's** bow back and forth, pushed logs and limbs to the sides of the channel. We were in constant danger of getting a limb entangled in the propeller.

We relaxed only when we could once again move to center channel where, for a few miles, we had easier going because most of the debris had been pushed aside.

At mile 100 we met three successive tows in less than one mile. **The Alliance Baron** pushed two chemical barges, the **Theresa Seley** twenty-two empty grain barges
176

and the **Robin B** and **Tom Smith** in tandem pushed four heavily laden petroleum barges.

By 3:30 we had met or passed fourteen tows, had dodged or attempted to dodge thousands of floating objects, and had taken a picture of Tower Rock.

Although grateful to see the jetty that marked the outer wall of the harbor at Trail-of-Tears State Park, we were dispirited to remember the tragic chapter in American history which this park commemorated - "Trail-of-Tears" was the name given the route traveled by hundreds of thousands of Choctaw, Creek, Chickasaw, Cherokee, Seminole, and other Native Americans as they were driven from their ancestral lands and forced to resettle in the unknown wilds of Oklahoma, Kansas, and parts west.

The chart showed the marina entrance to be at the lower end of the quarter-mile jetty. As we approached, our spirits were raised by the sight of several recreational vehicles in a campground atop the levee. Our elation was short lived, for as we rounded the end of the rock wall, we saw that the entire marina was filled with sand and mud. Not even a rowboat could have entered. Apparently the Trail-of-Tears marina had been no more wisely conceived and executed than the tragic events which it commemorated. We were about ready to shed a trail-of-tears of our own.

In vain I searched the area below the harbor for a sheltered spot to land or anchor. Like the Indians before us, we were forced to keep moving. "It's fifteen miles to Cape Girardeau," said Dee, as she looked at the chart again. "I hope we can stay there."

"Everybody says that's really a rough dock. It's right on a bend that gets the full brunt of the stern-wash of both upriver and downriver towboats."

As we turned toward the Sinclair gas dock at Cape Girardeau, I knew we would not stay overnight. The strong, log laden current hit the dock with full force. It was with considerable trepidation that I maneuvered against the current for a landing. "If I was sure we had enough gas I wouldn't stop at all," I said as I swung the bow out trying to bring the boat in parallel to the dock.

Just as I thought I would make a successful docking, the current swung the bow hard over against a metal cleat, then the stern came against the dock with a thump. I held her steady while Dee stepped off and made

177

the bow line fast. The force of the current held the stern in. We were secure, with only minor damage to the metal track which holds the rub rail in place.

I quickly scurried up the ramp and levee, then climbed a steep metal ladder over the top of the high concrete wall that represents the town's final protection when the river is in flood stage. On the other side of the wall was a wholesale fuel distributer who's long hoses ran up and over the wall to the pumps on the dock below. I was just in time to catch him before closing.

Logs bounced merrily off **Sol Seaker**'s hull. As our tank was filled , a limb became entangled in the out-drive, requiring considerable effort to remove. When the fueling was complete, the man asked, "You plan on staying overnight at the dock? 'Cause I'll have to charge you a dockage fee if you do?"

"No," we replied in unison, as another log bounced off **Sol Seaker** and floated downriver.

We had heard of a safe anchorage about five miles below town. We hoped our information was correct.

The sun was balanced on the edge of the horizon as we cautiously approached the backwater anchorage. About fifty yards inside, the depth suddenly changed from five feet to three feet. We backed up until five feet showed again. Dee always skeptical of electronic equipment double checked with our long boat pole. Satisfied, we secured **Sol Seaker** with two anchors and fell exhausted into our deck chairs, for our first anchoring out experience in such an isolated spot. Secretly we hoped that some other weary travelers would seek refuge and provide some company. None came.

As we sat on the deck, we watched the most glorious sunset yet, then moved inside to watch Milwaukee clobber the Cardinals ten to nothing in the first game of the world series. Before drifting off to sleep, we counted seven towboats on their way upriver. How happy we were that we were not out there facing them in the dark.

The sun was up and a mist rose from the water when we awoke next morning. A gentle breeze, aided by the sidewash of passing towboats, had drifted a collage of river debris into our backwater refuge. We were surrounded by logs, limbs, paint cans, bottles, styrofoam cups, broken ice chests, boards, a railroad tie, a sheet of green plywood and assorted odd bits of flotsam and jetsam all held together by giant clumps of detergent like foam.

178

The pale, early morning sun, the rising mist, and the floating collage, with **Sol Seaker** in the center, combined to give an erie, but magical, quality to our surroundings. Last night we had wished for company. In a unique way, the river had answered our wish by giving us, not man, but a wide assortment of his artifacts. Ole Man River left it to our imaginations to create the dramas to accompany these artifacts.

A worm box drifted into view. Instead of just an empty container, I imagined a father and son in a flat bottomed jon boat. The two had left early in the morning for a quick run across the river into a backwater slough. In that quiet place, the father had introduced his young son to the pleasure and solitude of angling. I could see the boy's eyes grow wide and hear the gleeful shouts as he landed his very first blue gill.

The bait container drifted away.

Behind the worm box came a sheet of plywood with nails protruding and bits of broken two by fours still attached to one side. The board was covered with peeled and cracked green paint. We saw this board as a part of one of the small floating fishing houses that were so common upriver. Rain and melting snow were turning the rapidly rising river into a raging torrent. Some yards upstream from where the small floating house was being buffeted by water and logs, a large tree stood on a small point of land being undercut by the rushing river. Inch by inch the soil was torn away, adding its ocher to the already muddy-brown water. The tree tilted, swayed, then pirouetted slowly. A root snapped. The tree spun around faster. Two more roots snapped. The tree lurched crazily and crashed into the river below. In a last feeble effort to pull itself upright, it clung tenaciously by two remaining arm-like roots. Slowly the strength was sapped from its "arms" and the tree let go.

The master river swung the uprooted tree around, making triumphant sounds as he did. As though by some nefarious plan, he hurled the tree into the small green house that was already struggling to maintain its place by the shore. The force of the collision shattered one side of the house. The boards to which its restraining cables were attached, broke loose. The shore-ward wall remained with the cables anchored to trees high on the bank as the rest of the house and the tree became intertwined. Like a giant food processor, the river spun the two until the house was torn to bits.

179

Here and there along the banks as later the water
receded, men had salvaged the broken boards. Just this
one piece had avoided sandbars, wing dams and man until
last nights passing tows had nudged it into our remote
backwater chute, where it could rest at last. The plywood drifted by.

Then something came into view which produced one of
those instantaneous poems Bob Smith and I had talked
about at Lansing. I grabbed my pen and wrote:

ADRIFT

I did not choose to be here.
Not Me!
To lie beside this road was not my idea.
To float on this stream,
To sink or drift to shore.

I did not want to destroy the beauty of this place.
Not me!
It was not my doing,
It was you!

You drained the life from me 'til I was dead.
You discarded me and left me here.

If I had had my way,
I would have returned from whence I came.
To be full of life again.

You made me lie along the road.
You made me drift along this shore.
Battered,
Barely recognizable,
As what I once was...

A can of Schlitz Beer!

As we pulled anchor and pressed the starter button
Sol Seaker's engine sprang to life. We realized. as we
pushed slowly through the flotsam and jetsam, that without the engine we too would be but a part of the debris,
waiting for someone to salvage us from among the river's
refuse.

LOGS AND LIMBS

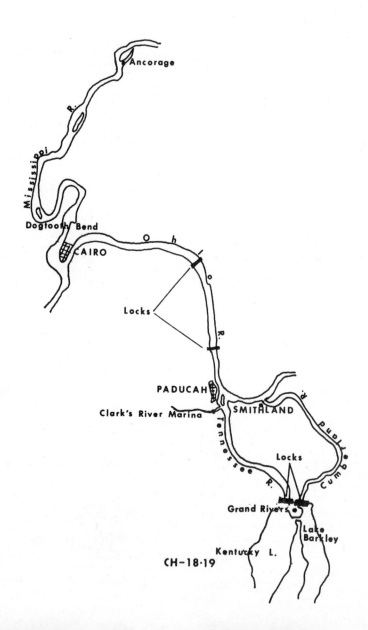

Ancorage

Mississippi R.

Dogtooth Bend

CAIRO

Ohio

R.

Locks

Locks

PADUCAH

Clark's River Marina

SMITHLAND

Cumberland R.

Tennessee R.

Locks

Grand Rivers

Lake
Barkley

Kentucky L.

CH-18-19

18

SOUTHERN POLISH

Around the sharp bend between Gray's Point and Rock Island (actually a small cape), we came face into the breeze which had filled our anchorage with the treasures of the river. The strong breeze, which had an almost straight upriver path for twelve miles from the Thebes Railroad Bridge to the bend at Billings Island, created those pesky waves which cause wallow and roll if you run too slowly, or jar and jerk if you run too fast.

After trying several speeds we settled for wallow and roll. About half way through the straight, we met the **Cooperative Ambassador**, a tow capable of pushing fifty empties, but with only fifteen. She had all engines churning full speed and was chewing up the river. Unfortunately for us she was also discharging it from her stern in great peaks and valleys. The combination of a large sandbar on one side of the channel, several wing dikes on the other, and the strong upriver wind served to intensify and agitate the rowdy river. We slowed further and braced ourselves for several hundred yards of yawing, rolling and saltating.

A half-mile below the tow, the river had quieted enough for us to enjoy the scenery, when suddenly Dee pointed downriver and exclaimed, "Look at that! There are breakers going clear across the river."

"What the hell is causing that?" I gasped, as I slowed and began to search for a break in the rolling surf ahead. "It looks like the giant 'potato patch' that occurs near the Golden Gate Bridge when the incoming tide crashes into the out-flowing Sacramento River."

The sternwash of the **Cooperative Ambassador** had somehow hidden beneath the water, then suddenly erupted again to crash against the waves caused by the wind. In our concern over the unruly waters, we had taken our eyes off both chart and channel markers. "Isn't that a black can up ahead on the left?" Dee asked as she picked

up the binoculars to double check.   "Yes it is. We're
out of the channel."

Joe's warning, "If you don't watch him all the
time, he'll get you," flashed through my mind as I swung
Sol Seaker to port.   The depth sounder read a constant
nine feet as we moved toward the black buoy, jumping to
eighteen feet as we re-entered the channel.   We were
lucky - this time.

At mile 25 we entered Dogtooth Bend.   During the
next two hours our compass directions changed from
Southeast to Northwest then back to Southeast as we
negotiated first Dogtooth then Greenleaf Bend.   We traveled a distance of twenty miles, but land-wise were
only three miles closer to our destination, the Gulf of
Mexico.

The wind dropped suddenly, and the river became
more placid as we turned to the last page of our Upper
Mississippi River Navigation Chart.   A great milestone
was soon to be reached.   Where the mighty Ohio joined
the Mississippi we would arrive at mile zero, the demarcation between the Upper and Lower Mississippi.
There on a narrow peninsula pinched between these two
great streams was the town of Cairo, Illinois. We had
assumed that Cairo would be a celebration of the meeting
of these historic rivers.   We visualized riverside
parks, marinas, floating restaurants, pageants, keelboat
and towboat races and such other events and monuments as
befitted a city of Cairo's unique location.

Our first disappointment had been the official
Chamber of Commerce brochure we had received in the mail
before leaving California.   On the front of the brochure, the name CAIRO appeared in giant print and in
letters of almost apologetic size ". . .where the Ohio
and Mighty Mississippi Rivers meet. . ."   Inside there
were pictures of such exciting points of interest as a
classroom addition to Washington Junior High, six churches, St. Mary's Hospital and the Armory. We were duly
impressed by Magnolia Manor, ". . .the scene of a bril-
liant reception for President Ulysses S. Grant, a great
friend of the builder. . .," and the City Office Building which ". . .houses the Police Headquarters, the City
Jail and city offices. . ."

As we came downriver, we had learned that we
probably couldn't even stop at Cairo.   This latest information had come from the captain of the towboat **John
MacMillan**, when·we first met it about eighty miles up-

182

river. It drew special attention because of a small towboat being deadheaded among the empty barges. As was our custom, we had waved as we passed. A crewman returned our greeting by spreading his arms wide apart. Not understanding this gesture, Dee went below to call on the radio. "Oh, that signal is just an old river greeting," came the answer to her query. "Where are you folks headed?"

"To New Orleans."

"Well, I might see yall down there. I'm goin' to New Orleans later. You'll probably beat me though."

"I don't know," replied Dee, "we're going very slowly - stopping along the way."

"Not much to see along the lower river. If I was you I'd head straight for New Orleans. Yall have a good trip."

"Thanks. You too."

Before leaving our anchorage near Cape Girardeau, we had spotted the **John MacMillan** again, this time heading downriver. We might not have realized that it was the same boat except that the tiny towboat was still nestled among the, now full, grain barges. Again Dee had called on the radio. "I talked to you yesterday," she said.

"There was a different crew aboard yesterday," came the reply.

"Oh, I was just wondering if you knew if there was a place for a pleasure boat to tie up at Cairo."

"I don't think so. They don't much like pleasure boaters, but when you get there you call Cairo River Base on channel sixteen. They can tell you if there's a place."

"Thanks."

"We'd better get off before we get bad mouthed fer talkin' on this channel."

About three miles above the confluence of the Ohio and Mississippi, I called Cairo River Base. The reply was short and preemptory. "There ain't no place fer pleasure boats at Cairo. You'd better watch out for the towboats, they don't pay much attention to pleasure craft."

"What would you like to do?" I asked Dee. "Head on down to Hickman, or go up the Ohio to Paducah. Quimby's guide says there's a marina and gas dock at Paducah - forty miles upriver."

"We're really making time since St. Louis, and it

183

looks like we'll go even faster on the lower river. Why don't we take the side trip."

"Sounds good to me. The only problem I see is that we don't have charts for the Ohio."

"Oh, I never thought about that."

"Well, let's start up the river; if it looks too complicated we'll turn around," I said as we passed beneath the Cairo Highway Bridge. Ahead was a sight we would not soon forget.

The meeting of the Missouri and Mississippi had reminded us of two youthful pranksters who, freed from parental restrictions, joined forces to see how much mischief they could create. They boiled, eddied, frolicked and foamed. Any new stream that joined their "gang" had to live by their rules. The tiny Kaskaskia tried to add its placid, muddy personality to the gang, but found that almost instantly its identity was consumed, as it conformed to the will of these powerful leaders.

From our vantage point on the flying bridge, we could see the wide, clear, "Beautiful Ohio," as she pushed against the muddy, roily Mississippi. No great battle for supremacy occurred here, as the mild mannered Ohio allowed the rumbunctious Mississippi to push its muddy boils and eddies over the top of her clear waters.

As we swung around the junction buoy and headed up the Ohio, two new realizations surfaced. We realized, immediately, that the Ohio was not as mild mannered as she appeared. Although there was little debris and no boils and eddies to grab and spin **Sol Seaker**, there was great strength in the relentless current. To make the forty miles to Paducah before dark, we must significantly increase our speed, with a concurrent increase in fuel consumption.

We also realized that each time we took a side excursion, we better understood the character and personality of the Mississippi. The broad, strong, but even tempered Ohio, contrasted sharply to the untiring unsettled, unpredictable, unrelenting, often unmanageable, unreasonable, unsafe, unsympathetic and sometimes untidy Mississippi.

There is a seriousness about the Mississippi. Even when the boils and eddies appear bubbly and innocent, there's a kind of underlying somberness that prevents him from being completely frivolous and gay. He is tolerant of man's intrusions only to the extent that man heeds his seriousness and power. Man has altered, polluted, and used him, but never conquered him.

If you trespass on the Mississippi - and all who venture there are trespassers - you must constantly reaffirm his permission to let you do so. The moment you think you own the river, he will push a log in front of you, ground you on a sandbar, or drift you over a wing dam. And he does not work alone. Over aeons, he has formed covenants with wind, rain, thunder, lightening and fog. These allies he calls upon to drench you, toss you about unmercifully, or hide from you the navigational aids and landmarks essential to a safe passage. But, if you maintain a constant vigil and are blessed with a measure of good luck, you may complete your trespass without major mishap.

The first of the two Ohio River locks we traversed was under repair. The gates were open, and we slowly made our way up the swift flow between the lock walls.

Good fortune was with us at the second lock, lock fifty-two, which we shared with two small tows without a wait. This ancient lock did; however, prove to be the slowest we encountered, requiring thirty minutes to lift us ten feet. Later we learned that lock fifty-two was known as the busiest lock in the world, to which we would add, "and the slowest."

We asked the lockmaster about a Marina at Paducah. "Call Walker Dock at Paducah, he replied, "They'll tell you how to get there."

Three miles below town I called. "Come on up. Take the Tennessee to the right and go past the second shipyard. When you get closer, call again and I'll guide you in."

"They're sure a lot friendlier here than in Cairo," Dee asserted, showing a definite relief. It had been a long push against the current, our fuel supply was dwindling, and the sun was setting. Lights were beginning to show on shore as we spotted the first shipyard, a dry dock for barges and towboats. I turned on our running lights. To our right was the sleek metalic hull of the once proud cruise boat, **Admiral**.

I called Walker Dock again. "This is the pleasure craft **Sol Seaker** calling the Walker Docks."

"Walker Dock. Go to eleven. Yes Cap, what can we do fer you?"

"I'm located just east of the island where the **Admiral** is moored. Where do I go from here?"

There was a chuckle. "Well, Cap, where do you want to go?"

Suddenly realizing I wasn't talking to the same person I had contacted before, I said, "I'm a pleasure craft looking for a place to tie up overnight."

"Oh, you can go into the Clark's River Marina. Just come on up the Tennessee past them tows and the dry dock. Look close, and you'll see the Clark's River to your right."

We found an extremely narrow, dark, stump choked, opening a few yards in front of a rusty barge. "Do you suppose that could be the Clark's River?" I wondered.

Cautiously we entered, with depth sounder reading fifteen feet. Ahead we could distinguish a floating house, with two small boats, against the left bank. On the right, around a slight bend, was an old wooden boat attached to a large floating dock, holding a small building - all were in disrepair. On the dock beside the building were four fuel pumps, two without hoses and two with worn-out hoses. Beyond the gas dock and behind the house we could see the sterns of three houseboats covered with a mantle of twigs, leaves and dirt.

The Clark's River Marina could have been a ghost marina left to rot away in this spooky backwater. After tying to the gas dock, a quick look around confirmed our growing suspicions that the Clark's River Marina was closed. The building was empty. Doors were ajar and windows broken. Bags of garbage lay here and there, and gaping holes in the dock made walking hazardous.

Several electrical outlets proved to be dead; broken wires hung loose. As I was about to abandon hope for shore power, I spotted a long electrical cord extending from the far corner of the building to the old wooden boat. Closer inspection revealed that someone had been using power tools to repair the boat. I tried the outlet. It worked! Following the "live" line, I found it attached to an outlet closer to **Sol Seaker**. This, too, had power. Soon lights were ablaze and the erie quality of Clark's River Marina was shut outside our snug cabin.

That night St. Louis won the second game of the world series 5 to 4, tying the series at one game each.

Although exhausted from the long day's travels, eighty-eight miles, half of it against the strong Ohio current, our sleep was frequently interrupted by loud metalic clanks, barking dogs, car lights shining from

186

the hill opposite the marina and a mysterious pickup which drove with lights out down to the floating house across the way, then after about twenty minutes just as mysteriously drove away.

Added to these identifiable sounds and events was an occasional bumping, thumping sound, seemingly coming from our rear deck. Twice I peered through the glass door, but saw nothing. The third time I was awakened, I took the flashlight to the rear of the cabin and shined it through the locked door, again I saw nothing. But I should have seen the bag of stale bread Dee saved for duck food. The empty bag was laying next to the gunwale and a few crumbs were scattered about. Among these were the damp tracks of small animals.

"Rats!" I exclaimed. "Rats have been jumping on the boat. They've eaten all your bread." With the mystery solved we finally dropped off to a more peaceful sleep.

Morning inspection of Clark's River Marina removed some of the creepy quality, but did little to change our "ghost marina" opinion of this dilapidated dock.

While Dee did some housekeeping, I climbed the steep river bank and headed down a four lane highway to the first business I saw, a liquor store. Two men customers were buying cases of beer. One of them said to the lady clerk. "You're not from around here, are you?"

"No," answered the lady.

"I didn't think so. That's a strange accent you have. What is it?"

"Polish."

"I knew it wasn't from around here."

Amused by the conversation. I smiled inwardly as I listened to the combination Polish and deep-south speech of the lady proprietor. I thought, "If she's Polish, surely she's Southern Polish."

"Do any of you know about the marina?" I asked when there was a break in the conversation.

"It's closed. Closed on Labor Day." replied one of the men.

"Do you know where we can get gas for our boat?" I continued. "We came into the marina last night."

"Which way you headin'?"

"Up the Tennessee to Kentucky Lake."

"Well, you can get gas right below the dam. Just before you go through the lock. On the right side."

"If you need gas," broke in the lady, "I got a

pickup out there, be glad to give you the keys so's you could go fill some cans. You got some cans?"

"Yes, but I think we have enough gas to make it to the dam."

"Yore shore welcome to use my pickup, long's you bring it back."

"Thanks, but I'm sure we have enough. If you're positive we can get gas at the dam," I looked at the man.

"Yeah, got it there lots a times."

I looked over the wine selection and told the lady I lived near where most of the wines were made. "Don't have many wine drinkers 'round here," she said. "Beer. Ever'body drinks lots a beer. Weekends comin' up. Cain't hardly git enough beer in my cooler fer the week-ends. Takes a long time to git beer good and cold. Beer drinkers around here, 'n whiskey now that the weather's gettin' colder. Cold weather they drinks whiskey, but in summer it's always beer. You shore you don't want to use my car? You're shore welcome to it."

"No." I thanked her, bought a bottle of wine, and headed toward the door.

"Now yall come back if you git in a pinch fer gas. Glad to let you use my pickup."

As I walked toward the marina, I marveled once again at the trust these river people put in a total stranger, from the acceptance of personal checks to the offer of cars, pickups, even beds to sleep in.

"There's civilization up there," I called to Dee, holding up the bottle of California wine.

On our way up the Tennessee, we encountered several "shelling" boats. These shell fishermen drag the river bottom for valuable mussels that are shipped to Japan, where they are broken into tiny pieces and implanted in pearl oysters, to become the nuclei of beautiful cul-tured pearls.

Below Kentucky Dam we saw a busy boat ramp. Many small outboards were plying the fast water below the dam. Beyond the ramp was a new, but deserted looking gas dock. A large sign said "Closed."

At Clark's River we had emptied our last reserve can into the main tank, and now the needle was getting close to the empty mark. Dee called the lockmaster to inquire about locking through and about gas above the dam. "There's a big marina, open year round just about a mile above the dam, you can get gas and supplies there.

188

It'll be 'bout three hours before I can lock you through though. Got several tows waiting," came the prompt reply.

As we watched and waited, the **Edwin L. Kennedy**, with eight barges, eased up along the far bank, and the **George Barker**, with fifteen barges, tied off to the mooring dolphins in mid-river. We remained by the radio to make sure we didn't miss our turn. The **Margaret Igert** was entering the lock when her base station called to inquire about her location.

"I'm in the lock now," replied the Captain. "Had to wait a long time."

"Can I put the **Doodlebug** in with you?", the lockmaster broke in on the conversation.

"Shore," came the reply.

There followed precise directions to both Captains on how and where each should tie up in the lock.

When Dee became concerned that we had been forgotten, I used some of our precious fuel to move out beyond the **George Barker**. Dee called the lockmaster, hoping we could lock through with the **Margaret Igert** and the **Doodlebug**. "I don't want to put you with the commercial tows," came the reply. "I've never done that before."

"We've locked through with towboats before."

"The only way I could put you in is if you could go in last and leave first. Can't do that with these tows. I'll come back down an get you as soon as these tows are out. Now I'd like for you to move back downriver. I'm gonna have the **Edwin Kennedy** come on the wall. When it's your turn I'll blow the horn and you can move around the **Kennedy**."

As we drifted downriver, the **Edwin Kennedy** moved slowly past the **George Barker** and stopped on the wall below the gigantic lock doors.

"This is the **Edwin Kennedy** calling the sport boat."

"This is the **Sol Seaker**," replied Dee.

"What channels do you have?"

"All."

"How about 68?"

"Okay, 68."

"I'm all tied up here on the wall. You can ease on up behind me. I've left plenty of room for you to go on past into the lock. There's a whole barge length opening."

"Great," replied Dee. "How long do you think it will be?"

189

"They haven't let all the water out yet, but pretty soon. I'm tied up here so it's safe for you to go on in soon's the gates open. I'm out and standing by on 14."

"**Sol Seaker** out and standing by on 14."

"This is the lockmaster calling the **Edwin Kennedy**."

"This is the **Kennedy**."

"How big are you?"

"Four long, two wide, plus the tow."

"I could put you in with that sport boat if you're in a hurry. I've never done it before, but there's room and I think it would be safe."

"Well, I'm in no hurry. I'd rather be safe than sorry. When I get through the lock I'll be layed up four days before I come back so I'm in no hurry."

"Well, I thought you might be. I'm sure I could put you in with that sport boat. But if you're in no hurry, then better safe than sorry. What do you think?"

"Well I'd rather be safe than sorry and if one of these barges got loose in there and hit that fiberglass boat, there'd be nothin' left. Better take them up alone."

"That's the way we'll do it then."

The gates began to open, slowly discharging the last swirles and eddies. As we started forward, the lockmaster said, "Go all the way up to the last barrel on the starboard side. Hook your rope over near the center and hold on tight, cause the stern may try to swing out." What an isolated feeling to enter this gigantic fifty-four foot high, damp, musty chamber all alone. We were relieved when the boiling and swirling of the incoming water ceased and the upper gate opened freeing us to move out onto beautiful and clear Kentucky Lake.

CITY BUILDING - CAIRO

19

CANOE ANTIQUE AND CHILI PARLOUR

Grand Rivers Marina had boats, people, gas and a waiting berth. Suddenly came the realization that this was the first truly protected and well lighted marina we had seen since Hannibal, Missouri, some four hundred miles and a century of time away.

The next day we unfolded our bikes for the first time in almost three weeks, and spent the morning riding through the beautiful and peaceful country of the "Land Between the Lakes."

At the small town of Grand Rivers, we heard a friendly and hearty laugh coming from inside the Canoe Antique and Chili Parlour. "Let's go in," Dee said. "If the food's as friendly as the laugh, this is a good place to eat."

"All I have is hamburgers and cheeseburgers. If you want vegetables, go to the Iron Kettle. If you want steaks go to Patti's," said Linda Ray, the proprietor.

"How about Chili?" Dee asked.

"Yes, but I want you to know I put noodles in my chili, and I wouldn't want to do you wrong by not tellin' you I put noodles in my chili. I never used to put noodles in, but one day I tried it and a man told me, 'that's the best chili I ever ate.' Well that's the best compliment a little ole country girl like me could ever git, so I been puttin' noodles in ever since.'"

As Linda went to the back to "fetch" our chili, Dee noted that she had a short haircut, very much like Dee's own. "Where can I get a hair cut?" Dee asked, when Linda returned."

"Fantastic Sams. But I'll tell you the best haircut I ever had. One day four laughing ladies come into my shop." Linda laughed, then continued. "They had this hearty laugh you know. Just my kind of people." She laughed again. "One of the ladies said, 'I just love this town. I wish I had the money to come here and open a shop!'"

"'What kinda shop would you open,' I asked. 'I'd open a beauty shop,' she said."

"'Well hon', I replied, 'I wisht you had your scissors and razor with you now. I need a haircut so bad. I'd shore put you to work right now.' Well, she opened her purse and said, 'I got my scissors right here, an' I got my razor right here. I'll give you a haircut.'"

"So I got me a chair and set it up right out front. And I got me a old sheet and put it around me an' she give me the best haircut I ever had. People was stoppin' and lookin'. Best haircut I ever had. I asked her where I could git haircuts like the one she give me. 'At Fantastic Sams in Paducah,' she replied."

"She was from Virginia," laughed Linda.

Linda was called away to show a couple a beautiful hand made quilt, draped over an old table in front of the store. When she returned she said, "I make quilts. About a week ago a couple come here lookin' for a quilt. 'We've been looking for a special quilt in these parts for about a week,' the lady said."

"'Did you see the ones out there?' I asked. 'Yes they're not what we're looking for,' she replied."

"'I have more up at my other shop,' I said. 'Won't take but a minute if you want to go up and see them.' They looked at each other, then the lady said, 'No, I don't think so.'"

"I said, 'It don't cost you nothin' to look.' The lady looked at the man again. He said, 'well, like the lady said, it don't cost nothing to look.'"

"When I opened the door to my other shop, I saw her eyes git bigger and her mouth fly open about that wide." Linda gestured with her hands about a foot apart. "'There it is!' the lady exclaimed. 'Will you take a check for it?'"

"'Yes,' I said."

"They showed me all their identification, then told me my quilt would be on exhibit in Chicago at the Chicago Quilt Guild's annual quilt show."

"I said to my husband, 'I ain't gonna make a cent on that dude 'cause I'm gonna fly up to Chicago to see that dude on display. It ain't ever day a little ole country girl like me gits her quilt displayed in a big city quilt show.' I haven't cashed that check yet. I'm gonna make me a photo copy and frame it and hang it right up there."

We congratulated Linda, but as we left, Dee

whispered to me, "I hope that check doesn't bounce. They sounded like a couple of con-artists to me."

That night St. Louis' rookie Willie McGee got his first two world series hits, both home runs. The Birds' pitcher Joaquin Andujar was hit on the right knee by a Ted Simmon's line drive, and although in great pain, he suffered no broken bones. As was so often the case during the regular season, Cardinal bull pen ace Bruce Sutter came on in relief. In the last of the ninth, Willie McGee went high on the center field wall to rob a Milwaukee batter of a home run, as St. Louis won game number three, taking a two to one lead in the series.

"Do you realize it's been two months since we left Clearlake," Dee said, more as a statement than a question, as we rode our bikes toward town for breakfast the next morning. On our way we stopped to say good-bye to a California couple we had met the day before. They were preparing to leave the campground next to the marina. The final preparation was to hook a tiny Toyota to the back of their large motor home.

The man drove the car slowly forward, while his wife directed his approach to the hitch. "More this way, a little that way, more forward," she was saying in a small voice that her husband was unable to hear.

As the husband inched forward, I signaled directions and distance with my hands, unknown to the wife, but visible to her husband. The car stopped in the perfect spot and the wife set the towbar on the hitch.

"Well," she said, "I finally did something right!"

Her husband and I looked at each other and smiled.

We stopped at the Iron Kettle for breakfast, only to find that our visit with the California couple had made us too late. The buffet table was already set up for lunch, although it was only 10:40. The delicious smell and tempting sight of the food prompted Dee to say, "Why don't we eat a big meal now, then not eat again 'til dinner?"

The Iron Kettle's country buffet was something to behold. On a long table were cold selections of all kinds - golden hominy, crisp lettuce, red and green jello, potato and macaroni salads, green pea salad, cole slaw, watermellon pickles, radishes, green onions, even fresh pineapple. Two large wood burning ranges held hot dishes of fried chicken, beef stew, chicken and dumplings, pot roast with new potatoes, macaroni and cheese, barbecue chicken, ham and white beans, black eyed peas,

cabbage, stewed tomatoes, baked beans, and fish. In the
warming ovens were "light" bread, plain corn bread, hot
pepper corn bread, peach cobbler, apple cobbler, and hot
apple sauce.

We gorged ourselves.

After walking around town, we purchased souvenirs
and jumping worms. Back at the marina, we met the local
boat broker, who wanted to know more about our trip.
After our brief explanation, he told us about his wife.
"She's got a masters degree in mathematics," he said,
"but after our six kids were raised she wanted to work
as a cook on a towboat. She's on thirty days, then off
thirty days. She's having a ball."

At 3:00 we headed **Sol Seaker** out of the narrow
harbor entrance, up Kentucky Lake about two miles, then
through a short canal connecting Kentucky Lake with
Barkley Lake. This canal creates a shortcut between
the navigable waters of the Tennessee and Cumberland
Rivers.

In Barkley Lake we found a quiet cove and anchored.
I removed the "jumping worms" from the refrigerator only
to find that they were no longer jumping. The refrigerator was apparently too cold for these worms that had
jumped often and high when I purchased them only a few
hours earlier. I fished with them, but caught only
small blue gills and one tiny catfish.

On the back deck we enjoyed the final rays of the
warm sun and watched the soft colors fade into evening,
before eating a light supper of cheese, crackers and
grapes. Milwaukee won the fourth game - the world series
was now tied two games each.

The next day was Sunday, October, 17. We were
quickly lowered in the fifty-foot Barkley Lock to the
peaceful and quiet Cumberland River below. Through the
trees lining each bank, we caught glimpses of farm
houses, barns, cornfields, mobile homes and small vacation cottages. We passed an occasional fisherman in a
small jon boat and observed two blue herons, three ospreys, several kingfishers and many, many vultures. "I
wonder if there are any turtles in the Cumberland?" Dee
asked, just before she spotted one sliding off a log.

"There's one!" she cried. But it was gone before I
saw it. "There's another one!"

I caught a glimpse of this one just as it, too,
slid into the water. "There are turtles everywhere!" we
exclaimed as we focused on the logs lining the river.

If Dee hadn't wondered about the turtles, I suspect we would never have noticed them. How much we miss in life because we aren't "tuned in."

"We should be nearing Smithland," Dee said, using our road map as a navigation chart. "It's where the Cumberland and Ohio join."

As Smithland came into view on the high left bank, the river began to act strangely. In addition to encountering many boils and eddies, we found ourselves pushing against the current even though we were traveling downstream.

"The river's flowing upstream!" I exclaimed.

More accurately, a rising Ohio was spilling water into the Cumberland and pushing "upstream" for about half-a-mile, giving the impression that the Cumberland was flowing backwards. The collision of the two waters was creating an unusual number of boils and eddies that were playing "push and shove" with **Sol Seaker**.

As we turned into the Ohio, the **Mis T Way**, a fifty foot Chris Craft, sped by, going upriver.

By 3:30, we were once again in the Clark's River Marina. Milwaukee won game number 5, to lead the series three games to two.

The next day was very cool as we started our seventy-five mile run to Hickman, Kentucky. We drove from inside. Above lock 52, tows and barges were "rafted" together three and four deep, waiting to lock through. The **Edwin Kennedy** was among the waiting tows. "There are nineteen towboats waiting," came the reply to Dee's inquiry. "We've been here since noon yesterday. Now we're fourth in line, should get through sometime after dinner, maybe 1:30 or 2:00."

"I thought you were going to be off four days," Dee said.

"I was only off two days, now I'm takin' this load of rock for the river banks down near Cairo."

"I bet you hate to see us pleasure boats when you've waited so long."

"No," he said politely, but without conviction, "We like to see the pleasure boats. You can probably go on down. They'll take you through first. I've gotta sign off now I'm getting another call."

The call was from the **Edwin Kennedy**'s home office, telling the captain that a small towboat was bringing out some more barges to add to his tow for transit downriver.

Dee called the lockmaster. "Come on down and wait behind the riverside wall until this six hundred foot tow clears the lock, then I'll lock you down with that other pleasure craft that's coming downriver."

We looked behind us and saw a white shape with spray flying. When the boat got closer, we recognized it as the **Mis T Way** from the day before.

After we locked through, the **Mis T Way** roared past creating a wake almost as big as some of the towboats. Before the wake disappeared a stiff breeze sprang up from dead ahead. The increasing wind churned up some very respectable waves sending spray crashing against the windshield. I turned on the wiper.

Soon the spray became sheets of water making the wiper useless. I slowed to idle speed and turned our bow on an angle toward the Kentucky shore in order to quarter against the oncoming waves. Sheets of water continued to hit the windshield, and spray went over the top of the flying bridge. Visibility became so bad inside that we had to move to the bridge helm.

For four hours we wallowed and pitched our way into the on-coming wind, keeping our heads down to avoid the flying spray. A few miles above Cairo the river turned south, and the surface, now free from the straight up-river blow, smoothed to a light chop.

After our struggles against the wind and water of the Ohio, the boils and eddies of the meandering Mississippi were a welcome sight. Even in the strongest gusts, the centers of the boils remained glassy smooth, as the river's own movement thwarted the winds efforts to master the water's surface.

What a reception we received as we nosed back into those muddy waters. The **A.M. Thompson,** pushing twenty-one empties was passing the slower **Jeffboat** with thirty-seven empties. On our left the tiny **Leo Bartel,** at full speed, was turning into the Ohio on some unknown but crucial mission. Behind **Jeffboat,** a smaller tow struggled against the current with thirteen empties and one loaded barge. Just below, the **Katie Whalt** was scurrying across the river in front of the **Dottie Fride-man,** which was coming off the Wickliff Revetment pushing one full petroleum barge.

The current, the wind and the stern washes of all these towboats created a composite action which seemed to say "welcome back."

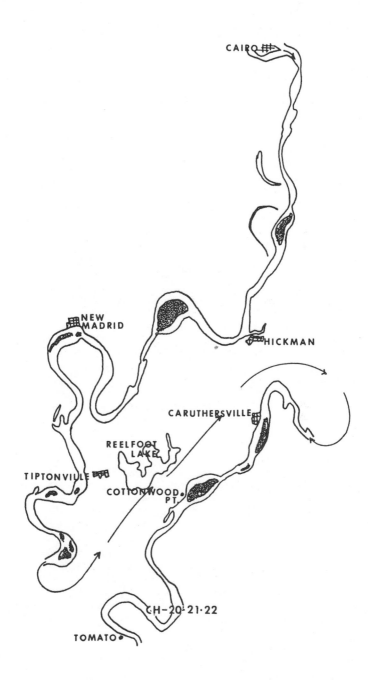

CAIRO

NEW
MADRID

HICKMAN

CARUTHERSVILLE

REELFOOT
LAKE

TIPTONVILLE

COTTONWOOD
PT.

CH-20·21·22

TOMATO

20

LIFE AND DEATH IN HICKMAN

At mile 953.8 we entered the Lower Mississippi River. We were now 847 miles from Minneapolis and still more than 950 miles from The Gulf.

After the welcoming towboat activity, the river quieted, allowing us to increase our speed to fifteen miles an hour. The rough trip down the Ohio had been very tiring, and we were anxious to get to Hickman as soon as possible. The river was kind to us; the mile markers and navigational aids slid quickly by. In two hours we were approaching Beckwith Bend, four miles above the entrance to the Hickman harbor.

Quimby's guide told us to ". . .call the motor vessel **Stephen L** on VHF-FM channels 68, 13, or 15 for directions." We tried several times without success. Finally an answer came, "This is the **City of Hickman**. Please stand by on Channel 68. Captain Ken Love of the fuel tow **Stephen L**. will call you."

Just before we reached the harbor entrance the radio came to life. "The **Stephen L** calling **Sol Seaker**."

"**Sol Seaker**," I replied. "We're looking for gas and a place to tie up overnight."

"How big are you, Skipper?"

"Twenty-six feet."

"How much fuel will you be needing?"

"Oh, about forty-five gallons I guess."

"Okay Skipper, we'll be ready for you."

"Good, we'll be there in a few minutes."

"This is **Sol Seaker**, W R W 2683, clear on 68."

"The **Stephen L** clear."

A few minutes later our tired boat and her exhausted crew nosed into the quiet backwater slough that was once the main channel of the Mississippi. On the hills we could see the buildings of Hickman, the most prominent being an imposing brick structure which could have been a church or government building. We passed the Coast Guard station, some barges, a large towboat with

197

engines running, the smaller **City of Hickman**; then, alongside the tiny derelict towboat, **Stephen L**, one of the most welcome sights of our journey. The opposite side of the **Stephen L** was occupied by **Mis T Way**.

A frail old man, called "Pops", marina operator Ken Love, and **Mis T Way**'s skipper, Tom Phillipi, helped make us secure.

We learned that Pops had limped into Hickman several days before aboard an equally fragil and leaky wooden boat, that was now tied stern in against the levee. He was on his way to Florida, then to some island off Central America. Aboard with Pops was an old black and white dog, which served as companion and as an extra blanket in cold weather. "I don't need a heater," Pops said, "if'n the weather turns cold I jist snuggle up to that old dog and we's warm as toast."

Ken told us privately that the day after Pops arrived, two Coast Guard officers had come by to see him. One of the officers said, "We've had complaints about you from several towboat captains."

"I ain't done nothin' wrong," the old man had replied.

"One captain says you cut right in front of his tow and he almost hit you."

"Thet were his fault," Pops had answered, "I was jist goin' along on my own side of the river, mindin' my own business, an' he jist kept edgin' over closter and closter to my side. I had to do somethin' so I run acrost to get outen his way."

After several more minutes of discussion, in which the old man had continued to blame the towboat captains for all his problems, the Coast Guard officers threw up their hands in exasperation. "You'd better stay off the river in that wreck," one officer said as they departed.

"He really doesn't belong on the river in that boat," Ken told us. "It has a leak. We've got it pulled in stern first so it won't sink. The engine's flooded and needs repair. Pops is too frail to handle a boat, and besides he has this flap in his windpipe to breath through, which sometimes gets stuck so he can't exhale. As if that isn't enough, he's on social security," Ken added. "Gets only $160 a month. He's already borrowed two months ahead for boat repairs from some marina owner upriver. I'm letting him stay here. When the water goes down I'll try to get his boat fixed, but I hate to see him go back out on the river. He'll

drown for sure if he does. Meantime I'll see that he
don't starve. Don't know what else to do."

The **Stephen L** was tied bow in against the levee.
Since the water level fluctuates so much, there is no
permanent walkway between boat and shore. A 2 x 12, and
a telephone pole with cross boards serve as gangplank.
Gas and diesel pumps, fuel and water hoses, assorted
bits and pieces of metal, wire, flotation material,
revetment rock, and bags of garbage, made our passage
from boat to firm land tricky, if not treacherous.

Once past the debris, we climbed the steep levee to
a dirt road running parallel to the shoreline between
the water and the inevitable concrete wall. Two openings
in the wall, which could be closed on short notice, gave
access between river and town. We turned right, walked
past the Coast Guard station then turned sharply left up
the levee and through one of the openings.

Beyond the wall, we could see the lower parts of
Hickman. While there were some vacant buildings, the
town seemed more alive than some of the small river
towns we had visited. The levee dropped steeply down to
a street below, where a man about the same vintage as
Pops, but on crutches, was attempting to cross the
street. We could see that his ragged and dirty pants
were also very wet in the seat and down both legs.

With each step the old man would stumble backward,
hitch up his pants, gain his balance, then move his
crutches forward for his next step. Sure that he would
fall at any moment, I hurried ahead to assist him. As I
approached, he lost his balance and collapsed into a
heap at my feet. I let out an involuntary gasp as I saw
him land on his left leg, which was now pointing off at
an oblique angle.

"Oh, my God his leg's broken!" Dee shouted.

"It's artificial," I said as I quickly bent down
to help. The fall had caused the straps to slip. I sat
beside him, the odor of urine so strong that I had to
muster all of my humanitarian convictions to grasp the
sopping leg, straps and long underwear.

During the repair operation, the old man kept talking, but his speech was so garbled I couldn't understand
a word he said. I kept nodding and working on his leg.
After several minutes, I effected successful repairs,
got the old man to his feet, and helped him across the
street. Once across, I concentrated on his attempted
communication - still without much success.

Finally I said slowly, "My name is Weldon Parker. What's your name?"

"Ish Floogd Lugdmoonds."

"What?" I repeated, as I strained to hear.

"Ish Floogd Lygdoomdis," He said more slowly. "Floogd," He repeated.

"Floyd?" I asked.

"Yesh."

"What's your last name?"

"Ligeduns."

I took out my notebook and wrote "Floyd Ligeduns" and showed it to him. He indicated that Floyd was correct but Ligedons wasn't. After some time I finally got "Floyd Ligons."

He nodded.

He continued to jabber as we walked across a vacant lot, but no matter how hard I tried I could not understand anything more than his name.

We were to the center of the lot when an elderly, arthritic, but neatly dressed man came to our rescue. "Where are you headed?" he asked.

"Darnell's Restaurant," Dee replied as I continued to try to communicate with Floyd.

"Are you on a boat?"

"Yes, we're on our way to New Orleans."

"Wait here. I'll get my car."

Dee protested, saying that we could walk.

"I need to get out in the evening," he said, as he hurried off toward a tidy yellow house across the street, reappearing quickly in a shiny new car.

"That old man's a town drunk. Has a nephew just about as bad, on drugs and everything. The least I could do was get you away from him."

"Thanks," said Dee, obviously relieved.

"You going to be in Hickman long?"

"Just tomorrow. We have motor bikes, and want to ride around town and see the countryside. We heard there was an Indian site near here."

"That's north of town. When you finish your ride tomorrow, stop by and meet my wife, Lucille. We live in the yellow house. Moved here from Evansville ten years ago to be near Lucille's parents. They're dead now, but we're all settled here, so I guess we'll stay. We go out to Las Vegas once-in-a-while, to just get away. I have a son there. Ray's tone said he didn't care too much for Hickman, but to move would be a big chore.

At Darnell's we thanked Ray again, promised to drop by the next day, then I rushed into the restroom to wash the urine off my hands and arms.

We had been in Hickman less than an hour and already we had had two unusual experiences. We must have been on a roll, for the restaurant provided the setting for the Hickman saga to continue.

We learned, early in our trip, to pick out a table or booth which provided us with a full view of the restaurant. In Darnell's we sat at a table in the front corner from which we could see all other tables, the counter, into the kitchen and in addition catch the last rays of the setting sun.

At the booth across from us was an attractive and expertly coiffured blond lady, dressed in a stylish white pants suit. With her was a distinguished looking man. When their food arrived, they bowed their heads for a moment of silent prayer before beginning to eat.

A handicapped boy in his teens entered, ordered a coke at the counter, then sat three tables down from us. He had enlarged joints, a misshapen left arm, irregular gait and puffy face with large bulging eyes. In a few minutes a man came in, sneaked up beside the boy, and took his drink in an affectionate tease. Although feigning displeasure, the boy obviously enjoyed the attention. The man sat across the table from the boy and they began to converse.

Suddenly, the front door burst open. Dee and I gasped as a tall, rough, unshaven desperado came through the door looking, more than anything, like the bad guy in an old western movie. The "villain" glanced around as though anticipating a fight. A shiver went through me as his cold eyes caught mine for an instant.

He strode toward the counter, then stopped and sat heavily in a booth near the center of the room. Once again his cold eyes surveyed the room - this time more slowly. He spotted the handicapped boy. Suddenly his cruel, whiskered face went soft, and he broke into a wide grin showing two rows of large, uneven teeth made even larger by diseased and receding gums. "Tim," he said in a voice which completely destroyed the sinister image. He moved over, put an arm around the handicapped boy, and sat down beside him.

At the booth next to the blond lady and distinguished gentleman, sat a quiet, short lady in her mid-thirties and an older woman. The younger lady had a

201

pleasant face and neat auburn hair. As they rose to leave, we noted that, despite her high heels. the younger lady was even shorter than she had appeared when seated.   She wore a red plaid, wool skirt and a red blouse.

After dinner, we stepped out into the chill night air, on an unfamiliar street, in an unfamiliar town. As we hurried along the dark sidewalk, barking dogs, erie shadows, and low hanging limbs added fuel to the fires of anxiety that had been kindled by the events of the evening. What a relief it was when we were finally safe and snug aboard **Sol Seaker**.

The next day we searched without success for the Indian Mounds that were listed on our river chart. One farmer said, "There usta be mounds hereabouts. but they've all been plowed and the stuff picked up. Yall lookin' fer arrow heads?"

"No, we're just interested in archeology," we replied.

"Well you might find something if you look around in them fields over there. That usta be an Indian site." He obviously thought we were "pot hunters."

In East Hickman we wandered into a neighborhood market which contained a wide variety of "soul food." We were especially intrigued by a shelf filled with cans of Pork Brains with Gravy. We bought Cokes, and asked the clerk what we should see in town. "Up on the hill you can see where all the fancy, fine folks live," she replied.

As we were leaving the store we noted that a clerk and the store manager were in animated conversation. The clerk gestured toward the parking lot. Outside, we spotted the object of their concern. A grizzled old man with only half-a-mouth of teeth, and these stained a mustard brown by a chaw of "tobaccy" that would choke a horse, was selling the largest most beautiful apples, tomatoes, turnips, and sweet potatoes we'd ever seen. As we passed, he asked if we'd like to buy some turnips or "sweet 'taters."

Just as we were declining, the store manager appeared. Although we couldn't hear the subdued conversation, obviously the old man was being unceremoniously evicted from the stores property. Later in the day, as we again rode past the store, we noted that the old man was doing a lively business on an empty lot next door.

In Hickman, as in other towns, our bikes drew a lot

of attention. On Holy (pronounced Holly) Alley we were
hailed by an elderly but spry looking man, standing in
the front yard of a modest house. Beside him, tail
wagging, was a medium sized dog of questionable paren-
tage. We returned his wave of greeting as we rode slowly past. About a block down the road Dee said, "I'll
bet that man has a story to tell, let's go back. Besides, I think we're lost, and he can tell us how to get
back to the main street."

That's how we met Loyd (one L).

"I'm eighty-two years old. I was a paper boy in
Hickman fer years. Used to be some niggers livin'
across the road. One day I give them the wrong paper.
All the niggers take the Nashville paper. Maybe yall
didn't know that but they does. I don't know why but
they nearly all takes the Nashville paper."

"Well, when I growed up I worked for a man owned a
hardware store and a furniture store. I used to drive a
great big truck to get loads of furniture. Wunst I
drove to Nashville to pick up a load of wood cook stoves
and heaters. Heavy they was. That old truck could
barely go up hill."

"On the way back I come up a steep hill with trees
growin' along both sides of the road, limbs hanging way
out. At the top of the hill I met this Greyhound Bus.
We could barely pass. Next day I read in the papers
where a panther jumped out of a tree and smashed through
the windshield of a Greyhound Bus. I figured it was the
bus I met. There was a wreck, but wasn't nobody hardly
hurt, according to the paper. 'Course it killed the
panther."

Loyd paused to fill his pipe with Elks Tobacco.
"Main crop around here used to be tobacco. Now its
beans - soybeans. When the farmers used to get a dollar
a bushel fer beans they thought they was in tall cotton.
Now they figger they can't make it on less than seven
dollars a bushel. 'Course you don't see none of them
walkin'. They all drive great big cars and pick-up
trucks."

"Me, I think the T-Model Ford was good enough for
anyone. Where you folks from?"

"California."

"California! I got sister-in-laws in Fresno. One's
a nurse. The other's a wino." He chuckled. "She don't
drink wine, but I call her that 'cause she works in a
winery."

203

"Now, when I was drivin that big truck, I always wanted to git back before bad traffic." Loyd stopped talking suddenly as though it was time to "git back" to some important chore "before bad traffic."

"Does this road lead back to town?" Dee asked.

"Yall kin take a right at the corner. Goes down a steep hill then out by the courthouse. From there you git the best view of the river in these parts."

"That must be the brick building we saw from the river," I commented to Dee as we rode away.

On our way to the courthouse, we stopped by a bank for Dee to cash a traveler's check. While inside, she asked where she could get a hair cut, as she had been unable to stop at Fantastic Sams in Paducah. "They's a new beauty shop in town," answered the teller with short brown hair. "Lady used to own Darnell's restaurant, now she has a beauty shop."

Hoping to get an appointment for later in the day, we went directly to the beauty shop, to find that there were no other customers. "I can take you right now," said Pat, the "well coiffured" blond we had seen in Darnell's. "My husband and I've been married three years. He owned Darnell's restaurant when we got married. He wanted me to give up the hair business to be a cook and waitress in the restaurant. I did, but every night I said, 'Dear Lord you know how much I like to fix hair, so if you can find a way for me to do that I'll be so thankful.'"

"Well, last spring my husband became a policeman. He sold the restaurant, and now I have my own shop. I show my appreciation to the Lord by puttin' bible verses on the ceiling. Now my customers can lean back and take comfort in the Word of God. We belong to the Full Gospel Church, and we know everyone."

"I like living in Hickman. When my friends come, I like to take them on a tour of the town. One day I got confused and turned the wrong way on our one-way street. I got stopped by a policeman. Boy did my husband get razzed 'cause his wife got caught drivin' the wrong way on a one-way street."

"I don't have much business yet. I guess I'll have to advertise. When I finish your hair, I'm gonna' close up shop because my three step-grand-children are coming over for the evenin'."

"You might get business from boaters like me if you put a notice down at Ken Love's marina," Dee commented.

"That's a good idea. I never thought of that."

As Pat was finishing, Dee asked her about Tim, the handicapped boy. "That's a very sad story. He was perfectly normal until about two years ago. Then he got this disease. I don't know what it is. They've had him to doctors in Memphis, but now he's very handicapped. He's a good boy too. Always has been. He still has a good attitude. Everybody likes him. It shore tears us up to see what's happenin' to him."

At the courthouse we met the short lady in red from the restaurant. She had a janitor take us up to the bell tower for the 'best view of the river.' "Yall have to hurry though, 'cause them bells go off on the hour, and you don't want to be up there when they ring."

From the courthouse we rode up a steep hill to where the "fancy fine folk" live. Half-way up, my bike ran out of gas. By the time I pushed it to the top, I, too, was "out of gas." As we coasted down toward the main street, we spotted a small bait store. "Let's stop," I called to Dee. "I want to get some worms."

"Ain't got no more worms, 'cause catfishin' is about over," we were told by the proprietor. "Now ever'one's fishin' for crappie. I got lots of crappie minnows. You folks ain't from around here are you?"

"No, we're on a boat trip down the river," I answered as Dee searched in her purse for a picture of **Sol Seaker**.

The man looked enviously at the picture, then pointed to a large, brick house down the street. "I live there," he said. "I been trying to sell my house but not many people buyin' houses 'round here."

"That's true all over," Dee replied. "How much are you asking for it?"

"Well, the askin' price is $55,000, but the takin' price is $45,000."

Dee and I chuckled inwardly, partly because of the low price here, as compared to California, and partly because of the naive confession that he was willing to take much less than the "askin' price."

"Do you know how much a house like that would sell for in a place like Saratoga, California?" Dee asked.

"Prob'ly mor'n a hundred thousand," he replied.

"More like $300,000," Dee said.

"Ooooh Whee. Guess I better see if I can find me somebody who can move a house that big, hadn't I? You want some crappie minnows?"

205

"We don't have our bucket with us, and it's a little hard to carry a bucket on these bikes. Maybe we'll come back later," I answered.

Our last stop before returning to the boat was to see Ray, and meet his wife Lucille. The car was in the driveway, but no one answered our knock at the door of the yellow house. We walked around to the back, where we noticed a police car and two policemen at the house behind Ray's. We knocked at the back door. There was still no answer.

A lady came out of the house where the policemen were, said something to one of them, then headed across the unfenced yard in our direction. "Can I help you?" she asked. Her voice was strained and there was a look of despondency in her eyes.

"We're looking for Ray," Dee replied. "We're on a boat. We met him yesterday, and he asked us to drop by today."

As the lady opened the back door and called, "Ray, Ray," we noticed that she wore two large rings on each hand. An answer came from inside. "He's on the phone; come on in. I'm Lucille, Ray's wife. Everybody calls me 'Cille (pronounced seal). Sit down, Ray'll be off the phone in a minute. I'm sorry I seem upset, but the boy in the house back there just shot hisself. The ambulance took him away a few minutes ago but I think he's already dead. Put the gun in his mouth and shot hisself. He never was quite right. Thirty-three years old. Never worked. Jist stayed in the house all the time."

"That was my house. Was my parent's house. We moved here from Evansville to be near my family. My brother lived there, and we looked after him. One day I had supper fixed and Ray went to git him. Found him dead. I was so upset Ray said, 'Let's go away for a little while.' So we went away for five weeks. When we come back, I was still upset. Ray took me away for three more weeks. Finally I got over it."

"Now, Cyril has shot hisself. I know he's dead. He was sittin' in a chair in his room. Stuck the gun in his mouth. They was a big pool of blood on the floor. His head was turned way over to the side and his eyes was open, jist starin'. I closed his eyes and cleaned up the blood. His mother was hysterical. She went with him to the hospital in Union City, but I know he's already dead."

Ray was off the phone. "Come on 'Cille let's talk about something else, ain't nothin' you can do now. Maybe they'd like a coke or something."

As we sipped our cokes, Lucille became calmer and began to talk about her and Ray's life together. We listened both from genuine interest and because we knew that talking would help Lucille get through the trauma of the moment. "Ray and I have been married for twenty-three years. My first husband died. He had given me a beautiful diamond ring."

We glanced at the four rings on her fingers, wondering if they were real diamonds.

"That ring was lost for almost eight years. One day I was goin' through an old purse I found in the back of the closet. There was a wad of Kleenex in the purse, and something hard in the Kleenex. Well, it was my lost ring. I had that ring cleaned up an gave it to my niece. I told her to always wear it an' never put it away. I like diamond rings," she said holding out her hands.

"When we were younger, Ray and I both drove school busses. At one time we owned eleven busses and contracted with the schools. Later we decided to just have and drive two busses. At the same time Ray ran a restaurant and cocktail lounge. He didn't allow no profanity or drunks. Even though he's little, he would throw people out if they got too loud or had too much to drink. I like diamonds and Ray likes new cars. We've had eighteen new cars since 1954. We got a new one now."

Ray, who had been sitting quietly, entered the conversation. "I never could hold on to money so I figger I better buy something worthwhile. So I buy diamonds and cars. I never carry more than two dollars with me or I'll spend it. We also had horses. Had twenty-five horses since we been married."

Ray continued, "We go to Las Vegas every year to visit my son. He's married to a Thai. They have a nine year old son who is Thai and a six year old son that's half caucasian and half Thai. Last summer they come to visit us in Hickman. Them two little boys sure love their Grandma."

Lucille broke in, "When my stepson was here from Las Vegas, I showed him all the valuable things in the house - a cane with a gold head, a tiffany lamp, and all my jewelry. I'm always afraid someone might steal our stuff so I wanted him to know what's here. A lady down the street was robbed in her own house. They tied her up and poured hot coffee on her. You never know what kids will do when they get on drugs. Like everyone else, we keep a loaded gun, and we'd shoot to kill if anyone tried to rob us."

There was a knock at the back door. Ray answered the door. We could hear him telling someone about the tragedy. A male voice filled with grief said, "He's been talkin' about doin' this, but nobody thought he was serious."

Ray went outside with the visitor. Several minutes later he returned and said to Lucille, "That was Cyril's nephew. He took the news hard. He's goin' over to the Union City Hospital."

Meanwhile, Lucille had told us about three other Hickman residents who had shot themselves in the past few years.

"You do any fishin' on your boat?" Ray asked, again trying to change the subject.

"A little. We stopped by a bait shop to get some worms, but they were out. We talked to the man for a little while."

"Was it the old man?" asked Ray.

"No it was a younger man."

"Oh him," said Lucille, "I've knowed him since he was tiny. I always believed children should mind. One day I was takin' care of him and he didn't mind. Well I switched him good and never had no more trouble outa him. He used to be the police chief here for about five years. Then, rumor has it that he got caught doin' somethin' illegal and was asked to resign."

"If you folks like to fish," Ray said, "I bet you'd like to see Reelfoot Lake. It's the purtiest lake in the world and it has the best fishin' too. When are you planning to leave?"

"Tomorrow," we answered.

"Sure wish you'd stay another day. We'd like to drive you down to Reelfoot Lake."

"You ever seen bow-facing oars?" Lucille asked.

"No," we replied.

"Well, tomorrow you come with us to Reelfoot Lake, and we'll show you bow-facing oars."

Intrigued by the prospect of a beautiful lake and these mysterious oars, we agreed to stay over another day.

"We'll pick you up about ten."

Back at the boat, I looked up toward the courthouse where we had enjoyed the local version of the "best view of the river." "We saw the best views at Redwing, Alma, Fountain City, Lansing and lots of other places," I said to Dee. "Which one do you think was the best view?"

"This one!" she said as she climbed to the flying bridge and made a sweeping gesture toward the river.

That night as the rains came down on Hickman, St. Louis built up a 7-0 lead in the sixth game of the world series. When the game was temporarily halted by rain, I fell asleep, but Dee stayed awake to see St. Louis win the game 14-1 and tie the series at three games each. Tomorrow's game would decide the championship.

HICKMAN COUNTY COURTHOUSE

21

LAKES, QUAKES AND POTATO FLAKES

Although the rain had stopped, clouds still hung heavy the next morning, as Dee reached for her clothes in the storage space beneath the helm seat. "They're all wet!" she exclaimed. "The boat's leaking!" We removed the clothes from the area. All were soaked. A quick inspection showed that the wetness extended the full length of **Sol Seaker**'s starboard side.

As Dee removed a large box of potato flakes from the food storage area, the moistened bottom of the box gave way, and damp potato flakes flew all over the loose shag carpet. The sight of soggy clothes and the mounds of moist potato flakes on the dark brown carpet would have evoked laughter, had we not been convinced that the boat was sinking.

The water seemed to have entered from the stern. The weight of our bodies in the bed caused the bow to ride lower than the stern, allowing the water to work its way forward, soaking everything in its path.

I quickly checked the bilge and found it dry. "The water must be from the rainstorm," I said, "not the river." **Sol Seaker** wasn't sinking after all. However, my inspection failed to reveal how the water seeped in.

We wrung the clothes as best we could, and draped them over table, steering wheel, and stove. Dee scooped up most of the potato flakes with a spatula, and we were ready for our trip to Reelfoot Lake when Ray and Lucille arrived.

The drive south from, Hickman toward Tennessee, was through a landscape of harvested fields and rolling, tree covered hills. As we approached the Tennessee border, Lucille told us the story of Reelfoot Lake.

"Lots of people I know are afraid to go to California because of the earthquakes," she said, "but the biggest earthquake in the history of the United States happened right here, where Kentucky, Tennessee and Missouri meet. It happened in 1811. The shock was felt as far east as Boston. They don't know how far west it was felt because there weren't many settlers there. In Missouri some lakes were drained, and the lake beds raised ten to twenty feet in the air. New lakes were formed in Arkansas, Louisiana and Tennessee. The biggest lake formed by the earthquake was Reelfoot Lake, which is just over the Tennessee line."

"They called it the New **Mad**rid quake (we noted that she pronounced the word **Mad**rid rather than Ma**drid**) because New **Mad**rid was the largest town in the area at that time. Before the earthquake, the place where Reelfoot Lake is was a swampland, covered with cypress trees. When the quake hit, it is said that the Mississippi actually ran backwards and spilled over its banks. The lowlands sank even lower, and the waters of the Reelfoot and Mississippi Rivers flooded an area of about twenty thousand acres - up to twenty feet deep in some places."

"No one knows exactly how this all happened, because there weren't any white men living in the area. In fact, the lake wasn't discovered by white man until fifty years after it formed. But the Indians in the area had a legend about how the lake was created and named."

"If I can remember it all - Let's see - It seems Reelfoot was a Chickasaw Indian. He was called Reelfoot because he was lame and had a bad limp, which made him reel when he walked. Reelfoot was handsome and strong in spite of his handicap, and his father, who was chief, selected him to be his successor. When the old chief died, Reelfoot became a fair, respected leader of his people. But he was lonely because he couldn't find a suitable mate among the maidens of his own tribe."

"Reelfoot took a few of his trusted braves and headed down the Mississippi in search of a princess. After many days, they came to a large Choctaw village. The Choctaw chief greeted Reelfoot warmly as he stepped from his canoe. Reelfoot looked around at the people who had gathered along the bank, and his eyes fell on a beautiful girl arrayed in regal finery. He loved her instantly, and that evening informed the chief of his desires."

"The chief became angry, telling Reelfoot that the young lady was his only daughter, Laughing Eyes. He would never permit her to be wed to a club-footed foreigner, but only to a Choctaw Chieftain."

211

"So struck was Reelfoot by the maiden that he offered the older chief many valuable gifts for his
daughter's hand. The old chief sent for his medicine
man asking him to call upon the Great Spirit to determine his wishes in the matter."

"The Great Spirit told Reelfoot to go home at once,
forget the chief's daughter, and seek a bride from his
own tribe. If he disobeyed, the Great Spirit would
cause the earth to tremble and shake. Reelfoot and all
of his people would sink into a watery grave. Heart-
broken, Reelfoot kneeled before the Great Spirit and
promised to abide by his wishes."

"Back home, Reelfoot became more and more lonely
and despondent. The face of Laughing Eyes haunted him
day and night, until finally he could stand the torment
no longer. The warning of the Great Spirit was forgotten, and Reelfoot called together his bravest and
strongest warriors, and set out on a secret mission to
capture his princess."

"Laughing Eyes was quietly seized and carried to
the canoes, which were quickly paddled upstream. The
maiden had heard the edict of the Great Spirit and was
terrified for herself and Reelfoot and his people."

"Upon their arrival at Reelfoot's village, festival
fires were lit and great quantities of food were prepared for the nuptial celebration. As the wedding cere-
mony began, a fierce trembling started. The earth
rumbled and giant cracks formed. The Indians tried to
run to safety, but the shaking earth threw them down,
and the Great Spirit called upon the Father of Waters,
whereupon the water of the Mississippi overflowed its
bank, ran uphill and covered the place where Reelfoot's
village had stood."

"Reelfoot, Laughing Eyes, the warriors, and all the
people of Reelfoot's tribe were covered and vanished.
Where they once stood, there is now a beautiful lake,
mirroring from its depths the glint of royal beads, the
rich colors of the maiden's robes, and the everlasting
sparkle of the princess' eyes."

When Lucille had finished the beautiful legend of
Reelfoot, Dee said, "The Indians were a very romantic
people, at least in their legends. Everywhere we go we
hear about Indian braves who risk life and limb for a
beautiful maiden. Or about a young warrior and his
lover who end it all because the father forbids them to
marry. I wonder how many "lover's leaps" there are in

212

the world? I know we have one along the Russian River in California. The high rock formation even looks like the head of an Indian when viewed from a certain angle."

"I noticed that you pronounced New **Madrid** with the accent on **Mad**. Is that just a local pronunciation or is there a reason for it?" I asked Lucille.

"There's a story about that too," she said, "but I don't know if it's true or not. It seems a man named Morgan, Colonel George Morgan of Virginia, had this big plan to get a bunch of people from the east to come out here to settle. That was in the late 1700's when Spain was in control of this area. The Spanish Ambassador to the United States promised to support Morgan's plans. He would see that Morgan would be granted 15,000,000 acres that stretched three hundred miles along the Mississippi River."

"Morgan started advertising free land for the first six hundred settlers to come west. He then built cabins and laid out hundred acre garden plots. In addition, farms of 320 acres could be bought cheap."

"So attractive were the terms, and grandiose the plans for New **Madrid** that many Easterners said that the people who followed Colonel Morgan were **Mad**-rid indeed. And that's how the pronunciation got the accent on the first syllable."

"Morgan's advertisements were a bit premature as he had to get final approval from Miro, the Spanish governor of Louisiana. Unfortunately for Morgan, Miro was involved in schemes he hoped would destroy the American Union. He saw Morgan's plan as strengthening the union. Also fearing that Morgan would bring a lot of protestants west and weaken the Catholic Church's position in the area, Miro denied Morgan's request."

Despite the build-up, we were not fully prepared for the unique beauty of Reelfoot Lake. Giant cypress trees lined the shore and many stood "knee" deep in the greenish brown water. Dark shadows and sparkling reflections were mirrored on the water's cool surface.

"It's easy to see how the Reelfoot Legend came about," said Dee, as a slight breeze ruffled the rich dark watery robes of the now vanished Laughing Eyes, and created a string of sparkling jewels between two cypress trees.

As we drove along the shore, we came to places where entire sections of the lake were filled with small cypress trees, each standing on its own shimmering reflection, like a fairy Christmas tree land. In other spots, huge logs and burned stumps were scattered helter-skelter over the lake's surface.

Ray turned the car into one of the many small fishing marinas that line the lake shore. "Now you can try the famous bow-facing oars, that were patented by the Calhouns nearly a hundred years ago," he said, as we emerged from the car and walked toward several canoe-like boats, whose bows had been pulled into a neat row along a small canal.

My eye was caught by the strange contraptions on each side of the boat. Regular oar locks consist of a simple movable ring through which the oar is placed. The rower tips the blades up, moves the handle forward, drops the blade into the water, and pulls. The force of the blade against the water causes the boat to move in the direction that is behind the rower. The problem with this action is that it is very difficult for the rower to see where he is going.

Since Reelfoot Lake is very shallow and infested with sunken logs, limbs and stumps, being able to see where one is rowing has a distinct advantage. The Calhoun bow-facing oars are the answer. Each oar is cut into two pieces. The pieces are attached to hinged oar locks which change the direction of the movement of the blades. Thus, when one pulls back on the handles, the boat is propelled forward, allowing the rower to see ahead.

We pushed a boat into the water, and Lucille got in to demonstrate the technique. It looked easy, but I soon found that my many years of rowing with a standard set of oars made this new experience akin to driving on the left side of the busy streets in London. Everything worked in reverse.

I asked Ray about the small motors I saw in some boats. "Why don't you try one out," he suggested.

We rented a boat for an hour. We should have known something was wrong when Ray and Lucille insisted on watching from shore as we cranked up the Briggs and Straton engine and headed out into the lake. A wooden lever controlled the rudder, and a small metal one controlled the speed. After cruising around slowly for a few minutes, we turned the bow toward the center of the lake and opened up the throttle. The cypress and fiberglass boat slowly gained speed. Suddenly the bow shot out of the water, the boat teetered for an instant then

214

the bow came down, and the stern went up and followed the bow down with a splash.

"My God, we've hit a log," I exclaimed, as I jerked the throttle lever into slow position. "I probably ruined the propeller."

We looked toward Ray and Lucille, and saw that they were laughing hysterically. We had just had our first lesson in boating on Reelfoot Lake.

Still a bit shaken by the experience, we returned to shore where we learned that Calhoun had designed metal skid plates to fit beneath the propeller so that the boat could go over logs or hit bottom without damage to the propeller or shaft. This little boat was virtually indestructible.

"What a fantastic boat this would be for Anderson Marsh!" Dee exclaimed, thus planting a seed of interest that was, over the next few weeks, to grow into a tree of reality. And a Calhoun boat has now taken its place among the fleet which surrounds the floating dock under our Clearlake, California home.

A whopping meal of catfish, ham, pork chops, potatoes, peas, onion rings, hush puppies, coleslaw and applesauce provided an appropriate, if somewhat belly bulging, climax to a memorable excursion to one of the most beautiful lakes in the world.

It wasn't until we were almost back to Hickman that Dee and I remembered the soggy potato flakes still covered Sol Seaker's carpeted floor. "We have a small vacuum cleaner," Lucille said. "I bet it'll pick up them potato flakes."

"Either that, or we could add water and a little butter and get down and eat them," Ray chuckled.

"Ugh!" said Dee, "I'll opt for the vacuum, I couldn't eat another thing after that meal at Gooche's."

"Our boat isn't usually this messy," Dee explained, as Ray, Lucille, and their welcome vacuum entered the cramped quarters. The vacuum worked and in a few minutes, except for the still damp clothes, our little floating house was almost presentable.

We thanked Ray and Lucille for their hospitality, promising to send them a card from New Orleans, and to keep them informed about the progress of our book. Thus one more entry was added to our ever growing list of Mississippi River friends. But more than the new names, was the addition of the memories of the fellowship with another couple in the seemingly endless number of warm, hospitable, sharing, human beings that people the revetted and leveed banks of America's mightiest river.

That evening two sailboats anchored in the backwater beyond the **Stephen L**, and St. Louis wrapped up the championship by defeating Milwaukee in the seventh, and final, game of the world series. True to form, Pa Pa Joe had lost his $5.00 bet with Harvey Boone, Cindy's ancient next door neighbor - a bet Joe had made with Harvey before St. Louis had even clinched the league championship.

REELFOOT LAKE

22

SMITH TOWIN' SERVICE

To our right, fog blanketed the backwater anchorage; to our left, the sun made sparkling yellow-brown "Tiger Eyes" out of the gently ruffled, muddy waters of the moving river. While we were preparing to say farewell to Hickman, the ghostly forms of two sailboats broke through the veil of mist, slid past the Coast Guard Station, and turned downriver.

A chill remained in the air. After a few minutes at our upper helm, I turned the wheel over to Dee and went below to add extra socks, rubber boots, Winona sweater and gloves. Dee, always wiser than I about the weather, had already bundled up against the lingering cold.

At Island Ten, we passed Everett's Light which, in addition to serving as a navigational aide, marked the point where less than a mile of land prevented Ole Man River from making a cut-off that would by-pass the nineteen mile long Hotchkiss-New Madrid Bend.

On this huge loop, we met the **Lexington** with fourteen empties and two petroleum barges, passed and waved a greeting to the two sailboats, skirted New Madrid, met an Army Corps survey boat, that had just put a crew off on a small sand island, and met the **John C. Byrd** with four petroleum barges. One hour and forty minutes after entering the bend, we met the **Rita Barta**, with thirty empties - at the other side of the narrow strip of land that kept New Madrid an active river town, rather than just another village whose connection with the Mississippi was but a memory.

At mile 879, Darnell point appeared on our chart. We wondered if there was any historical connection to Darnell's Cafe in Hickman.

It was a moderately busy day on the river. During the next thirty miles we passed the trawler, **Fairbound**, and met the tows **Dot Miller**, **Bayou Couba**, **Dixie Challenge**, **Joseph Patrick**, and **Thomas Hines**. The last two were in tandem, moving thirty-five empties upriver.

217

At three o'clock, we rounded the sharp, Little
Prairie Bend, and headed down a long straight stretch
toward Caruthersville, searching in vain for a place to
tie up for the night.

Fifteen miles below town, where the channel hugged
the Missouri shore, we spotted three small towboats
moored against the bank, at a spot our chart called
"Cottonwood Point". Three young men were sweeping dirt
and gravel off a rusty rock barge. "Any place we can tie
up for the night?" I yelled as we came into hailing
distance.

The three men talked among themselves, then one
gestured for us to come alongside the barge. "You can
stay here; we're cleaning this barge so we kin paint it
tomorrow. We jist got a little more to do before quitting time," he said as he helped secure our lines to the
large bollards, while the other two finished sweeping
the barge.

"I'm William Smith. This here's my brother David,
and our side kick Buddy Ward," he added, as the other
two arrived. "My daddy, brother and me run these towboats, Smith Towin' Service. We own four boats. Three
small ones and one bigger one."

"If yall got time I'd like to show you our boats,"
said David, with obvious pride.

"Great!" Dee exclaimed. "I've been wondering how we
would ever get aboard a real towboat.

"Well, these ain't much like them big towboats,"
David replied. "They got livin' rooms an' T.V. an'
ever'thing jist like at home. That little boat's the
Slave II. That was my Daddy's first towboat. Before
Slave II, he worked for a towboat company in Memphis."

"What kinds of jobs do you do with your boats," I
wondered.

"We do whatever's at hand. Any kind of small tow
job that is. Our bread-'n-butter jobs are adding and
takin' off barges from the big tows, as they move up and
down river. See that grain loading dock acrost the
river? When they need empties, Smith Towin' will take
them from tows that are movin' upriver. 'Course the tow
companies keep track of which barges go where. Each
barge is numbered. When there are full barges, we add
them to tows that are goin' down to Baton Rouge or New
Orleans. We add and take away while the tows are on the
move. They never stop."

"Sometimes we work for The Army Corps of Engineers
218

on rock barges like the one you're tied to. Usually just between Caruthersville and Memphis. Once in a while we take two barges as far as St. Louis. Right now things are slow so we're cleanin', repairin' and paintin' rock barges for this one company."

"Our business is really a family affair," David continued. "Some big companies have tried to buy us out, but Daddy's afraid we'd lose control. Other little companies have sold, and the big companies say, 'You can keep your name,' but one day you see the old name on the tow, then the next day it's gone."

"This here's our pride and joy," David said as we stepped aboard the **Harold Joseph**. "It's named for William's son Jody. The **Elizabeth Ann** there is named for William's little girl."

"Was this once a regular tugboat?" I asked, noticing the pointed bow to which had been added the "knees" used for pushing barges.

"No," answered David, "It was originally a mine layer built in 1945. Here's the brass plaque that tells where it was built. It wasn't never used to lay mines 'cause the war got over. The Army Corps used it for a long time. Then when it was up fer sale my daddy bought it. It's got a lot of the original stuff still on it. We even have the original wheel. 'Course we changed to power levers fer better control. But if'n the power ever fails, we can put the wheel on an' steer her that way. It's even got the original engine. On paper it's rated at six hundred horse power, but it's more powerful than all three of the other boats together. Must really be at least a thousand horse power."

When we returned to the barge, Buddy and William joined us. "You must have had some exciting times on the river," I said.

"I guess we've had our share," William answered. "One time we were crossin' the river right over there." He gestured. "We was in the **Elizabeth Ann** when all of a sudden our engine quit. We was right in front of a bunch of tied up barges. The current swept us right into the barges. I was on the front, so I jumped onto a barge jist before we hit. Buddy an' David grabbed holt of each other. The impact threw them clean acrost the deck and skinned them up pretty bad."

"One of the pushin' knees was broke off the boat, an' the bow was bent up pretty bad," David added.

"Another time," William continued, "we was movin'

a barge in the Memphis harbor. David was runnin' the boat - he runs it better than I do - an' I was handlin' the line. The line was a one and three-forths inch rope. Well I got on the barge an' looped the line around a bollard. It wasn't holdin' good, so I made a turn around the second bollard. As I did, I stepped into the coil of the rope. I still couldn't hold it and the line came out of my hand. As the barge and tow separated, my foot and leg were dragged into a figger eight around them two bollards. Broke my leg in four places. They say you could a heard my yell a mile away."

"A black feller heard me and come a runnin' to help. As he was a comin', he was a reachin' in his pocket fer his knife. When he got there my leg was free from the rope, but he immediately cut my boot laces and got my boot off. I shore give him credit fer that. They say if he hadn't got my boot off when he did they'd a had to burn it off. My foot swole up that fast."

"You were laid up almost a year weren't you?" said David.

"More'n six months at least," William replied.

To us, David said, "Despite that accident, William's a lot better at working the lines than I am."

"Yall need anything from the store?" William asked. "I'll be glad to take you. I'm goin there anyway."

"I guess we could use a few things," Dee answered, happy to get the chance to see Cottonwood Point.

On our way William pointed toward two houses that set back from the levee. "David lives in that house and my folks in that one. I live about half a mile down the road. See that big tree? My grandaddy planted that Indian Pear tree."

"What's an Indian Pear?" asked Dee.

"Well, it has fruit about the size of an apple, but it's bitter. I think they sometimes use it to make preserves."

When we returned to the river, David was standing on the levee with William's son, Jody. "Debbie brought Jody; said to remind you she's goin' to a doin's, and you're supposed to fix sandwiches for you an' Jody."

"I near forgot," responded William.

As David was leaving, Dee said to William, "I don't know when I've seen two brothers that have so much pride in each other, and in their family and business."

"Yes, I guess we are kinda proud. It's a good feeling to work together an' not be scrapin' like some."

William and Jody walked down to **Sol Seaker** with us.
They sat on the edge of the barge and Dee and I on our
rear deck. "I guess you heard my wife, Debbie, is goin'
to a doin's at the neighbor's. I wisht she was goin' to
be home cause then you could come home with us fer a
good home cooked supper."

All the while, Jody sat holding to his father's
arm, looking very much like he would someday carry on
the family enterprise.

William looked tenderly toward Jody. "We almost
lost him wunst. There was a rock barge like this one,
an' Jody accidentally backed off the upriver side, and
completely disappeared under water. I jumped in an
grabbed, and luckily I got holt of him. When we got out
of the water a friend said, 'You know you're lucky he
didn't go clean under the barge.' Then I started
shakin'. It happened so fast I hadn't realized that
both of us could have been swept under and drowned."

Before William left, he related one last river experience. "We contracted for this job in St. Louis for
the **Harold Joseph**. The night before we was to leave, we
filled all of the boat's fuel tanks. First time we ever
filled all the tanks, because we was never going that
far before. Well, we got up early next morning, and
when we got down here the boat was sunk. It was settin'
on the bottom listin' way over to one side. Well, we
lost the contract an' about $4,000 worth of fuel. An'
we had to raise and repair the boat."

"You know the reason it sunk? 'Cause someone before
us had put in a new bathroom. Where the old pipes went
out through the hull were holes that they didn't patch.
These were always well above the water so we never noticed them. But when we filled them tanks, the old
'Harold Joseph' floated so low that water came in them
holes, an' by mornin' it just sunk!"

"Well, I better git Jody home and git him somethin'
to eat. If you hear a noise in the night, don't worry
none. I generally come down to check on the boats most
ever night."

After William left, Dee and I commented again about
the strong family pride that was creating so much human
"sunshine" here on the banks of the Mississippi, at the
tiny village of Cottonwood Point, Missouri.

"I'm glad we stopped here," Dee said.

I was too.

It was early, and very cold, with wisps of mist

rising from the river, when William and Buddy came down the levee and started **Slave II**. We hurried over to say good-bye and get William's address.

"I didn't git down last night," William said. "I slept right through. First time I've done that in a long time."

After exchanging addresses, Dee told William again how impressed we were with the closeness of his family. "You just don't see that much anymore," she said.

"We're gonna have a busy day today," said William, as he and Buddy walked back to **Sol Seaker** with us, while **Slave II**'s engine warmed. "We got seven empties to remove from upriver tows and one or two full ones to add to other tows."

Buddy and William helped us add the fifteen gallons of gas from our portable cans to **Sol Seaker**'s fuel tank.

"We came eighty-nine miles yesterday," I said. "Our next gas stop will be Memphis. I don't know if we'll make it today. We want to stop at Tomato."

William's eyes opened. "Debbie's from Tomato," he said. "I don't know if you'll find a place to stop though. There ain't nothin' there."

"Do you know the postmistress in Tomato?" I asked. "Her name's Emily Lee."

"Debbie would. I'm shore sorry you couldn' have a meal with us."

Buddy and William wished us well, and once again we headed down our Magical Mississippi. Below Cottonwood Point, the state of Missouri was replaced by Arkansas on our starboard side. Our thoughts turned to Tomato, Arkansas.

SOL SEAKER AT SMITH'S TOWIN' SERVICE.

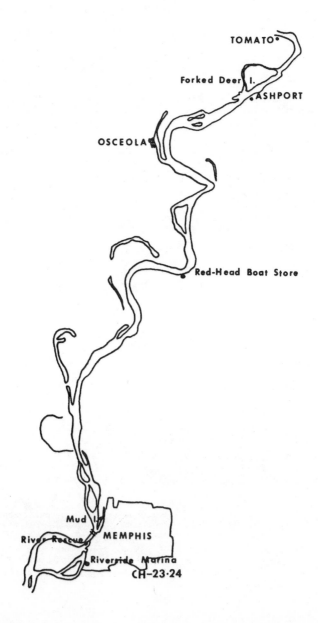

TOMATO

Forked Deer I.
ASHPORT

OSCEOLA

Red-Head Boat Store

Mud I.
River Rescue MEMPHIS
Riverside Marina
CH-23·24

23

SOUL FOOD

When planning our Mississippi River adventure, the name "Tomato" had intrigued us. Postmistress Emily Lee had answered our inquiry with a letter that peaked our interest even more. In her last paragraph she stated, ". . .There's not much left of Tomato now. Like all small places it has gone down. Just our people and a small fourth class post office left."

"I sure hope we can stop at Tomato," I said. "I just have to know who 'our people' are. Besides we told everyone we would pick up mail there."

"We also told people we'd pick up mail at Cairo," Dee replied. "And you see how far we got with that."

The day was uneventful until we were approaching Barfield Bend, just above Tomato. At the head of the bend we overtook a downriver tow. As we increased our speed and edged past the towboat we realized it was the **Rita Barta** a boat we had met the day before going up-river with empties. Now, it was already on its way down with twenty-four loaded grain barges.

"They must have worked all night," Dee exclaimed. "How else could they have delivered those empties and got here with these full barges?"

By the time we had put a mile between ourselves and the **Rita Barta**, we approached the place our chart called "Tomato Landing." The entire bank along this section had been thoroughly revetted with large rocks. Tomato Landing turned out to be a semi-flat place in the rocks, just large enough to launch a small jon boat.

Our hopes of landing at Tomato grew slimmer and slimmer as we moved slowly downriver, searching for any kind of stopping place. We had all but given up, when suddenly the rock revetment ended, exposing a small cove carved into the soft levee by the swirling waters. Cautiously I eased into the pool of slowly circling water. The depth was fine.

"When I get about forty feet from shore, drop the
223

stern anchor." I said to Dee. "Let the line out as I ease up to the rocks, so you can get off with the other anchor. Carry it up on shore and wedge it in the rocks. I'll tighten the stern anchor and get off too. I think if we use a third line and walk along the end of the revetment we can swing the bow out where she'll be held in place by the three lines, like the center of a spoke wheel."

Much to my pleasant surprise, the maneuver went smoothly and worked perfectly. Even the passing **Rita Barta** created only a gentle rocking motion, as the lines held fast. "Tomato here we come," Dee said, as we scrambled up the steep revetment.

"Man, these banks are even higher than they look," I panted, as we reached the top.

Beyond the bank lay broad fields of recently harvested soy beans, broken by rows of cottonwood and willow trees, and by shallow ditches. In the distance we could see buildings that we supposed were Tomato. "It would be closer to go across the fields than around the road," Dee said.

"What if one of those ditches is full of water?" I asked. "Then we'd have to come all the way back to the river. I think we'd better follow the dirt road around the levee to the landing. There must be a road from there into town."

Our sense of excitement rose as we walked along the dusty road. The sun was finally removing the chill from the autumn air, and unidentified birds sang from the tops of the tall cottonwoods that lined the roadway.

When we reached the landing, our dirt road joined a gravel one that came down the levee from upriver and turned toward town. We had gone only a few yards on the gravel road when we came to three large, idle harvesters. A young man standing near the machines turned away shyly as we approached.

When we drew closer he raised his eyes from the ground and said a timid, "howdy."

"We're looking for Emily Lee," Dee said.

He pointed to the first house a few hundred yards ahead. "She lives right there."

"We also want to know where the post office is," I added.

"It's right there too," the young man answered. His eyes dropped once more to the ground, as he shuffled his feet self-consciously in the dirt.

224

"Thanks," we said. We could feel the boy's relief as we left him to tend his machines.

Next to the modest house stood a small white building with the words, UNITED STATES POST OFFICE, TOMATO, ARKANSAS, painted above the door. A sleeping dog "guarded" the door to the screened entry porch. As we approached, the door opened and a man in his sixties appeared.

"Are you Mr. Lee?" Dee asked.

"Yes."

"Is Mrs. Lee at home?"

"Yes."

"We're the Parker's from California. We're here on a boat. It's tied up below the revetment. We wrote to Mrs. Lee several months ago. She may not remember."

"Come on in. Emily'll be happy to see you."

We were quietly amused when we learned that Emily Lee's husband was Robert E.

"We've lived in Tomato for a long time," Emily told us. "Robert is a commercial fisherman, but he had a heart attack a few months ago. He hopes to get back to fishing soon though. Most folks left here after the 1972 flood. You see, we're on the river side of the levee so there's nothin' to keep the water out like other towns have. Ever year our place is surrounded by water. In 1972 there was a bad flood. Here's an article about it."

I read aloud from "Rural Arkansas," 1972: "The Mighty Mississippi River didn't stay away from the doors of Tomato. In fact it absorbed houses, gins, blacksmith shop, two stores, a cemetery and the post office. People just picked up what they could and started over a little farther back from the river bank."

"We're on a little rise here so's we didn't get much water in the house," said Emily, "but sometimes we're surrounded an' can't get out for days at a time."

"How long have you been the postmistress?" I asked.

"Only a year now," Emily replied. "I don't know how much longer we can stay open. Not many folks use the post office. I'm only open two hours a day now. I got a letter for you folks!" Emily suddenly remembered. "Came several days ago. I was wonderin' if you was really gonna come to get it!"

She got up and led us to the post office and gave us a letter from Al and Nancy, friends from San Jose.

"This buildin' used to be a smoke house," Emily

225

said. "I guess it's the only post office in the United States that was once a smoke house. We used to think we had the smallest post office in the country, but then our former postmaster, Joe Jones, heard about one in Florida that is smaller. He wrote to them and measured the outside of our building, and they measured theirs, and theirs was just small enough it could fit inside ours. Ochopee, Florida it is. I got a picture of it right up there." On the wall was a post card of a tiny white building, much like the one we were in, but located in Florida on the Tamiami Trail, between Naples and Miami.

"Would you like to see what used to be our town?" asked Emily.

"Yes!" we replied.

The tour was short. Down the road was an old, weathered building with broken windows and unhinged doors. "That was our grocery store," Emily said, a note of sadness in her voice. "Just didn't pay, so folks just up and left it about three years ago. Now we have to drive eighteen miles for just a loaf of bread."

She then led us across the street. Beneath an over-growth of brush and vines we could see parts of a once proud sign: TOMATO BAPTIST CHURCH. A faded, blue, frame building stood back from the road. The roof over the small porch was askew where a board had rotted allowing one of the two support posts to drop down about a foot. Inside, a vase of artificial flowers still stood on the simple alter. To the right an upright piano waited for someone to play an old hymn from the books that still graced the racks behind each dark stained pew.

On a chalkboard at one end of a tiny Sunday School room were half erased bible verses. Children's "lessons" were stacked on a shelf, and several bible pictures were still pinned to the wall.

Two pigeons, startled from their roost inside the small back room, escaped through broken windows. Their droppings had made small white mounds on top of several bibles stored on a shelf below their perch. "We just got to get them windows boarded up," Emily said, a deep sadness in her eyes and voice. "It don't look like much in here now," she continued, "but we sure used to have some good preachin' an' singin' in here. Lots a souls found Jesus in this little ole church. I don't know if it'll ever be used again or not. The piano's probably out of tune now. It sure is heart breakin' to see ever'thing goin' down. The only folks left in Tomato is us poor folks," she said, half to herself as we left the church.

"So that's who 'our people' are," I thought as we headed back to the Lee's house.

"How did Tomato get its name?" Dee asked as we sat comfortably in the Lee's living room.

"Well, there's two stories about that," answered Emily. She showed us an article in which both versions were mentioned.

I read aloud from the article:

"One version goes that in 1895 a postal representative came here to officially record the name of this place. It had always just been called 'Canadian Reach' by the river men. Letty Coleman and her father had the store here, and Letty was putting groceries on the shelf when her father and the postal representative were trying to decide on a name. It was late in the day, and Letty's father turned to her and said, 'Letty what do you think we should call our town?' Letty had just picked up a large can of tomatoes and looking at it said, 'Oh, why don't you just call it Tomato.'"

"The other version says that originally there was a large wooden tomato packing box nailed to a tree that was used to place the mail delivered by the steamboats. The box had a large picture of a tomato on it, and the name just seemed natural."

"I think the second version is probably more likely," Emily concluded.

As I skimmed further down the article I came to the following passage:

"Living in Tomato is like a tranquilizer. . . A place to step away from the hurried life. . . To listen to the rustle of the giant cottonwoods. . . To see the kids playing as they used to play. . . Listening to the songs of the birds as you look down the street into yesterday."

Robert and Emily drove us back to the boat and waved as we left.

"I'm afraid that as we looked down the street into yesterday, we were looking down a street where there's no tomorrow," I said dejectedly, as we waved a final good-bye to two people whose lives were perhaps more memory than reality.

We rode in reflective silence for a long time, each of us thinking about the many people, places and events

227

that had, in just two months, provided a life-time of affection, concern and adventure.

Finally Dee broke the silence as she said pensively, "If for some reason we had to end our trip right now, the experience would have been much more inspiring than I ever imagined it could be."

"Amen," I replied feeling that somehow this religious expression was most appropriate for the mood which had enveloped us since we first stepped into the Tomato Baptist Church.

But life and responsibility must continue - a realization that hit us as we saw a tow approaching from downriver. She was six barges wide and her bow was swinging relentlessly toward us as she passed the Ashport Landing light, which marked a point where the channel swung quickly from the left bank across to the revetment on Forked Deer Island.

We continued on the one whistle side, moving as close as possible to the black buoy marking the end of a long wing dike. When the tow was no more than a hundred yards away, the swing of the bow ceased. We were almost in touching distance when the lead barge slid past, setting **Sol Seaker** into a moderate rocking motion that continued until all forty-eight barges and the tow had passed.

"That's the biggest tow yet!" Dee exclaimed.

"And the closest," I added, as we wallowed in the sternwash of **Miss Kae D**, whose six barge width and eight barge length was, indeed, the largest tow we had yet encountered.

William Smith had told us of several places between Cottonwood Point and Memphis that we might find a friendly tow operator who would let us tie up for the night. One of these was the towboat **Mary Ann** just below Osceola.

"Just call him on the radio and tell him William, of Smith's Towin', sent you. He'll let you tie up."

As we passed Island Thirty we could see a barge with a small crane working on some new mooring dolphins, about a hundred yards up the backwater slough which ran toward the town of Osceola, about a mile away. We turned into the channel, monitoring our depth sounder as we moved slowly past the working barge. Two hundred yards up the slough we suddenly found that the bottom of the channel and the bottom of **Sol Seaker** decided to occupy the same space. I raised the stern drive and

228

slowly backed off the mud, switching to neutral so we could survey the situation. The men began to move the barge away from the dolphin with a small outboard boat. They pushed it against the bank, and secured it with cables to trees high on the levee.

"Looks like quitting time," I said. "Maybe they'll let us tie up to their barge for the night."

The man we asked consulted the foreman, who said, "Yall can tie up here."

"We'll leave early in the morning," I said, "so we'll be out of your way when you come to work."

"No need," replied the foreman, "it's Friday. We won't be back 'til Monday. Stay as long as you like."

As two of the men helped us secure **Sol Seaker**, the foreman directed another man to lay a 2 x 12 "gangplank" for us to get to shore.

The men then gathered up coats and lunch pails and scrambled up the levee to their waiting pick-up trucks. The foreman disappeared into a metal building.

As Dee and I started up the levee road on what would be about a mile and a half walk to Osceola, the foreman emerged. "Yall goin' to town?" he asked.

"Yes."

"It's a long walk and part is through a bad neighborhood. I'll take you to town. An' I think there's an old man with a taxi you can git to bring you back."

"Where should we eat?" Dee asked.

"Well there ain't really no decent restaurants in town but yall can probl'y git a hamburger or somethin'."

We had eaten very little breakfast and lunch, so were famished. "It doesn't look like much." I said, as we approached a tired brick building with a faded sign that said simply "Cafe." Inside, the eatery was decorated in "early poverty". Tables, counters and booths were worn and torn, but clean. The simple menu included a choice of beef stew or pork steak, vegetables, slaw, rolls, butter and German Chocolate cake, but did not list the price.

I had generous portions of stew, rutabagas and brown beans, along with the slaw, rolls, butter and German Chocolate cake - actually, yellow cake with chocolate-coconut frosting. Dee had pork, mashed potatoes, and carrots. The total bill was five dollars, for both meals. For two dollars more we got a taxi back to the boat where we were safe and snug away from the wash of passing tows.

It was still and cold when we cast off for Memphis,
so cold that we decided to run from inside. After re-
entering the main river, we spotted the **Mary Ann** busily
moving an empty barge toward a grain dock. I called the
captain on the radio and brought him greetings from The
Smiths.

"One thing about us here on the river," he said,
"we always try to work together an' he'p each other."

"I wish I could take that attitude back to some
people I know in California," I replied.

With steaming cups of hot coffee in our hands, we
settled into an easy pace. The river was smooth, and
the channel meandered casually between the Tennessee and
Arkansas shores.

At mile 780, we encountered a flock of swallows
that must have numbered in the thousands. Then we saw
Chickasaw Bluff number one, and speculated that these
cliffs probably were home for the swallows. Just as we
rounded the bend and headed into Sunrise Towhead Chute,
we passed the **Cooperative Ambassador**, a tow we remembered seeing upriver, but couldn't recall where.

At the end of the chute, we came to Chickasaw Bluff
number two. The sunlight glistened on the pale pinkish
cliffs, providing a welcome contrast to the miles and
miles of rock revetment and low sand islands that were
the distinguishing vistas of the lower river.

We remembered that Chickasaw Bluffs was one of
several locations that lay claim to being the spot where
De Soto first viewed the broad and muddy Mississippi.
For the dramatic effect of a proud explorer standing
atop impressive cliffs with a panoramic view of miles of
winding river and virgin forests, Chickasaw Bluffs certainly got our vote as the most likely discovery spot.

By now the sun had warmed the air, and we moved to
our favored bridge helm. As we glided past Morgan
Point, where the river turned sharply to the right, we
could look straight up at the towering bluffs. Beyond
the bend, the river was constricted into a narrow channel between the bluffs and Island Thirty-four. As if to
protest this sudden change in direction, and the constriction, Ole Man River responded with the most spiri-
ted series of twisty-turny boils and eddies we were to
encounter.

In the last two hundred miles, we had come to realize that no matter how menacing boils and eddies
appeared, they constituted no threat to our twenty-six

foot boat, unless we were trying to maneuver in close quarters. Since there were no towboats in sight, we let our spirits join those of the magical river. We allowed the swirls to turn **Sol Seaker** at will, letting out a war whoop as one particularly violent boil spun us around in a wild carnival ride.

As the bow swung toward the Tennessee shore, we spotted two men standing on a ramshackled floating dock just below the narrowest point in the river, the Red Head Boat Store. They stared at us, not knowing whether we were in need of assistance, or just two more idiots trying to conquer the Mighty Mississippi River.

Our second war whoop, and giddy wave of greeting, dispelled all doubt.

At mile 755, we met the **Cooperative Spirit**, pushing forty-two empties against the fast current, her propellers pushing up mountainous wheelwashes. Grabbing my camera, I leaned over the railing to get a water level shot that would give our friends back home some idea of the size of these monumental waves.

Some minutes after I had resumed my place at the helm, we, for the second time, experienced breakers on the Mississippi River. The conditions here were similar to those where we had our first experience - powerful upriver tow and a deep channel which became shallow, and constricted by a wing dike, and a sandbar.

After bouncing through the "surf", we glided down the long reach of Brandywine Chute - From Tennessee to Arkansas, back to Tennessee, and then back to Arkansas, in a distance of less than five miles. But no, we didn't really go back to Arkansas on our last crossing. We had crossed the river, but our chart showed that we were passing one of the many places where a cut-off had stranded a little chunk of one state on the opposite shore - a piece of Tennessee three miles long and three miles wide had been deposited on the Arkansas side.

At mile 740, we caught sight of the Memphis bridges, and once again passed the two sailboats that had left Hickman just ahead of us.

The Memphis skyline loomed ahead as we turned into the quiet waters of the old Wolf River channel, motored past Waterway's Marine, and headed for the new Yacht Club Marina at Mud Island. It was with mixed emotions that we were leaving the isolation of the river and returning to the "civilization" of a big city.

24

RIVER RESCUE

W. C. Handy, Beale Street, Birth of the Blues, Elvis Presley - Memphis Tennessee. Graceland, St. Judes Hospital, Danny Thomas, Chucalissa. The Peabody Hotel, with resident ducks that waddle down the stairs, through the main lobby and into the gift shop, with its duck do-dads of all descriptions.

Memphis, Tennessee, founded in 1819 on Chickasaw Bluff No. 4 , was home to the Chucalissa Indians until Hernando De Soto "discovered" the Mississippi and usher-ed in the inevitable.

On June 6, 1862, Union forces captured Memphis, as thousands watched the battle from the bluffs. In the 1870's, Memphis experienced three yellow fever epi-demics. The one in 1878 is still regarded as one of the worst urban disasters in United States history, infect-ing more than 17,000 people, killing 5,000 and causing 30,000 to flee the city.

Perhaps Memphis is best known for its place in musical history. W. C. Handy made Memphis famous as the birthplace of the blues, and Beale Street followed. Sun Studio artist Elvis Presley gave the world rock and roll. Other famous Sun Studio artists include Johnny Cash, Jerry Lee Lewis, and B. B. King. In the 1960's the Memphis sound was that of Booker T and The M G's, Wilson Pickett and Aretha Franklin. Memphis can also boast of Mignon Dunn, Ruth Welting and Marguerita Piazza.

It was to this, the fourteenth largest city in the U.S., and the hardwood lumber capitol of the world, that **Sol Seaker** and the Mississippi had brought us on this Saturday, October 23. We were assigned an inside berth at the new Mud Island Marina.

It was soap, towels and a steaming hot shower at the new, clean Memphis Yacht Club. Upon our return to the dock, we found that the smaller of the two sailboats we had first seen in Hickman was moored next to us. Ed and Rex Whitaker, father and son, greeted us. Father,

Ed, was accompanying Rex as far as New Orleans, then he would return to his home in Cincinnati. Rex planned to continue on to Florida, then perhaps to the Bahamas. Like most parents, Ed wishes his son would get married, settle down and live a "normal" life.

"Rex and I have always been close," Ed said. "When my boys were growing up, I'd take time off from work and we'd go fishing or camping. I guess that's why we're close now. But I've learned a lot about Rex on this trip. I've learned that he has a real, caring interest in other people. Maybe he got part of that from me, too. I used to sell cars. But every morning I had to look at myself in the mirror, and finally I had to give it up. Now I'm getting my real estate license. I retired once, then inflation caught up with me, and now I have to work. Until I get my license, I do maintenance work for my girlfriend, who sells real estate and has several rentals."

"What are you folks doin' for dinner?" Rex asked.

"We thought we'd try one of the restaurants here on the island," I answered.

"Would you like to go together?" Ed wondered. "Rex and I have to go into town to do some shopping. We'll be back in about an hour."

"Good," Dee replied. "We're going to walk around Mud Island for a while, why don't we meet you back here about 6:30?"

When we started across the ramp to shore, Dee tripped and bruised her knee. As I helped her up she asked, "You remember that fortune: **Leave your boat and travel on firm ground**?"

"Yes."

"Well I don't believe it. This is the second time I've tripped on firm ground. I think I'm safer on the boat."

We laughed, as we continued up the stairway to the top of Mud Island. A quick tour made us realize that it would take several hours to see the quarter-mile long River Model, containing information on every important bend, chute, curve, cut off, sandbar and town on the Lower Mississippi River.

At dinner we learned that Rex has eighty-seven acres in Wisconsin, where Ed helped him build a two bed-room cottage that has no electricity. Rex picks apples during the season to make money to travel. He bought the sailboat after it had been wrecked, then altered the

keel so it now has only a thirty-two inch draft. They
came down the river without charts, radio or depth
sounder. Once they accidentally cut a black buoy and
ran aground. Rex had immediately jumped overboard and
pushed the boat back into deeper water. After that,
they got a long stick to use to measure the depth.

After sharing a glass of wine with Ed and Rex, we
slept soundly despite the continuous noise of the big
city across the Wolf River.

The next morning Dee's knee was a bit stiff, as we
made our way slowly up the steep steps to the top of the
island. Ahead of us was a man who, like Dee, was favor-
ing an injured knee or foot.

At the top of the stairs we met Norm. "I fell on
the dock up at Hoppie's Marina," he said, "skinned my
knee and bruised my side."

Norm and Dee compared knees. Soon we were joined
by Norm's petite wife, Patti, carrying portable video
tape equipment. Patti, a smartly dressed, neatly coiffured blond, was panting under the weight of the heavy
equipment. "We were part way up when I realized I'd
forgotten the equipment," Norm said. "I want to make a
video tape of the river model and the museum. My side
hurt so much Patti went back for the camera."

"Which boat are you on?" I asked.

"The **Patricia B**," Norm replied, pointing to a
gleaming white, forty-eight foot yacht with a bright red
stripe circling the hull. I sold my scrap metal business in Illinois, and we're going to Florida to live on
the boat."

Norm connected the video equipment and said, "Look
at the monitor." He pressed the button, but nothing
happened. "Darn, I forgot to charge the batteries last
night." He looked sheepishly at Patti, who was still
breathing heavily.

I helped Norm return the camera to his boat.

We went our separate ways to tour the islands
attractions. At noon, Dee and I arrived at the model
Gulf of Mexico, where one could rent paddle boats for a
boatride on the Gulf or eat at Crawdaddy's. We opted
for lunch. Norm and Patti were in the restaurant, where
we joined them for Jambalaya, gumbo and fried fish.
"We're eating at the Riverside Terrace tonight." Norm
said. "We'd like to have you join us."

"Our car and trailer are down at the Riverside
Marina on McKeller Lake, they're expecting us," I

answered. "It's about fifteen miles, so we plan to leave about three o'clock."

"Well, if you change your mind just come knock on our door."

After lunch we toured the Mississippi River Museum, with its excellent displays of Indian artifacts, history of trapping, logging, riverboat shows and gambling. A life size and life like Mark Twain told the story of each display. Other highlights of the museum included an 1870's steamboat and a Civil War battle, in which we were first on land with the Confederates, and then aboard a Union Gunboat.

At four o'clock we said good-bye to Norm, Patti, Ed and Rex. We ran slowly down the long row of new slips noting the names of the many boats - **Broker Two**, **$econd Mortgage**, **Southern Lass IV**, **Sand Castle**, **Scape Two**, **Hummel Hummel**, and finally the **Patricia B.**

As we left the marina behind, we increased speed slightly, still observing the "no wake" rule past the Waterway's Marine Service. We gained more speed as we re-entered the strong current of the main river.

The Mississippi had been kind to us for several days. He had given us a place to stop at Tomato. He hadn't thrown a lot of logs in our way. He hadn't caused us to be drenched by rain or blown about by wind. He had even frolicked with us at Chickasaw Bluff No. 2. We felt as though the "Ole Man" had accepted us into the inner fraternity of "River Rats."

We should not have assumed so much. After passing beneath the old Memphis bridges, our engine began to sputter. "Good God," I exclaimed, "We're running out of gas."

The engine hit a few more licks, then died.

The thing we always knew could happen, but never expected to happen, had happened. We were adrift in the middle of the shipping channel of the rushing Mississippi River.

As I turned to go down off the bridge, I saw great white clouds billowing out of the engine area beneath the aft deck. Had **Sol Seaker** been a steamboat, I would have been sure a boiler had erupted. I quickly checked the engine temperature gage - two hundred forty-five degrees - the highest possible reading.

Dee held the fire extinguisher at ready, as I slowly lifted one of the panels that covered the engine. As a breeze cleared the cloud of acrid steam, I could

235

see that a small hose had broken. Was it, I wondered, a part of the internal system, which had merely sprayed coolant on the engine, or was it a part of the system which picks up water from outside and pumps it through the heat exchanger? If it were this latter, river water would be flooding the bilge, and we could sink if the intake valve wasn't closed right away.

Inspection revealed that there was no water rushing into the bilge - and that there was a broken belt. The sequence of events was clear. Almost immediately after the weakened belt broke, the engine had over heated causing the small coolant hose to break. Coolant had escaped through the break and flooded the hot engine, turning into foul smelling steam.

Dee, realizing there was no need for the fire extinguisher, ran to the radio to call the Coast Guard, while I scanned the river for towboat traffic. There was none. We were in no immediate danger.

As Dee gave the Coast Guard a description of our boat, our location, and the nature of our problem, a voice broke into the conversation, "This is the Memphis River Patrol. A boat is on the way."

"Check the river each way," said the Coast Guard operator. "If you see a towboat, call the Captain on 13 and tell him your problem."

"There are no towboats coming!" I shouted to Dee. "I should have this belt changed soon, but I don't know what to do about the broken hose. Maybe I can clamp it 'til we get to the marina."

We were in mid-channel at the head of a sweeping curve when the engine stopped. We were still near mid-channel, but moving closer to the Tennessee shore, when I lowered myself into the engine compartment with spare belt and tools in hand. Immediately I realized that the job would take longer than I first anticipated, as the broken belt was located behind another belt that would need to be removed first. I worked to loosen the bolt that would allow me to free the front belt. The bolt refused to budge.

"How are we doing?" I asked Dee.

"We're drifting toward the Memphis shore," She replied. "But it's still a long way off, and there are no towboats coming."

Finally the stubborn bolt was conquered.

"With a little luck I should have this changed in time," I said, as I slipped the belt off the forward pulley and loosened the bolt that held the rear pulley. I didn't have a little luck. The spare belt didn't fit. Try as I might, it was just too short. "Check the depth," I said to Dee. "We may have to drop anchor."

"Fifty-two feet" came the reply.

"Damn!" I exclaimed, "Our anchor line isn't long enough to hold at that depth in this sandy bottom.

"There's a boat coming!" Dee shouted.

I looked up to see a small outboard, with four people, racing in our direction. Then I looked toward the Tennessee shore, where a row of moored rusty barges was directly in our path - and the gap between us was decreasing rapidly. "My God, how did we get over here so fast?" I asked of no one in particular.

Hurrying around to the bow, I began removing the anchor from its chocks. Before I finished, I heard a man yell frantically, "Get ready to catch this line and make it fast - anywhere!"

As **Sol Seaker** rotated slowly in an eddy, Dee and the stern came close to the rescue boat. Dee grabbed the line and, expertly, made it fast to a stern cleat. Our rotation had placed the tiny outboard directly between us and one of the large rusty barges. If we didn't move quickly, the small boat, with her four passengers, would be smashed between **Sol Seaker** and the barge. "Full speed astern," shouted the man who had thrown the line to Dee.

The small boat moved backwards. The line grew taut and held. Slowly our stern swung downriver and away from the barges. As it did, the bow came around toward the barges. Clutching the bow railing I looked up at the large, rusty object, now less than ten feet away.

The little outboard continued backwards, struggling to pull a much heavier **Sol Seaker** across the swift current. When we were a short distance from the barge, the man directed Dee to remove the line from the stern cleat and fasten it to the bow for easier towing. She traversed the narrow walkway, holding tenaciously to the line with one hand, while clinging to the railing with the other. At one point I was sure she was going to have to let go of the line or be pulled into the water.

I suddenly realized that I had been a spectator in this entire drama. Dee called the Coast Guard. Dee held the fire extinguisher ready. Dee grabbed the rescue line and made it fast to the cleat. And Dee walked the line around to the bow. "Thanks," I whispered.

"I'm a member of the River Patrol," said Buddy Chapman, who had thrown the line. "We're a part of the Memphis Police Department and the County Sheriff's Department. We'll stand by until Don Lancaster gets here in the **Sand Castle**. It's a large Gibson houseboat with powerful engines. He'll tow you back to the harbor."

William Smith had told us how his fear and trembling set in after the danger was over. We now understood this phenomenon. As the events are happening, your mind is so occupied with the "now" that it is incapable of anticipating what might happen in the next instant. But, when you are freed from the immediate, your mind rushes to fill in the, "What could have happened", it was denied during the height of action.

Don and the **Sand Castle** were soon on the scene, and we were called into the action of securing lines and placing fenders in preparation for the slow run against the current back to Mud Island. The trembling slowly subsided.

We were less than two miles out of the harbor when the engine stopped. The strong current had drifted us more than two additional miles. It took an hour for the **Sand Castle** to tow us in. "You're our third rescue today," Don shouted over the roar of the engines. "They all happened about the same place, but one of the boats drifted into the sandbar on the Arkansas side. I think the Ole Man is just being cantankerous today."

"I guess we've earned a place in history," Dee commented, as we moved slowly upstream.

"What do you mean?" I asked.

"Well, I think it was just above Memphis that the worst steamboat disaster in history occurred. After the Civil War, the **Sultana** was overloaded with two thousand Union troupes anxious to get back home. About two in the morning, the boiler exploded and she caught fire and burned. More than fifteen hundred people died. It was just about as bad as the **Titanic**."

"So, how does that give us a place in history?"

"Well, today just below Memphis, while floating along easily with the current, a half inch coolant hose broke on the tiny **Sol Seaker**, with two people aboard. Both people survived without a scratch, making this about the least disastrous boat incident in the history of the Mississippi River."

As we laughed, the last vestige of lingering fear disappeared.

Back in our old slip, we walked over to the **Patricia B** to tell Patti and Norm we would be delighted to join them for dinner. Tonight we were very happy to be eating at all.

The next morning, I inspected our engine further and found that in addition to the broken belt and tiny coolant hose, a larger coolant hose was damaged, where the belt had rubbed against it. This new discovery created a problem which kept us at Mud Island two extra days.

We took a taxi to the Riverside Marina, where we explained our problems to James "Buttercup" Butler, the owner, and told him we would bring our boat in as soon as possible. "We got some dredgin' goin' on in the harbor," he said. "But, I'll find a place for yall when you git here."

After a trip to the post office, where we had welcome letters from several friends and relatives, we set out to find belts and hoses. What we thought would be a simple quest turned out to be not only difficult, but impossible. The hose that had been damaged by the belt proved to be a special hose available only from a Mercruiser dealer. No local dealers had one in stock, and to order one could take up to two weeks.

We purchased a belt, but were unable to locate a coolant hose. At four o'clock, exhausted from our search, we returned to the boat, relaxed a while then revived our spirits with a night out at Blues Alley.

Norm and Patti joined us.

"And now ladies and gentlemen," the announcer was shouting over the raucous noise of the crowd, "Introducing that seventy-five year old bombshell - Little Laura Dukes!"

> Call the Po-leese
> Hurry Hurry
> Call the po-leese
> Hurry Hurry
> Call the po-leese
> Hurry Hurry
> Somebody stole my man away.

Little Laura was tiny, probably four foot ten and weighing no more than eighty-five pounds soaking wet, but she could belt out a song that hushed even this boisterous crowd.

```
            Ain't gonna marry
            And I ain't gonna settle down
            Ain't gonna marry
            And I ain't gonna settle down
            Ain't gonna marry
            And I ain't gonna settle down.
```

Little Laura continued to sing, as she slipped her belt down around her hips and began to move sneakered and bobby soxed feet. Slowly, she turned her back to the audience and rotated her hips in a "sexy" gyration that caused youth, and senior citizen alike, to howl their approval.

```
            When I git the blues
            Git me a rockin' chair
            When I git the blues
            Git me a rockin' chair
            When I git the blues
            Git me a rockin chair...
```

As soon as she finished one song, she burst into a new one.

```
            Flip, flop and fly
            It's ok if I die
            Flip, Flop and fly
            It's ok if I die
            Flip, flop and fly
            It's ok if I die.

            Like a Mississippi Bullfrog
            Sittin' on a holler stump
            Like a Mississippi Bullfrog
            Sittin' on a holler stump
            Like a Mississippi bullfrog
            Don't know which way to jump.

            Flip, Flop and fly...
```

Little Laura flipped her rear in a final gesture as she concluded her last song.
"And now ladies and gentlemen," the announcer again, "don't forget the great Blues Alley souvenirs that are on sale right over there. There's Blues Alley T-shirts in all sizes and colors. And there's Blues
240

Alley baseball caps. And don't forget to have the famous Blues Alley blue drink, only $5.95 with a souvenir glass.

During the brief pause, we ordered Blues Alley drinks and dinner, then were bombarded by the songs of "Don McMann, the Boogie Man" a white blues singer who told us how to make moonshine.

> Git you a copper kettle
> Git you a cob of corn
> Git you a copper kettle
> Git you a cob of corn
> Git you a copper kettle
> Fill it with new made corn mash.
>
> Jist lay there by the juniper
> While the moon is right
> Watch them jugs a fillin'
> In the pale moonlight

"Yes sir, folks, we still got lots of them Blues Alley souvenirs. Now let's hear it for a little lady from Kansas City. She's only five-feet tall, and weighs maybe ninety pounds, but you're gonna love her song. It's her first record, a 45, which she'll be sellin' at the next intermission. Here's Little Cindy Carr." A tiny blond singer with a big voice boomed out:

> Oh my mello' man
> Oh my mello' man
> Cain't no-body thrill me
> Like my mello' man can...

Little Cindy was followed by the grand old lady herself, the "mother" of the Blues, Ma Rainey. Although seventy-six years old, wearing a pacemaker, and seated in a wheel chair, Ma Rainey captivated the audience with:

> Got my Mo Jo workin'
> Got my Mo Jo workin'
> Got my Mo Jo workin'
> Got my Mo Jo workin'
> But it jist don't work on you...

"Let's see how many saints we got in here tonight,"

she said, as she held up a large container. "Whils't I
sing this next song, all yall saints jist march right up
here and put sumpin' in this here kitty fir the
musicians."

Oh, when the saints go marchin in
Yes when the saints go marchin in...

"Come on yall, march right on up."

Lord I want to be in that number...

"Come on all you saints."

When those saints go marchin in...

"I shore can see there ain't no saints here
tonight."

As we emerged from Blues Alley, we were "wrung dry"
from the non-stop sound and fervor of the place. "That
was an experience," commented Norm.

We spent the next day improvising repairs to our
boat. A man at Central Auto Parts found a hose with a
bend that matched the bend at the damaged end of our
large hose. He showed me how, by cutting our hose in
two, I could discard the damaged end and replace it with
a piece from the new hose. By clamping the two pieces
over a short pipe, I successfully made a temporary repair. I used the same technique to repair the smaller
hose. We crossed our fingers as we started the engine.
No leaks. The new belt wasn't rubbing against the
spliced hose. The temperature gauge slowly climbed to a
cool one hundred forty degrees, and stayed there. We let
the engine run for several minutes. When we were confi-
dent that all systems were go, we once again left the
Mud Island Marina.

Norm and Patti had already headed downriver, and a
new boat was occupying the Patricia B's old slip. Hummel
Hummel was also gone.

We held our collective breath, as we approached the
spot where our engine had stopped. This time she continued to "purr" smoothly, and all gages displayed
proper readings. "There are the barges we almost hit,"
Dee said, pointing toward the Tennessee Shore. "We
should go over and take a close-up picture of them."

I maneuvered across the swift current. As we got closer and closer to the rusty barges, my heart began to climb into my throat, a position it maintained until the pictures were taken, and we were once again well out in the channel. I heard Dee give a loud sigh, and realized that she too had been affected by our second approach to the barges.

We arrived at Riverside Marina just as "Buttercup" was about to go home. He showed us a slip and said we could wait until later to pay.

Since we had our car, we decided to stock up on supplies that had been dwindling, including food, toilet paper, porta potti chemical, film, stove fuel, alkaselzer, and sanitary napkins. We found everything but the right kind of sanitary napkins. We also toured "Graceland," the home of the late Elvis Presley. Although not big Elvis fans, we were impressed by the numbers of loyal worshipers that were making the pilgrimage, even on this cold, rainy day. Perhaps their devotion is summed up in this excerpt from the poem "Memories of Graceland Mansion," by Janelle McComb:

> . . .I've seen his fans come up the hill,
> And stand at windswept graves,
>
> I, too, would cry along with them;
> I'd tire of being brave.
>
> Today my columns seem more erect;
> My pride shows within these walls.
>
> My life has taken on new meaning;
> His friends have come to call.
>
> I knew that one day you would come;
> I've waited and counted the minutes.
>
> Even though my owner is away just now;
> His heart is still here within it!

Later in the afternoon, as we sat on the back deck watching the activities around the marina, we couldn't help but note the contrast between the Riverside and the Mud Island Marinas.

Mud Island had been new and spotless. It's boats were mostly large houseboats or yachts which gleamed

243

bright and clean. The boat owners, likewise, were neat
and clean. There were turtle neck sweaters, sport blaz-
ers, captain's hats, high heels, and poodles.

By contrast, The Riverside Marina consisted of a
hodge-podge of rusty floating docks and uneven walkways.
Buttercup had apologized to us for the tilting walkways.
"The water fluctuates as much as fifty feet here, putting a lot of strain on the docks and equipment. Sometimes the river rises overnight, and causes docks to
break apart, or knocks out flotation material. We do
the best we can to keep them repaired, but the cost is
high."

The large floating building that housed the marina
store, restaurant, storage rooms and fuel pumps had been
repaired many times with makeshift materials. Occasionally a rat could be seen poking its head up between the
uneven boards near the fuel pumps. One of the marina
cats was usually in hot pursuit.

The boats at Riverside Marina were of all sizes and
shapes. Many were homemade or had been significantly
altered from the original. At several places along the
outer dock, unique living arrangements had been constructed, consisting of large covered floating U shaped
platforms, enclosed in front to form a small apartment.
The back consisted of the boat slip which formed the U
in the platform. This was also covered. The boat could
be used as an extra bedroom.

There were many "live-a-boards" at the Riverside
Marina, but few at Mud Island. One Riverside resident
reminded us of Pops, at Hickman. He, too, had wandered
in with boat troubles. Buttercup had allowed him to
stay in a back room of the marina store in exchange for
doing odd jobs.

"I shore wisht he'd go," we had overheard Buttercup's wife say. "He don't ever clean the shower or pick
up his clothes. An' he ain't much help neither."

"Which marina do you prefer?" I asked Dee.

She thought a minute before replying, "I really
like those clean showers at Mud Island." She thought
again, then continued, "But you know some of those
people over there seemed a little snobbish. Remember
that man who said, 'I'd never leave my boat at the
Riverside Marina.' I guess I like both marinas for different reasons. Mud Island is for the more affluent and
Riverside is for people that like boats and the water,
but aren't so wealthy. I'm just pleased that there are

places like the Riverside Marina where people of limited means can enjoy the same kinds of things that the 'rich folks' have. I guess if I was going to live aboard, I'd choose the Riverside, but if I had a boat that I came to on weekends, I'd choose to leave it at Mud Island. Mud Island is the best place for transients, because most transients are looking for clean restrooms and showers, good restaurants, and easy access to stores. I'm really happy we were near Mud Island when our engine failed," she continued. "If that had happened a hundred miles above or below Memphis, there wouldn't have been anybody to call for help."

As we were talking, Buttercup came hurrying down the dock toward us. "You folks still plannin' to leave in the mornin'?" he asked.

"Yes."

"Would you mind if we move you around to the fuel dock? You can stay there tonight. I just got word that the city has approved a hundred thousand for more dredgin', and I want to git the dock moved before dark so's they can start first thing. I've gotta move the whole west dock around to the east end. That'll block off this part of the marina."

"That's fine," I answered. "How will you move that long dock, with all those boats moored in the slips?"

"We got a towboat on it's way right now. He'll move ever'thin' at once. Jist go real slow."

We moved to the gas dock, then watched as a small towboat slowly pushed the entire fifty yard long dock, boats and all, from one end of the marina to the other.

Before he left for the night, Buttercup put fuel in our tanks, and we settled our account so that we could get an early start. Tomorrow we would try to make Rosedale, Mississippi, more than a hundred-fifty miles downriver.

RUSTY BARGE

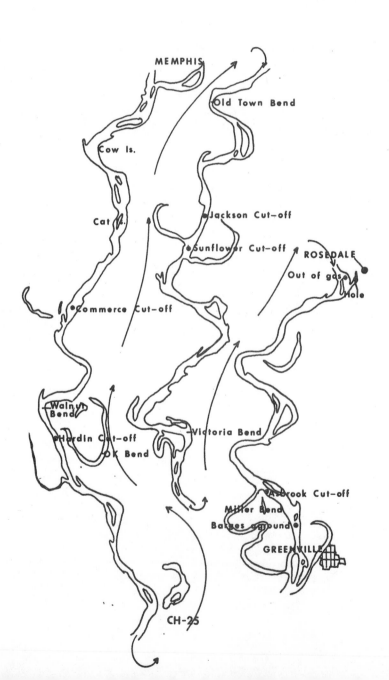

MEMPHIS

Old Town Bend

Cow Is.

Cat Is.

Jackson Cut-off

Sunflower Cut-off

ROSEDALE

Out of gas

Hole

Commerce Cut-off

Walnut Bend

Victoria Bend

Hardin Cut-off

OK Bend

Asbrook Cut-off

Miller Bend

Barnes aground

GREENVILLE

CH-25

25

BENDS, CHUTES & CUT - OFFS

On October, 30, a cold, cloudy, Saturday, we left Memphis. After two months on the river, we were still 733 miles from the Gulf. Our plan was to complete our voyage, return to Memphis for our car and trailer, clean and store **Sol Seaker**, then drive two thousand miles to Clearlake before Thanksgiving. We wanted to make Roseville today, which would be a run of ten hours at an average speed of more than fifteen miles an hour. Even with our early start, we might arrive at that unfamiliar destination after dark.

As we cleared Tennessee Chute, I eased the throttle forward until the RPM meter read 2200. To accurately gauge our over-the-bottom speed, we timed our progress for five miles by checking the markers posted on the lights and daymarks. We were traveling at just under sixteen miles an hour.

During the second five miles, we rode silently, watching the shoreline pass, and listening for towboat conversations on the radio. There were no conversations. Since Memphis, the river had been deserted.

Finally Dee said, "If we don't get a little more action we're going to have a hundred and fifty miles of nothing, to write in the log tonight." She sat a few more minutes, obviously in deep thought, then said, "I have an idea. I'll use the historical information we got from the model at Mud Island to give you a conducted tour of this part of the river."

"Great!" I answered, unnecessarily, as she was already pulling out our notes. In her best "tour guide" voice, she began to indicate the points of interest. "On our left for the next eight miles. . ." Her commentary was suddenly interrupted by towboat conversation on the radio.

"This is the **Charles Southern**. I'm headed down at Cat Island, checkin' on any upriver traffic."

"**Charles Southern**, this is the **W.T. Toutant**. I'm

comin' up with twenty-four empties, just enterin' Commerce. I'll catch you on the one whistle."

"Roger, one whistle. I'll be lookin' for you."

"**W.T. Toutant**, come in. This is the **Tom Smith**."

"**W.T. Toutant** back to **Tom Smith**."

"I'm jist ahead of the **Charles Southern** a little way. I'll be on the one whistle."

"Roger, one whistle."

"This is the **John H. McMillan Jr.** callin' the downriver boats. I'm right behind the **W.T. Toutant**. Catch you on the one whistle."

"Roger, the **Tom Smith**."

"Roger, the **Charles Southern**."

"This is the **Lily Freeman, Lily Freeman**, headin' downriver at Commerce with thirty full. Checkin' on upriver traffic."

"**Lily Freeman**, this is **Jeffboat**. I'm in Moon with twenty empties. Catch you on the one."

"Roger, **Jeffboat**, the **Lily Freeman** standin' by."

"**Lily Freeman**, this is the **Lois H. Meese**, I'm right behind **Jeffboat**. Got twenty-four empties. Guess I better stay on the one whistle too, seems to be a lot of traffic. There's another boat right behind me."

"This is the **Al Tonian** callin' the **Lily Freeman**. I'm behind the **Lois H. Meese**, just leavin' Walnut. Catch you on the one."

The radio fell silent and Dee said, "It looks like we're going to see a lot of traffic after a while." She started her narration again. "On our left, for the next eight miles, we'll be passing Cow Islands, also known as Islands 47 and 48. Although now joined together and attached to the eastern shore, they used to be separate. In 1866, the **R. J. Lockwood**, allegedly involved in a steamboat race, exploded and burned in Cow Island Bend, killing a number of passengers. Cow Islands straddle the Tennessee-Mississippi boundary."

"Good-bye Tennessee," she said a few minutes later, then continued our tour. "We're now approaching Norfolk Landing, established in 1861 as the first steamboat landing south of the Tennessee-Mississippi boundary. As a customs inspection point for the new Confederate States of America, the landing inadvertently worked to the disadvantage of the South. Many previously neutral people, outraged by the idea of regulating traffic on the river, became Union supporters. They believed that supporting the Union would help free the Mississippi."

"One thing I've learned already," Dee said, as she searched the chart for the next point of interest, "None of the places they call islands are really islands. They're all attached to either the left or the right shore."

She continued the narration, "We're now approaching Buck Island, which isn't an island, but was during the Civil War. Confederate smugglers ferried arms across the river here. Just after the war a steamboat called **City of Memphis** exploded and burned off Buck Island. She had been so popular during Antebellum days that a newspaper was published on board, which was widely read up and down the river."

As Dee finished her latest spiel, I was maneuvering **Sol Seaker** to starboard to pass the slow moving **Charles Southern**, pushing three gigantic petroleum barges. Ahead I could see many eddies and waves, where the water was boiling around the ends of two dikes and overflowing the downstream rush in center channel. Since the **Charles Southern** was going our same direction, she could not have caused this new turbulence.

When we were safely past, Dee resumed our tour. "Ahead and to our right is Council Island, named for important meetings between the Chickasaw and Choctaw Indians that used to take place here."

"I wonder if this is where Reelfoot captured his princess," I added.

"On our left, and away from the river, is the site of Commerce, Mississippi. In Antebellum days, this thriving community was running stiff competition to Memphis for the delta cotton trade. Just before the Civil War, the river began to wash away Commerce's waterfront. Residents built a levee in an effort to save their town, but the river breeched the levee and carried away much of Commerce. In 1874 a cut-off occurred at Council Bend, across the river, causing more washouts at Commerce, and the town finally disappeared. The cut-off is now known as Commerce Cut-off."

During the middle of Dee's dramatics, I realized that the turbulence we were encountering was the result of a very fast current combined with the deflection of masses of water by the dikes on the right. I also understood why the speed of the current had increased so dramatically. Before the Commerce cut-off occurred, the river had traveled almost twenty miles around Council Island to get from point A to point B. Now point B was reached in just four miles. This shorter distance created a significantly steeper drop, with a concurrent increase in speed of flow.

After seeing only one towboat in twenty-eight miles, we now met three in the four agitated miles of the Commerce cut-off. One of these was struggling against the current with thirty-six empty grain barges. Her powerful diesels added a six foot sternwash to the already unruly waters. "That was the **John H. McMillan Jr.!**" exclaimed Dee. "Isn't that the same boat we saw near Cape Girardeau?"

"I thought that was the **John McMillan**," I answered. "I don't remember the H or the Jr."

Dee tried to radio the towboat to clarify the situation, but was unable to make contact. A search of our log indicated that we had written **John McMillan** but neither of us could say whether we had just ignored parts of the name, or whether these were two different towboats.

A few minutes later we passed a very slow **Lily Freeman**, with thirty full grain barges, then, almost immediately, met **Jeffboat** coming up with twenty empties. "I know we saw that boat before," Dee said. "It was one of the tows that met us when we returned to the Mississippi from the Ohio."

As soon as we were past **Jeffboat**, we entered Moon Bend, where we met, in rapid succession, the **Lois H. Meese** and the **Al Tonian**. Three miles farther on we entered sharp Walnut Bend, and passed another slow moving tow with twenty full grain barges. We were so intrigued by the skill with which the captain was maneuvering the large load around this tight bend, that we forgot to look at the name.

When we were past, Dee returned to her historical tour. "Back where we passed that last tow is the site of the Whitehall crevasse, which occurred in 1927."

"What's a crevasse?" I asked.

"It must be a levee break. It says in our notes that the levee broke just below Whitehall, Arkansas." She continued, "This was one of thirteen major crevasses that occurred in the great flood of '27. After the river broke through, the gap grew to a width of 1400 feet. The crevasse came as a complete surprise to the residents, who were forced to take refuge in trees and on roof tops. Some weren't rescued for several days. In the '27 flood, more than 300,000 people were rescued from such perches along the river, and 700,000 were forced to evacuate."

"Just ahead is the Hardin cut-off. This was the last of thirteen artificial cut-offs made by the Corps of Engineers between 1933 and 1942, between Memphis and Baton Rouge. The Hardin cut-off removed the O.K. Bend. An oxbow lake formed by the old river bed is now called Tunica Lake. In 1858 a boiler explosion on the Steamboat **Pennsylvania**, in O.K. Bend, killed one hundred sixty passengers and crew members. Among the dead, was the boat's clerk Henry Clemens. Henry's brother Sam, who was the boat's cub pilot, was not on board at the time, thus saving the life of Mark Twain."

About mid-point of the Hardin Cut-off, we met the **Carole Brent**, then in rapid succession, the **Conti Susan** with thirty empties, and the **Rose G**, an Army Corps snag barge. Beyond these, the river narrowed, and we entered a stretch of rough water.

"The St. Francis River rises in the Southeast Missouri Hills," Dee continued, when the water had quieted a little. "It flows roughly parallel to the Mississippi for 475 miles. The first Frenchmen to explore the lower river were well received by the Arkansas Indians who lived near the mouth of the St. Francis. In the early 1880's, long distance navigation was impossible on the St. Francis because it was blocked with a huge tangle of driftwood, probably caused by trees toppled into the river by the New Madrid earthquake of 1811. The logs were finally removed, and the river is now open for log towing during high water."

Just above Prairie Point, the radio again crackled to life.

"This is **Bernard F**, checking for upriver tows. I'm above Flower Lake Bar comin' down with thirty full."

"**Bernard F**, this is the **Martha Trotter**, upbound at Montezuma with jist one."

"Cap, I think we better take you on the two whistle side. Yall better git way over, 'cause with this load, when I git started, there ain't gonna be no stoppin'. There ain't gonna be nothin' but behind an' elbows."

"That's a Roger, Cap. I think you'll be through that fast water afore I git there. We'll catch ya on the two. Yall have a good one on down."

"Roger, yall have a good one up. Clear and standin by."

At Prairie Point, we passed the **Bernard F.** and

spotted a large flock of ducks who, like us, were flying south with the sun.

"Helena, Arkansas is coming up on our right," Dee noted from our chart. "It's one of the places we can get gas in an emergency, but I think it's the place you have to pay for a hundred gallons no matter how much you actually need."

"I'm glad we have enough to get us to Rosedale," I commented.

During the next several miles, we interrupted our tour to have lunch, pass three more tows, take a potty break, wave to three fishermen in orange hats, and to move to the bridge helm to enjoy the weather, which had turned sunny and warm.

Dee took a turn at the helm and I became tour guide. "We're now in Old Town Bend. Until 1830, when Shreve's snag boat **Heliopolis** removed the snags, this was one of the most hazardous spots on the river. Sandbars continued to be a menace until the flood of 1858, which filled up the channel behind Island 62. In the 1860's dikes were constructed to further narrow and stabilize the channel. This bend was named for the "Old Town" of the Arkansas Indians. When Marquette and Joliet visited this tribe the Indians warned them of Spanish forces to the south, so the two French explorers headed back upstream."

"Early in the Civil War, Island 63 was a favorite spot for Confederate snipers to harass Union gunboats. After one attack had inflicted heavy casualties, the Union landed infantry on both sides of the island. They defeated the snipers, burned buildings and crops, then turned the island into a large wood yard for Union gunboats. When it was discovered that some of the ex-slaves running the wood yard for the Union were still loyal to the South, and were conspiring to hide explosives in the wood in an effort to disable the ships, a garrison of Federal troupes was placed on the island to protect the fuel supply."

After meeting three more tows, I continued our historical narrative. "We're now entering Jackson Cut-off, which, combined with the Sunflower cut-off, shortened the river by more than twenty miles. These were both Corps of Engineers' projects. In 1845, an overloaded steamboat ran aground in the Old Jackson Bend channel. To lighten the boat, the captain asked a hundred German emigrants to disembark and walk across the narrow strip of land, to be picked up above the bend. When the boat was once more under way the captain cured his overload by steaming right on by the band of bewildered Germans. Fortunately, they were later rescued by another boat."

"In 1852, the **Martha Washington** caught fire and sank in Jackson Bend, losing several lives and a heavily insured cargo. When divers later discovered that the crates were filled with bricks and stones, a number of people were arrested for fraud, arson and murder. But the evidence was deemed insufficient for conviction."

"Sunflower Bend was another favorite ambush spot for Confederate militia. Two artillery pieces were placed at the head of the bend. After bombarding Union boats, the Confederates would quickly haul the cannons across the narrow neck to give the boats a second bombardment, as they emerged from the downstream end of the bend."

"In 1830, a government Commission was appointed to determine where De Soto had really discovered the Mississippi. After some study, they named Sunflower Point as the spot. Later archeological studies, however, seem to refute this claim."

Below Sunflower cut-off, we met more towboats, some in rather constricted areas. We also began to see sand islands with straight steep banks. As I looked toward one of these a large chunk of the island collapsed into the muddy waters below. "Wow! Look at that!," I exclaimed. "Now I can see why people have warned us to stay away from the sand islands on this part of the river. Half an acre just disappeared into the water."

Along the shore we saw an occasional grain loading dock. Almost always the word "Bunge" was printed on the large round metal storage building.

The sun was dipping below the horizon when we emerged from Victoria Bend and headed down a six mile straight-away that would bring us to Log Loader Chute and the Rosedale harbor. Dee was at the helm, and I was tallying the towboats we had met or passed in the last hundred miles (thirty-one), when the engine coughed and sputtered. Dee immediately swung **Sol Seaker's** bow toward the red nuns marking a large sandbar just above Rosedale Bend. Twenty yards from one of the nuns, the engine coughed again and died. Our momentum and the current drifted us to a spot about thirty yards below the buoy and fifty yards off-shore from the low sandbar.

Moving to the bow, I dropped anchor into thirty feet of water. The line grew taut. Slowly the bow came around to face against the current. We were safely out of the main channel, holding fast on our anchor, and out of gas.

Later we would reflect philosophically about how our engine problem at Memphis had prepared Dee for her calm, efficient handling of this emergency. But at the moment the sunlight was fading, and we needed to add our spare gas to the main tank, re-start the engine, and get into the harbor before dark.

In the past we had added fuel while moored, where I could stand on a dock or barge and pour the gas into the opening located in the narrow four inch walkway along the outside of **Sol Seaker**'s cabin. Standing on the back deck, reaching far around the edge of the cabin with a heavy can of fuel, and tipping the can, while trying to fit the short pouring spout into the opening without spilling the gas, was more difficult than expected. But the hardest part of all, was balancing the heavy can in position as the fuel poured slowly into the tank. Each time a can was emptied, I had to give my arm and shoulder time to relax from the unaccustomed strain. Meanwhile twilight was upon us.

When the fuel was finally added, I hand choked the carburetor, while Dee tried, without success, to start the engine. Twilight was rapidly fading and so was battery number one.

Dee called the Rosedale Coast Guard. After several tries, an answer came. "This is Janoush Marine. There ain't no Coast Guard at Rosedale. Closest Coast Guard is at Memphis. You got trouble?"

Dee explained our situation.

"If you can't get started, call again. We can send a towboat out to bring you in."

"Thanks, that's good to know. Where can we tie up?"

"The safest thing is to go all the way up the chute to the hole. Towboats don't go up that far."

Dee thanked the man again, and returned to the rear deck. "I'm going to pour a little gas into the carburetor," I said. "I don't like to, because the fumes can settle into the bilge."

I carefully poured the last few drops from one of the cans. The engine sputtered to life and began to purr. "That's the sweetest sound I've ever heard," I said, as I quickly secured the gas cans, replaced the rear deck and pulled in the anchor.

It was almost dark when we approached Janoush Marine, where we spotted a man walking along the deck of the **Dixie Triumph,** one of three large red and white towboats moored near the drydocks. "Are you the man we talked to on the radio?" I asked as we came close.

"No. Musta' been someone at the office. They've all gone now. I'm stayin' on board here 'til the engines get replaced in this boat. Be here until Thanksgiving."

"Is there a gas station nearby?" I queried.

"No, 'bout a mile and a half. I got a car though. Be glad to take you for gas tomorrow. I'm Jerry. Just come knock on the door of the **Dixie Triumph.** I'll be here. I'm all alone on the boat."

"Thanks, we'd better get anchored before it's too dark to see."

As we left the lights of the service dock, we realized that it was already "too dark." Using our portable spotlight, we slowly motored to what we hoped was the "hole", then anchored far enough from shore to allow a full 360 degree swing around the anchor, in case the wind should change during the night.

When our eyes became adjusted to the darkness, we could see the outline of two sailboats tied to one of the commercial loading dolphins.

"I sure wouldn't tie up there," Dee said. "What if a barge comes in during the night?"

Since one of our boat batteries was down, Dee prepared a hasty meal on our alcohol stove by flashlight. We had just started to eat, when we heard the sound of a small outboard. As the sound grew louder, we could make out the shadowy figures of two people in the small, slowly approaching, boat. "I hope those aren't river pirates," Dee thought out loud.

"Yall need any gas?" a male voice inquired. "I talked to the man at Janoush and he said yall was comin' in and might need some gas. We kin git some fer yall."

We could now see that the occupants of the boat were two boys in their late teens. Still a bit leery of these strangers in the night, we thanked them, and explained that Jerry, on the **Dixie Triumph,** was going to take us into town tomorrow.

Obviously disappointed, the boys asked where we were from and where going. They were quite interested and envious as Dee told them about our journey. "I shore would like to do that," said one.

Dee gave her stock answer, "Work, save and wait until you have as much gray hair as we do."

"I wonder how much they charge," Dee said later, as we finished our corned beef hash. "I bet they do a pretty good business."

"Well, whatever it is it would be worth it if we hadn't already made arrangements," I replied.

We watched Love Boat and Fantasy Island on the tiny T.V. we had purchased from Bob and Jo, grateful that the T.V.'s internal battery was fully charged, making it unnecessary to use our boat battery.

The next morning we could see that one of the two moored sailboats bore the name **Salpicar**. We couldn't make out the name on the other, but written on the stern was Auckland, New Zealand. As we watched, a small towboat came close to the sailboats, tooted its horn loudly then headed across the chute toward several barges. "I bet he's telling them to move," Dee commented.

"They must think so too," I answered. "Look at them scurry to get untied."

As the sailboats pulled away from the dolphin, the little towboat was pushing an empty barge straight for the newly vacated mooring.

"I'm glad we didn't stay there." Dee said.

After breakfast we pulled up a muddy anchor and headed for Janoush Marine, where we found a strip of water between the **Dixie Triumph** and the shore, just wide enough for **Sol Seaker** to tie alongside the red and white giant. "Hello. Anybody home?" Dee called as we found the door to the spacious living-dining area. The T.V. set was on. In a few minutes Jerry appeared, obviously pleased to have visitors.

"I got lots of breakfast food if you don't mind fixin' it. I'm not much of a cook," he said, opening a large double-door refrigerator filled with milk, eggs, sausage, bacon, orange juice and assorted fresh fruits and vegetables. "I got cereal an' frozen waffles and lots a meat of all kinds. You're welcome to fix anything you want." He showed us the well stocked freezer.

We opted for coffee, orange juice and honey buns.

"I'm on twenty-eight days an' off twenty-eight days," Jerry explained as we ate. "We run from Texas City, Texas to the Monsanto plant on the Tennessee river in northern Alabama. We come up the Intracoastal, The

255

Atchafalaya River, Mississippi River, Ohio River and
Tennessee River with petro-chemicals."

"This is one of the newest boats, but the engines
just don't work right. They took some regular engines
and supercharged them, but they keep breaking shafts.
Finally they decided to replace them with new engines.
It'll take about two months. Someone from the Dixie Tow
Company has to stay on board all the time they're changing the engines. I'm the engineer, and I'll be on two
more weeks then I go home to Florida. I got a wife and
three kids. We live right on the banks of the Suwannee.
It's beautiful there. You could park your boat right
behind our house."

Jerry took us on a tour of the **Dixie Triumph**, a
medium large tow with two 4,000 horse-power diesels and
accommodations for ten to fifteen crewmen. Like all
towboats there was a long VIP sofa at the back of the
wheelhouse, four floors above the waterline.

Dee took my picture in the captain's chair, looking
intent as I guided an imaginary string of barges between
wing dams and sandbars. What a vantage point! But real
pilots were probably too occupied with controlling the
barges to enjoy the view.

As we returned to the main deck, Jerry said, "I've
got a good idea. Why don't yall stay here a few days.
I got plenty a room and all kinds a food. I'm not much
of a cook. Yall could stay on the boat and cook anything you wanted."

"That's the best offer we've had in a long time," I
said, "but we really have to go on downriver. We want
to get home for Thanksgiving, and we still have lots of
things to see."

Jerry took us to town with our three gas cans and
one of his own. When we had emptied them into our gas
tank, he once again invited us to stay a few days.

We noticed that Jerry was frequently glancing at
his watch. Finally he said, "I got only forty-five
minutes before my wife calls me. We can talk twenty
minutes for $4.50. I'll get to go home for Thanks-
giving, but I have to report back to work on December
23rd so I'll miss Christmas at home this year. Maybe
yall would like a hot shower before you go."

We thanked him for his help, hospitality and
friendliness, but declined the shower. As we pulled away
Dee whispered, "Now there's a lonely man."

Five miles downriver Dee said, "I wonder if we

should have gone back and filled our cans again. I certainly don't want to run out of gas before Greenville."

"I don't think we'll run out," I said. "I'm sure our problem yesterday was because Buttercup didn't fill the tank full. We took only fifty-two gallons and we were almost empty. It should have taken at least sixty-five gallons; I should have realized that when he put in the gas. Sometimes the pressure turns off the automatic nozzle before the tank is full, then you have to run it slowly to get the tank full. Besides, we drove at a bad speed. We should have alternated between ten miles an hour and twenty-five, because you get better mileage at both those speeds than sixteen miles an hour."

"How far is it to Greenville?" Dee wondered.

"About fifty miles. We have a least thirty gallons. At ten miles an hour we should be able to go seventy miles. I'm sure we'll be okay."

"I hope so," she said, still unconvinced.

"Why don't you do some more of the river history," I suggested, hoping to take her mind off the fuel.

Once again using our notes from Mud Island, we continued our historical tour, as we moved downriver through the Chaulk Neck Cut-off. "Coming up next is Cypress Bend. By the late 1700's the settlers in Louisiana had cut most of the highly prized cypress trees to the south. The loggers moved north and found excellent stands in this area. Huge log rafts were assembled and floated to market in New Orleans. After the Civil War, steam powered saw mills were built along the lower river to transform the logs into lumber. By 1916 the first stands of forest had been cut causing major changes in the ecology of the area, as many species of once abundant game and waterfoul disappeared from the area - some never to return again."

After meeting the **Melissa L** with four chemical barges and the **Bill Houser** with seven empties, Dee continued. "A disastrous levee flood occurred at the Mounds Crevasse in 1927. The levee collapsed at 6:30 A.M., April 21st, 1927. By noon the Crevasse was a half-mile wide and still growing. A wall of water quickly moved south to Greenville, Mississippi inundating the town with swift currents six feet deep. Waiting to be rescued, thousands took refuge on top of the Greenville levee. Their combined weight caused the levee to begin to sink, further endangering the town. When the river finally receded, more than two thousand square miles of land had been flooded by this single crevasse. When the water finally dried, it left a new sixty-five acre lake."

At Ashbrook cut-off an unusually bright sky coupled with just the right direction of sunlight, changed the normally brown water into a beautiful blue.

Below Miller Bend, we could see a towboat and barge ahead. "Is that tow coming or going?" I asked.

"I can't tell," Dee said as she peered through the binoculars. "Maybe it's coming up very slowly." She paused. "No, it's holding up waiting for an upriver tow. No. If it's a downriver tow it wouldn't hold up because it has the right-of-way. It's sideways!"

Below the sideways tow we saw another tow coming upstream with petroleum barges. "Where should I pass this sideways tow?" I asked Dee, who was still peering through the glasses.

"We'd better stay to our port, that's where the main channel is. No, what if we run out of gas? We'd be caught between the two tows. You better go around on the starboard."

As I steered toward the right side of the river, Dee suddenly gasped, "He's stuck on the sand! Don't go this way."

We now saw that there were actually two towboats, the **Sand Dollar** and the **Marlin** pushing on the side of a stranded barge attempting to get it off the sand. I quickly changed direction and passed between the upriver **Carol G** and the stranded barge.

I could feel Dee's relief when we were safely by, and back in the main channel. She continued the tour. "That was Tarpley Cut-off." She said. "There used to be a big bend there. It was called Spanish Moss Bend, because it was the most northerly location that Spanish moss occurred. Settlers used to harvest the moss for mattress stuffing."

We went boil hopping, then turned into Lake Ferguson, formed when the Corps of Engineers created the Leland Cut-off in the late 1930's. Five miles up Lake Ferguson lay the large Greenville Marina, and our first supply of on-the-water fuel since Memphis, more than two hundred miles upriver.

SOL SEAKER AND
DIXIE TRIUMPH

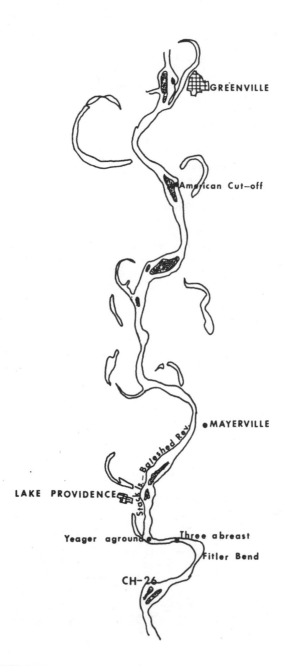

GREENVILLE

American Cut–off

MAYERVILLE

Stack &. Baleshed Rev.

LAKE PROVIDENCE

Yeager aground   Three abreast

Fitler Bend

CH-26

26

THE GREENVILLE CAUCUS

"You won't be able to git no gas at Vicksburg," said Greenville Marina's version of the old men we had seen at Hickman and Memphis, as he filled our tanks and spare cans to overflowing. The difference was, this old man carried a gun. "I'm an undercover narcotics agent," he said as he noticed Dee looking at his gun.

As we paid for the gas, Ed, the marina manager, told us there would be no place to tie up in Vicksburg. "Used to be a city barge there. The **Jefferson Davis** used to be tied to it. You see it's here now." He motioned toward a beautiful old tour boat that once provided excursions out of Vicksburg. "City got mad at the owner and told him he had to leave, so he came here. I hear they moved the barge, so there's no place to tie up."

"After tying to the revetment at Tomato, I bet we'll find some way to tie up at Vicksburg," a determined Dee declared. Looking up at the steep levee topped by the high wall, she continued, "It's too bad these levees have to be so high. It would be nice to have a house overlooking Lake Ferguson."

"Oh, there's lots of homes overlookin' the lake jist up from town a little. Fact is I have a home there myself. Last time we had high water, we had to move out. When the water went down we went back an' found a big old log had floated through a window right into the livin' room. It was so heavy we couldn't budge it. We had to git a chain saw and cut that thing up right there in the livin' room.

I used to run towboats," Ed continued, obviously proud of the time he had spent on the river.

Everyone who had ever worked on a towboat seemed to retain a sense of pride, regardless of how short their tenure, or how long ago it had occurred. "What was the most exciting thing that ever happened to you on the river?" I asked.

"The most exciting experience I ever had was just a few months ago. I was takin' a doctor, his wife and their two year old girl for a weekend outin' in my houseboat. There was a towboat comin' upstream, an' we was goin' down. Well, I talked to the captain and arranged on which side to pass. Then I got to talkin' and all of a sudden on the radio I heard a frantic voice saying, 'Are you tryin' to run me down?' I looked up an' was right in front of the tow. She had reversed her engines and was stopped dead in the water. Well I tried to stop, but the swift current took us right under the front of the lead barge. We caught there. I had to break the sliding glass door so we could get out of the boat. We climbed up on top and onto the barge. Luckily nobody was hurt. Well, the tow put a line around the houseboat and towed it to shore and tied it to a tree. Then he brought us back up here to Greenville. That night, passing towboats caused so much wake that the houseboat overturned. When we got back to it next day, there was nothing left but the metal hull."

Dee and I looked at each other. Partly because we had expected a story of towboat days, and partly because we wondered how an experienced towboat operator could have taken his eyes off the river long enough to get into such trouble.

"Be sure to sign our log book," said Ed as we got up to return to our boat.

In the log book we spotted the names of several boats we had seen upriver - **Shazam, Two Again , Mis T Way, Hummel Hummel, Patricia B, Prime Time** and **Salpicar**.

The next morning a man named Jack was at the marina when we stopped by the office on our way to breakfast. "Where should we go to eat?" asked Dee.

Jim's Cafe. Tell them I couldn't make it for my cup of coffee today, so I'm sendin' you."

We were impressed by the neat, clean look of downtown Greenville. Some of the older buildings had been converted to small shops, offices and a train museum. The streets were wide, and the main street had been landscaped into a shopping mall similar to ones we've seen in California.

At Jim's we selected a booth next to a table where Jim and several other men were conducting the day's round table discussion. Today's topics included politics, business, civic affairs, animals and hunting.

"Things shore is gittin' tight."

260

"Vote them democrats in, things'll git tighter."

"Yeah? Go ahead and put that republican Stennis in there. He cain't hardly even walk."

When the waitress brought our breakfast, I said, "Jack at the marina said he couldn't make it today. Was sending us instead."

"I been waitin' on Jack every mornin' fer fourteen years," she replied.

"We're leaving today, but someone upriver recommended a restaurant named Doe's for dinner," Dee said. "They told us to have the big steaks."

"Yall can git the same thing here at a lot lower price. Here, look at the dinner menu. Here's the T-Bone for $11.75. You'd pay $30.00 fer that at Doe's."

Jim, overhearing our conversation, said, "It's more'n a pound in that T-Bone. I cut them myself. I got a meat saw an' I cut my own meat. This last bunch was really good meat."

"If yall don't want them big steaks, yall can git good meat, two fresh vegetables an' dessert for $4.95. That's shore a lot better'n yall can do at Doe's," the waitress added.

We ate our breakfast slowly, continuing to listen to the "Greenville Caucus".

"We don't have the traffic Vicksburg has," Jim was saying. "They got that battlefield an' everything. 'Course the Sprague burned a long time ago. An' the 'Jefferson Davis' has been moved. They say they git over a thousand visitors a month."

"One thing, they got a strong City Council," came another voice. "When they renovate somethin' they jist go ahead an' do it."

"That's what we need here, a strong council."

While the waitress was refilling our coffee cups, the conversation changed to animals.

"You take a coon. A coon's a real survivor. A coon kin go in after a hornets nest an' come out with the whole nest."

"Coon'll take right out after a alligator."

"They forage around fer food. You'd be surprised how many coons they is right here in town."

"They's a lot of squirrels in town too.' Yeah, a feller could git himself a quiet pellet gun and git him a limit before dawn."

"I don't kere much fer squirrel huntin'. No, I'm a duck hunter."

"I'll tell you a tough animal. Fox. You know I had a old chow dog. Now a chow dog is 'spozed to be tough. Well, I tell you a fox come along. Fox had that dog's tail fer dinner."

"People makes pets outa squirrel an' coons, but I tell you them things'll bite you. Jist when you least expect it. Pet squirrels can be really mean."

"You wouldn't never make no pet out of a fox."

As we started to leave, Jim got up from the round table and presented a beautiful pink rose to a surprised and pleased Dee. "We grow all kinds of flowers an' fruit here. Sometimes we get a little snow but we kin mostly grow flowers year 'round."

It was 8:45 when we pulled away from the Greenville dock on our way to Vicksburg. We gazed in wonder as we passed under the highway 82 bridge, about ten miles below town. This was only the second bridge since Memphis, a distance of two hundred five miles. Below the bridge we passed the **Creole Queen**, then entered a reach that paralleled the American Cut-off, a natural Cut-off which occurred in 1858.

"I remember reading something about this cut-off in LIFE ON THE MISSISSIPPI, I said heading below to get the book, while Dee took the helm. Returning to the bridge, I turned to the page where Mark Twain describes his recollection of the **Pennsylvania**'s attempt to navigate the newly formed, snag filled cut:

". . .It was toward midnight, and a wild night it was – thunder, lightning, and torrents of rain. It was estimated the current in the cut-off was making about fifteen or twenty miles an hour; twelve or thirteen was the best our boat could do... the eddy running up the bank under the 'point' was about as swift as the current out in the middle; so we would go flying up the shore like a lightning express-train, get a big head of steam and 'stand by for a surge when we struck the current that was whirling by the point. But all our preparations were useless. The instant the current hit us it spun us around like a top. ...The sounding concussion and the quivering would have been about the same if she had come full speed against a sand bank. ...at the end of our fourth effort we brought up in the woods two miles below the cut-off. ...a day or two later the cut-off was three-quarters of a mile wide, and boats passed up through it without much difficulty, and so saved ten miles."

Cut-offs like the one at American Bend had occurred throughout recorded history, some natural and some helped along by a greedy plantation owner who saw a chance to increase the value of his property by changing it from "landlocked" to "waterfront" by plowing a ditch across the neck of a horseshoe curve at high water then allowing Ole Man River to do the rest.

In LIFE ON THE MISSISSIPPI, Mark Twain used the known facts of past cut-offs to record a startling "scientific" conclusion:

"In a space of one hundred and seventy-six years the Lower Mississippi has shortened itself two hundred and forty-two miles. That is an average of a trifle over one mile and a third per year. Therefore, any calm person, who is not blind or idiotic, can see that in the Old Oolitic Silurian Period, just a million years ago next November, The Lower Mississippi River was upward of one million three hundred thousand miles long. . . .And by the same token any person can see that seven hundred and forty-two years from now the Lower Mississippi will be only a mile and three-quarters long and Cairo and New Orleans will have joined their streets together, and be plodding along comfortably under a single mayor. . . There is something comforting about science. One gets such wholesome returns of conjecture out of such a trifling investment of fact."

After a routine meeting with the **Jefferson City**, moving thirty-five barges, Dee exclaimed, "Look there's a house."

Our chart showed us that about a half-mile from the river, beyond the levee, was the village of Mayersville. We wondered why this lone house was built outside the protection of the levee. We continued to look at the house until the current and a curve swept us out of sight.

We looked at each other and began to laugh. What a change this old river had wrought in these two wanderers. Once, meeting a towboat was the major event. Now, meeting towboats, even those pushing thirty to forty barges, had become common place. What did create excitement were bridges, fishermen, other pleasure boats and, above all, human habitation.

Perhaps we were becoming too complacent about the river, and the towboats. As we were gliding along the Baleshed - Stack Island Revetment, we spotted a large upriver tow.

263

The river here contained numerous shifting sandbars and islands along the inside of a sweeping left
bend that turned more sharply left where the backwater
entrance to Lake Providence Port turned off to the
right.

As we prepared for a routine two whistle meeting
with this behemoth, we spotted another tow about a mile
farther downriver. This second tow had been hidden by
the size and nearness of the first. "Keep an eye on that
second tow," I said to Dee. "It's sideways in the channel. It must be coming out of Lake Providence, but I
can't tell if it's going to turn upriver or down."

As we maneuvered through the inevitable bow wake
and wheelwash of the massive upriver tow, Dee attempted
to look through the binoculars at the second tow. "Will
you hold this thing still!" she said. "All I can see is
water and sky and some bouncing brown objects in
between."

"I'm doing the best I can!"

"I'll try to get him on the radio." said Dee, giving up on the binoculars.

"Find out which side to pass on," I said. In
response, I received a look that said, "You idiot, why
do you think I'm calling."

While Dee was trying unsuccessfully to make radio
contact, I noticed that a black can and a red nun were
fraternizing on the red nun's side of the channel. Further observation indicated that the fraternization was
widespread. "I think it's an orgy!" I exclaimed. "The
cans and nuns are all mixed together. I can't tell
where to go!"

By this time the river had calmed somewhat and with
the binoculars I could make out the name on the tow
ahead. "She's the **Yeager**." I said to Dee.

Dee tried twice to call the **Yeager** before an answer
came. The voice on the radio began asking where we were
from, and where we were going.

Thinking she had the **Yeager**, and in no mood to
chat, Dee said in a rather sharp tone, "We've got a
problem here. We need to know which way to go. The
buoys and nuns are all mixed up."

While Dee tried to get information from the **Yeager**,
I brought **Sol Seaker** around against the current. My
plan was to move back upstream until we knew which way
to go. As I turned, I could see that the **Yeager** was not
alone. A smaller towboat was in tandem with her, and

both were pushing against the sides of the barges, not the ends. "They're not turning upriver or downriver," I shouted, "They're aground!"

The reason for the confusion of buoys now became clear. A tow, perhaps the **Yeager**, had run aground. The current had swung the entire unit in a wide arc, picking up and depositing red and black markers willy-nilly as she spun slowly around.

As Dee was discovering that the voice on the radio was not from the **Yeager**, but from the pleasure craft, **Morning Mist**, a new voice broke into the conversation. "Skipper just head toward the right bank and you'll be fine."

I turned to starboard, passing well astern of the two towboats, still frantically trying to hold the grounded grain barges together. We now understood why the **Yeager** hadn't answered our calls. She and her companion boat were tuned to some little used channel so they could coordinate their efforts without interruption. Although we never knew who had steered us safely past the distressed barges, we suspected that it was the captain of the large tow we had just met.

For the second time in as many days, we had encountered barges aground. With all the "improvements" to the river by the Corps of Engineers, the "Ole Man" had to let it be known that he was still the master.

When we were once more moving easily downriver, Dee called the **Morning Mist**. "Where ya' comin' from?" came the question over the radio.

"Would you believe - California?"

"Ahh... okay...heh-heh... I believe that. How'd ya' git in the river?"

"Well this pleasure boat isn't the yacht variety. We're on a twenty-six foot cabin cruiser, and we drug it from California behind a Cherokee Chief, Jeep."

"Where'd ya' put in at?"

"Prescott, Wisconsin. We went up to Minneapolis and we've seen the river from Minneapolis on down."

"Tell ya' what. They ain't nuthin' wrong with that. Ya' plannin' on stoppin' in Vicksburg tonight?"

"We're hoping to stop in Vicksburg, if we can find out where to go."

"You turn up the Yazoo River. Do you have a chart?"

"We sure do have a chart. Where do we go when we get up the Yazoo?"

Okay. On the right hand side of the bank goin' up

the river - about one mile up the river you'll see a brown an' yellow barge. Prob'ly they'll be nuthin' tied to it. Right before you git to the barge, you can nearly step off the barge onto some little bitty wooden docks there that they use to tie up little jon boats an' so forth. If you don't need electricity you can tie up to that barge there. It's where the **Jefferson Davis** used to tie up. I think the **Jefferson Davis** is moved from there now. It was an excursion boat. The dock belongs to the city. About fifty feet up the river from that dock you'll see a bunch of work boats tied up there. You can also raft up to one of those. They got electricity an' water. They'll be a little yellow an' white houseboat tied in there. It'll cost you eight to ten dollars to tie up to that. Go ahead."

"Sounds great! We've had so many mixed reports on Vicksburg. Some say we can tie up - Some say we can't tie up. We were told by one person to tie up behind the **Jefferson Davis** at Vicksburg, then last night we tied up next to the **Jefferson Davis** in Greenville."

"Okay! I wondered where it went to. He had a fallin' out with the city there at Vicksburg, I think. We're a north bound pleasure boat. We're goin' to Oklahoma. We tied up there last night and its... uh... real nice."

"You were at Vicksburg last night?"

"Yes mam."

"That sounds good!"

At this point Dee's conversation was interrupted by two towboat captains talking about what happened to the **Yeager.** We listened. ". . .and uh... he uh...captain said 'he's lookin good, lookin' good,' and all a sudden ...uh... he... uh... called captain there an' said, 'cap'an I'm toppin' 'round'. They yelled, 'she is, she's toppin' 'round.' Nothin' to do... heh, heh... she was already broad side the sandbar. What it was - he was a hundred fifty feet off bank with him one hundred fifty-one feet wide - got out too wide. He hit an' was stuck an' you know that boat there she jist topped on around."

"Ah, yeah - Won't pick that stern up very good," 'specially in that turn, all right. Well, I got two more comin' up behind me, down in the bend there a little way."

"Okay, I don't think I got nobody behind me. We set there last night - **City of Greenville** come around with
266

five empties, Ain't heered no one behind since then."

The two boats signed off. About six miles below the stranded barges, we spotted a pleasure craft coming upriver around Fitler Bend. "That must be **Morning Mist,** Dee said.

We looked upriver and saw another pleasure craft coming downriver behind us. For several hours we had been hearing a boat named **Re-Run** call towboats we had met earlier. From the conversations we knew that **Re-Run** was coming behind us. We also knew that she was getting closer, because the intervals between our meeting a tow and **Re-Run,**s call to that same tow were getting shorter.

"That must be **Re-Run,** Dee said, pointing to the fast moving boat.

At mile 477, as if by some master plan, three pleasure boats were momentarily abreast on the river, crews waving to each other like old friends. "That's amazing," Dee exclaimed. "We haven't seen a pleasure craft since Memphis, and suddenly there are three of us at the same spot."

Before she could get the words out, the magic moment was over. **Morning Mist** disappeared around a bend upstream and **Re-Run** moved around Fitler bend downstream. After a short three-way radio conversation, we were once more alone on the Mighty Mississippi.

JEFFERSON DAVIS AT GREENVILLE, MISS.

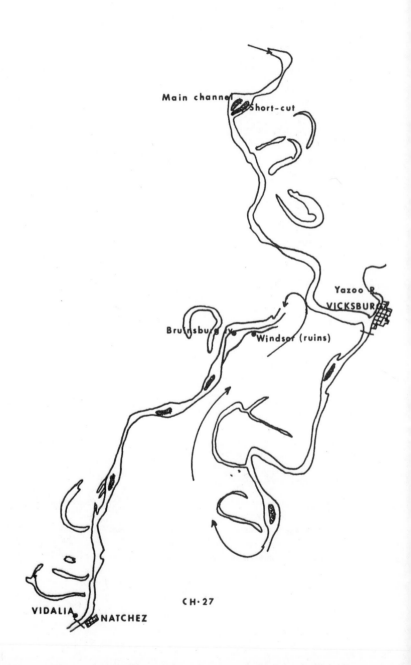

Main channel Short-cut

Yazoo R.
VICKSBURG

Brunsburg Windsor (ruins)

C H · 27

VIDALIA NATCHEZ

27

ON THE MISSISSIPPI QUEEN

"There's something strange on the chart," Dee said as we continued downriver. "The river splits into three channels. The main channel goes round a long bend, but on a cut-off you've written, 'Go here, twenty feet deep.'"

"Somebody upriver told us to take the short cut, but I can't remember who it was."

"Do you think we really ought to do that?" She asked hesitantly.

"We'll take a good look when we get closer."

Around Fitler Bend we again spotted **Re-Run**. "Let's see what she does," Dee said.

"Looks like she's going around the main channel," I commented just as **Re-Run** turned sharply to port and disappeared down the chute. "Wrong again!"

At the head of the chute we could see **Re-Run** about half way down. "The water's fast and there's no wind in the chute," I said. "I'm going to speed up. It's still thirty-five miles to Vicksburg and the sun is getting low in the sky."

Sol Seaker's bow came up as the tachometer rose to 2000, 2500, 3000 R.P.M. The bow slowly dropped as we reached full plane. I eased back on the throttle and we sped along at twenty-five miles an hour.

Re-Run, which had been growing smaller as she pulled away from us, now grew larger as we began to overtake her. Shortly after clearing the chute, we passed her and continued to plane for another fifteen minutes. Around Milliken's Bend we met a modest upriver breeze that turned the smooth river into an old-fashioned washboard. Before I could slow down, the bouncing waves had dislodged books, spices, shoes, and sundry other items, scattering them around the cabin floor.

At sunset, we cruised into the mouth of the Yazoo river and found the yellow and brown barge. A small work boat was slowly dragging the barge back into the water from where the falling river had left it stranded in the mud. When the move was completed, the pilot of the boat motioned us in to tie up.

A few minutes later **Re-Run** pulled in behind us and a German shepherd, overly excited at the prospect of "terra firma," sprang off the deck, ran across the barge and landed on all fours in the thick, black Mississippi mud. After an exciting chase, the dog's owners caught him and began the slow process of washing off his mud boots before allowing him back on the gleaming white, fifty-foot yacht.

When a second fifty-foot yacht, **Joi De Vivre**, came alongside, Dee and I took positions to help with lines - I at the bow and Dee at the stern. An older man stood on the stern of the boat, line in hand, looking nervously at Dee standing on the barge.

"Hand me the line," Dee said.

The man handed Dee the line - both ends and the middle - then continued to stand and look nervous. "You'd better keep one end to tie to the boat." Dee said kindly, but with a note of amused disbelief.

Later, when talking to the boat's hired captain, we learned that the man at the stern was a retired minister from England who knew nothing about boats. He was a friend of the owner, who was entertaining him and his wife in abstentia by giving them a two week cruise aboard his yacht. According to the captain, the minister and his wife had been bored ever since they came aboard. "We have all kinds," the captain confided. "About every two or three weeks we get new guests. Most of them don't know anything about a boat."

Feeling the need for some exercise, Dee and I walked around the lower part of Vicksburg for about a half hour before asking a drugstore clerk directions to the "Cookie Factory."

The clerk looked puzzled.

"Someone told us the Cookie Factory was a good place to eat," Dee said.

"Oh, you must mean the Biscuit Company."

A black lady-customer had overheard the conversation and began a contagious laugh that infected us all.

"Upriver two different people told us about good places to eat," Dee said. "One told us about the Cookie Factory and another about the Biscuit Company. I guess they're the same place. We're supposed to be sure to order the fried pickles."

As we approached the Biscuit Company, we discovered the source of the confusion. High on the wall of the ancient brick building were the faint words, "Cookie Factory." The fried pickles were excellent.

"The **Mississippi Queen**'s due in about midnight said the proprietor of the liquor store where we stopped for a bottle of Mogen David after dinner. "She'll be tyin' up right behind you. If you're awake you ought to watch her come in. It's quite a sight."

At midnight Dee was awakened by the sounds of engines and shouting. She peered out to see the majestic **Queen** inching toward shore. "Wake up!" she shook me.

Clad in pajamas and sandals, we braved the cool damp air to watch the slow, precise, process of docking this large sternwheel cruise ship against the steep levee. "I'm going to tour her tomorrow," Dee stated flatly as we shivered our way back to bed.

"Sure you are," I condescended.

The damp air had become a light rain by morning, as we carried our three empty fuel cans to the nearest service station. We left the cans there while we went to the post office for mail, then to the Corps of Engineers offices to get project information on the Lower Mississippi and the Atchafalaya River.

At Memphis we had learned that a number of years before the Corps built a huge concrete structure in the levee downriver at mile 315. This structure controlled flow from the Mississippi into the Atchafalaya River. At high water, twenty-five per cent of the Mississippi flow can be diverted to the Atchafalaya. Without this control structure, it was estimated that sometime between 1975 and 1995 an irreversible break in the levee would occur, sending the entire Mississippi River down the Atchafalaya, creating a new and shorter route to the Gulf, and leaving the huge ports of Baton Rouge and New Orleans forever cut-off from the Mississippi. The economic impact of such a catastrophic event is beyond calculation.

Even after construction of "The Structure," the river was almost lost when two large whirlpools began to dig deep holes on both sides of the structure. Before the holes were discovered they had undermined one end of a protective jetty, collapsing it into the chasm. Thousands of tons of rock were dumped into the holes before the structure was stabilized.

Since learning about the structure, we had entertained the idea of turning off at the Old River Lock and completing our journey via the Atchafalaya and the Intracoastal Waterway. "We don't have navigation charts for the Atchafalaya," said a very helpful man in the map department of the Corps' office. "The river's deep from bank to bank most places. We do have topographic maps. They have a lot of detail."

We picked up an arm load of brochures, reports and maps and headed back to the gas station. "Johnny," said the proprietor to a customer, "you don't have anything to do. Why don't you drive these folks back to their boat so they don't have to carry those heavy gas cans in the rain."

"Sure."

"Do you know where the remains of the **Sprague** are?" asked Dee, as we headed toward the river. "We toured it about fifteen years ago, then heard it burned."

"Yes. There ain't much left. She's on the banks of the Yazoo a couple of miles upriver. Yall like to see her? Be glad to take you there."

"That would be great!" Dee said excitedly.

"For a while there was a drive on to have her restored," Johnny told us. "But there just wasn't enough left. The cost would be too high. Soon, I'm afraid the old **Sprague** will just be a memory."

We took a picture of the large paddle wheel and rusty metal machinery that once was the world's largest steam powered towboat, then Johnny joined us aboard **Sol Seaker** for a cup of coffee. He told us he had moved here from Memphis four years ago to take over a glass business when his father died. "My taxes helped to pay for all that stuff on Mud Island, but I haven't even seen it. I like Memphis better than Vicksburg, but I guess I'm stuck here."

After Johnny left, Dee said, "Let's go tour the **Mississippi Queen.**"

"You go ask while I walk up the levee to get a picture before **Re-Run** leaves. I want to show the contrast in size between **Sol Seaker**, **Re-Run** and the **Queen**.

As I walked up the steep incline I saw a sign near the Queen that said "No Visitors." This didn't stop Dee. She walked onto the foredeck and talked to a young security guard. He shook his head, "no."

Dee gestured toward our boat then toward the **Queen**. The young man laughed, then stepped inside the Queen while Dee waited. In a few seconds an older man in

uniform accompanied the young man. Again Dee motioned
toward our boat. They all laughed, as Dee motioned for
me to hurry on down. She introduced me to Mike, the
younger man, and to Tom Murphy, the chief purser. "Look
around as much as you like," Tom said jovially.

"What did you say to them?" I queried, as Dee and I
climbed the broad curving stairway of the elegant boat.

"I just told them I'd let them tour my boat if
they'd let me tour theirs."

After our self-guided tour, Dee bought a silver
charm of the Queen. We searched unsuccessfully for Tom
to thank him, then returned to Sol Seaker. As we were
preparing to cast off, Tom came rushing over to our
boat. "You folks gonna be in Natchez tomorrow?" he
asked.

"Yes."

"We're havin' a big picnic aboard the Queen tomorrow. Why don't you join us."

"Great!"

Although I never said anything, I marveled at how
Dee could turn a "No Visitors" sign into an invitation
to an elegant meal aboard the Mississippi Queen.

Between Vicksburg and Natchez we met several upriver tows, but none of them were kicking up the high
sternwash we had seen before. Perhaps the depth of the
river here allowed the wash to remain buried below the
surface, or perhaps Ole Man River had decided that we
had finally passed our initiation of locks and dams,
wheelwashes, boils and eddies, logs and limbs, sandbars,
dikes, wind, waves and wing dams. Whatever the reasons,
the passage was smooth, with one disappointment - we
could not see the ruins of Windsor from our boat.

Fifteen years earlier we had traveled by car between Vicksburg and Natchez, stopping at Windsor.   A
descendent of the original owner had been running a
large bulldozer between the giant columns. "There are
rumors the house had a large basement and some of the
family treasures may still be down there," he had said.

We had watched expectantly as the blade cut deeper
and deeper with each pass. A bottle was turned up. The
family descendent took no interest in the small glass
object. Our son John, fourteen at the time, and very
much into bottle collecting, asked eagerly, "Can I have
it?"   Perhaps he was too eager, for the descendent
became more interested. He brought the bottle to us to
inspect for him. I guess he could see the disappoint-

ment on our faces, when we realized the bottle was not very old. "It was probably made about 1920," John told the man, pointing to the seam that came all the way up the neck to the lip of the bottle. "In older bottles the seam stops down here at the bottom of the neck. The neck and top are then hand turned leaving irregular marks around the neck. This is a medicine bottle, probably prescription since there is no embossing on it. We call that a 'zilch.'"

Impressed by John's knowledge, and unimpressed by a "zilch," the man gave the bottle to John.

While there, we had learned that Windsor was once Mississippi's most imposing mansion and was used by Samuel Clemens and other riverboat pilots as a navigation aid. We had hoped to share that bit of common experience with the great Mark Twain, but changes in the channel had left Windsor far away from the river.

We did; however, pass the ramp of the old Bruinsberg Ferry, but this is several miles from the original town of Bruinsberg where Grant landed troupes for his "back door" assault on Vicksburg. It was the subsequent fall of Vicksburg that gave the Union control of the Mississippi, effectively severing the Confederacy.

When we arrived at Natchez, **Joi De Vivre** and **Double Run**, a boat that had passed us a few miles upriver, were at Steve's Boat Dock. Steve's wife, Rita, directed us to a protected spot behind the long barge.

After dinner at Natchez Landing, we met the Votau's from the **Double Run** and La Habre Heights, California. Walt and Maxine bought the sixty foot motor yacht in Florida a year before. They had traveled up the East Coast to Nova Scotia, through the Great Lakes, down the Illinois and now the Mississippi. Their hired captain stays with the boat while they return home every three weeks to check on their machine and tool manufacturing business in Whittier.

A tour revealed that **Double Run** contains three state rooms, four bathrooms, a large aft entertainment deck, complete with bar and ice maker, and a kitchen with refrigerator-freezer and dishwasher. The twin 800 series Detroit Diesels use about $450 worth of fuel each day the yacht is running at full speed. "That's a beautiful boat," I said when we had returned to our tiny **Sol Seaker**.

"Boat? That's a small ship. I'd like to see you trailer that from California to Minnesota!"

273

Tuesday, November 2, election day. We watched the returns on our diminutive T.V. for a while, but sleep overtook us early. All during the night the wind blew the river into a frenzy, keeping **Sol Seaker** moving restlessly even in our protected location. We wondered how the Votau's were doing on the outside of the dock, where the full force of the wind tossed the sixty foot yacht against her large fenders with every new gust.

Next morning the wind still blew, the rain still came down, the weather was much colder, but Steve, turned paper boy, braved the elements to deliver a fresh, plastic wrapped copy of the Natchez newspaper to every boat in the marina. Hoppie had told us we would like Steve and Rita. Now we knew why. They had the same genuine concern for their guests as Hoppie and Fern, always ready to give a little extra to make you feel welcome.

This willingness to help really came to the fore in an unusual experience shared by Dee and Rita. Modesty and good taste dictate that this experience be recorded by Dee.

DEE: The first time my supply was low was way up-river in Prairie Du Chien. After dinner we had walked around town looking for an open store. We found one tiny market, but they were $5.50 a box. Refusing to be robbed, I decided to look farther. There were no other stores open in Prairie Du Chien.

The next day, in McGregor, I searched again. One market did not carry the kind I wanted. The lady clerk suggested another store several blocks away. When we got to this antique looking store, the door was locked, but small children were playing inside. I rattled at the door and a young man came around from the outside of the building.

"Are you going to be open?" I asked.

"What do you want?"

"Kotex."

He grumbled under his breath and opened the door. The price was the same as the store in Prairie Du Chien, but I had no choice. I bought it.

In South St. Louis I had experienced difficulty in finding the old fashioned kind. Many stores just don't carry them anymore. Now, my supply was low again, and our decision to take the Atchafalaya, where there might not be an easy place to stop, prompted me to stock up.

274

When Rita came to our boat and offered to take me to town to buy any supplies we might need, I said, "There is one thing I need, Kotex."

What a look of surprise she gave me. She couldn't believe that a fifty-two year old woman still needed Kotex. "I gave all that up when I was fifty," she said. "Am I glad to have that behind me."

Our first stop was an IGA store. Rita stayed in the car while I ran in. The shelves had lots of pads, but none of the napkins I use. I asked a male clerk. He blushed and said, "I don't know much about that sort of thing, I'll get someone to help you."

The lady that came to help suggested another store. Although I protested, Rita insisted on taking me to the next store. On the way she talked about intimate things that only friends share, then came in with me, curious about the "new" feminine items.

Fortunately this store carried the desired kind, and I bought two boxes.

"How much were they?" Rita asked me.

"A dollar sixty-seven a box."

"That's a lot," she replied. "Down at the dock the other day I heard two men talkin' 'bout gettin' oil out of their bilges. One said, 'I use Kotex to soak it up. It works real well an' I can just throw it away. But they're gettin' too expensive now.' I was jist wonderin' how expensive they were."

She was really shocked when I told her I had paid $5.50 a box in McGregor, Iowa. Well, I'll turn this pen back to my modest husband.

WELDON: At noon we braved the cold rain to walk to the **Mississippi Queen**, which had arrived during the night. The gala topside picnic had been changed to a buffet in the main dining room. Tom Murphy was not at the Purser's desk. We waited for a while then, thinking he might be at lunch himself, set out toward the dining room. Upon entering the beautifully decorated pink and white room, we found ourselves in the buffet line with an attentive waiter handing us empty plates and telling us we could sit anywhere.

After we each loaded one plate with salads and relishes and another with spare ribs, hamburger and baked beans, the waiter took our plates and led us to a comfortable table in the center of the dining room.

A charming young black waiter stood by waiting for

our drink order. When he returned with iced tea and coffee, Dee said, "We'd like to get our picture with you."

A fellow diner volunteered to take the picture. After the shutter snapped, the young black man said. "I shore am gettin' my picture took a lot. I only been workin' on this boat a week an' I'm gonna be on display all over the country." He beamed a sparkling white smile then headed to the dessert table to get us slices of warm apple pie.

"We're sure getting the royal service," chuckled Dee, "Funny thing is the meal's free, and if this is like other cruises, tips are saved until Thursday night, and we won't be here."

We had just taken our first bites of pie when we heard a faint voice over an outside speaker system. We missed most of the announcement but caught what sounded like, ". . .everybody aboard."

We looked at each other. "Oh my God!" I whispered. "We're about to sail!"

We gulped down our pie, took one sip of coffee and, in a degree of panic, headed for the main deck. At the top of the curved stairway, Dee paused long enough to extract two large golden delicious apples from a fruit basket, placed there for the passengers. When we reached the purser's desk we saw Tom Murphy, microphone in hand, announcing the last call for the bus tour of antebellum homes. The Queen wasn't ready to leave after all.

When Tom had ushered the last passenger aboard the waiting bus, we told him our story, much to his amusement. After giving Dee a hug and kiss, he said, "I have a few more chores to do here, then I'll meet you in a half-hour at the Under-the-Hill Saloon. You can buy me a drink."

"It's a deal," we responded.

While waiting for Tom, we toured the delightful Riverboat Gift shop where Dee bought the book, MISSISSIPPI RIVER FOLKLORE, a carved turtle, and two place mats with pictures of the Mississippi Queen.

At the appointed time a car drove up to the saloon. Out stepped Tom with a lady on each arm.

Inside, the saloon was packed with off-duty crew, and a few tourists. A loud country-western group made conversation impossible. When the group finally took a break, Tom said, "This is Mamie and Theresa."

Before we could begin a conversation a large female vocalist and her pianist took center stage. "We're entertainers from the ship," she said. "If you don't mind we'll rehearse for tonight's show by singing a few songs."

With the first notes, she had the audience spell-bound. Her style was somewhat reminiscent of the late, great, Ethyl Merman, albeit her song selection was a bit more earthy as reflected in some of the lyrics:

> "I just hate to give it away for free.
> You can look at my checkbook honey,
> But keep your hands off my purse!"

Between songs, Dee carried on a quiet conversation with Theresa, who seemed very nervous as she periodically added sprite to her glass of wine. After some time, Theresa leaned across and said to me. "You be careful. You've got a lot to be thankful for. You have a good wife. A good family. If you aren't careful you'll lose all you have."

Later Dee related to me the conversation that led up to Theresa's comments. "I'm from Morocco," she had told Dee. I got married to an American and moved to the states. I have three lovely daughters. After they were grown, I caught my husband running around with a Chinese girl. I couldn't stand it so I finally got a divorce four years ago. Now I also have two grandchildren."

"I worked for Ramada Inn, she had continued, "but I'm presently unemployed. My children help me financially while I'm looking for work. I have a house in Vidalia, across the river. It's a lot cheaper to live there. I don't go out much; I'm Baptist and I don't go in for this sort of thing." She added more sprite to her wine. "I wouldn't think of going out with a married man, not after what I went through when those other women went out with my husband. My kids keep telling me to go out and meet people, but I just like to stay home. When Mamie asked me to come with her today, I decided maybe I should. I'm sure glad I met you. I feel like I can talk to you. Like we've been friends a long time."

Later Tom disappeared back to the **Queen**, the music stopped, and the saloon emptied. We sat a while longer chatting with Teresa and Mamie. "I'm an interior decorator," Mamie told us. "I have a contract to come aboard the **Queen** every time it's in Natchez. I check all the curtains, draperies, and wall hangings to make sure there are no stains, tears or sags. You folks toured Natchez yet?"

"About fifteen years ago," Dee replied.

"If you've got nothing to do for the next couple of hours, I'd love to take you for a quick tour."

Our protests were weak, and we soon found ourselves in Mamie's car on our way to one of Natchez' many antebellum mansions. "What do you know about the Natchez-Under-the-Hill Saloon?" I asked as we rode along.

"Well, you know that used to be the rough riverfront section of town," Mamie explained. "Most of the buildings have been destroyed by floods or fire. Just a few left where the restaurants, gift shop and saloon are. Did you see the little back rooms in the saloon?"

"Yes", we replied.

"In the steamboat days those were used for prostitution. Later the roofs caved in and then they were like little open patios for overflow crowds. A couple of years ago we had a big rain storm. Rained for several days. The hill above the saloon gave way and the mud poured into those open patios and right through the building. Several people were injured and one waitress was killed. They rebuilt it though. Just like it was except they added new roofs to those little rooms."

"This is the first time I've seen it since the accident," Theresa added. "It made me feel nervous to be in there where that girl died."

During the next two hours we drove around the grounds of several antebellum homes, including Linden, Stanton Hall and Monmouth, where Mamie had done some interior decorating. She pointed out "Nellie's," a bordello which seems to continue to operate though technically illegal. "I'll have to remember how to get back here," I joked. But I noticed that Theresa didn't appreciate the humor.

Back at the dock, we showed Mamie and Theresa our little floating home, thanked them for a delightful and educational afternoon, and added two more names to our keep-in-touch list.

"Why don't you stay one more day?" Theresa pleaded. "I'd have you over for dinner. We could talk more."

I could see that Theresa really needed someone like Dee to talk to. "If the weather's still bad, we'll stay another day," I said. "I don't like going out on the river when it's stormy."

278

"I'll come by tomorrow and see if you're still here."

Before dinner, we sat on the large entertainment deck of **Double Run** chatting with Walt and Maxie Votau. "I always carry a loaded gun on the boat," Walt told us. "When we went to the Bahamas, I was glad I had it. We were anchored in this remote bay. Maxie and two women friends were sitting here on the back deck and I was fishing at the railing there, when a boat with three men came by the mouth of the inlet. When they saw our boat, they turned into the inlet. They kept drifting closer. One asked directions to a town to get gas. They kept coming closer. Finally I picked up my shot gun and leaned it on the railing in front of me and said, 'I think that's far enough!' They turned around and sped away."

"Walt wants to take the boat home to California," Maxine said. "But I would rather leave it in Florida where we can go and enjoy it together. I know if we take it to California we'll be entertaining on it all the time. That means I'll really be working and we won't be able to just enjoy it ourselves."

That night as we prepared for bed, Dee said, "I'll bet they have that boat in California before the year's over."

MISSISSIPPI QUEEN

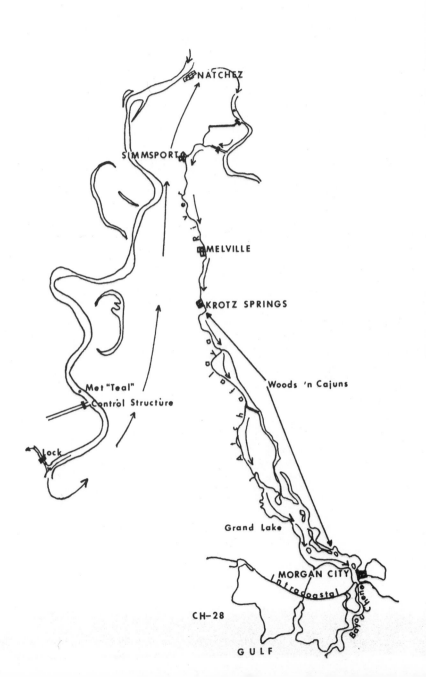

NATCHEZ

SIMMSPORT

MELVILLE

KROTZ SPRINGS

Woods 'n Cajuns

Met "Teal"
Control Structure

Lock

Grand Lake

MORGAN CITY

Intracoastal

Bayou Chene

CH-28

GULF

28

IN THE ATCHAFALAYA MUD

If Theresa came by to look for us, she found us gone.

It was cold, calm and clear, as Rita helped us with our lines and filled our tank with sixty-three gallons of gas, in preparation for our journey down the unknown Atchafalaya.

It was with no small degree of sadness that we began our last full day with Ole Man River. But we were resolute. We owed it to this sometimes cantankerous old waterway to follow **his** course rather than the artificial course to which man in his infinite intelligence, if not wisdom, had, for the present, confined him.

We met and passed a normal number of tows, with names like **Angie Golding, Lexington, City of Winona, Dick Conerly, Ginny Stone,** and **Lynda Ann.**

When we met the small towboat, **Teal,** with two petroleum barges, we didn't realize that she would be the final tow we would see before leaving the Mississippi. As we undulated in the **Teal,**s sternwash, Dee said, "Our chart shows there should be a warning sign about here. There it is!" She pointed toward the right bank.

WARNING
OLD RIVER CONTROL STRUCTURE
Very dangerous currents when structures are in operation. A flashing amber light on south point of inflow channel indicates structures are operational. The inflow channel is not a navigable channel; therefore, under no circumstances should any vessel attempt to enter. Tows and other vessels should navigate as far as possible from the area and as close to the left descending bank of the Mississippi River as safety will permit.

We had moved closer to the right bank in order to

read the sign. For some unexplainable reason, we read the sign then continued on our course along the right bank, looking for the structure. As we rounded a slight bend along the Coochie Revetment, the air was suddenly shattered by a voice saying, "Will the small cruiser please move away from the structure! Please go to mid-channel!"

At that moment the revetment ended and was replaced by a wide channel leading to a giant cement dam several hundred feet to the right. The water in the channel was boiling and churning. I turned quickly to port heading for the center of the river, and wondering how I could have failed to heed the warning sign.

From a safe distance we watched the Ole Man boiling a final protest at this structure which was controlling his urge to change course.

Below Fort Adam's Reach we turned right. At 3:15 P.M. on November 4, we left the Mississippi behind. Ahead the Old River Lock would lower us to the level of the Red, Ouachita and Atchafalaya River systems.

I tried to call the lockmaster on Channel 16. A voice broke in and said, "Call the lock on 14." The voice sounded like the man that had warned us away from the Structure. I could visualize him shaking his head in disbelief at these people who travel on the Missis-sippi without understanding warning signs or knowing how to contact a lock.

I shook my head a bit also. We had contacted more than twenty-five locks on Channel 14 on the upper river, but now had forgotten.

When the lockmaster answered, there was a strange inflection in his voice as he told us he'd be ready for us when we got there, and gave us simple and complete directions on how to lock through. "I bet the man at the structure called to warn him to look out for a small cruiser with an orange flying bridge," Dee said.

The **Salpicar** was tied near the lock wall, a man, lady and two children were walking along the top of the wall. We pulled over beside them to wait for the green light. "Why are you going down the Atchafalaya?" The man asked.

When we explained, he said, "We didn't know about this route. We'd like to take it to avoid the heavy ship traffic between Baton Rouge and New Orleans. Do you know if we can make it with our mast?"

"I'm not sure. The Lockmaster could tell you."

"That's where we're going now."

Later, as we were emerging from the lower end of the lock, we could still see the family high above us. "The lockmaster says it probably isn't a good idea for a sailboat to go down the Atchafalaya," They shouted down to us. "Perhaps we'll see you in New Orleans."

The **Salpicar** was the last pleasure craft we were to see, except for small jon boats and runabouts, until we reached Morgan City and the Intracoastal Waterway.

Seven miles below the lock we joined the Atchafalaya. Here, if we turned right we could travel three-hundred seventy miles to Dangerfield, Texas or four-hundred fifteen miles to Arkadelphia, Arkansas, if we turned left, in one hundred twenty-five miles we'd reach Morgan City, Louisiana on the Intracoastal Waterway. We turned left.

What a contrast the Atchafalaya was to the Mississippi. It reminded us a little of the Kaskaskia, but the Atchafalaya was larger and deeper than that tiny river, so many miles in the past. In the ten miles to Simmesport, we saw few buoys and no boats.

After searching unsuccessfully for a place to dock, we anchored in a small cove beneath the high railroad bridge, and spent a lonely and quiet night without towboat, pleasure craft, or people to break the silence.

Before going to bed, we studied the topographic maps of the Atchafalaya in great detail. There were only three possible places to get fuel before Morgan City. We already knew there was no marina at Simmesport. The map showed a ferry at Melville, the next town. "Where there's a ferry, there's a landing. We should be able to get fuel at Melville," I declared.

The next day we passed row after row of floating plastic jugs, marking the locations of fishing nets and "trot" lines. As we approached the railroad bridge at Melville, we spotted two small boat docks on the right bank. Several jon boats were pulled up on shore and two larger runabouts were tied to the docks. Atop the steep bank a number of houses appeared to be a tiny fishing village.

A large, sun-bronzed man, perhaps in his early forties, stood about half-way up the bank, watching as I slowed and headed toward him. Above him, near one of the houses, were several people, perhaps a family. There were two older people, two younger women and a child. The bronzed man walked out on one of the docks as

282

we approached. He motioned to us, then began to untie the lines on one of the larger boats as if to move it to make room for us.

A wiry older man came down from the house. Pointing to a spot on the bank between the dock and two of the small jon boats, he said, "He cain't talk, you couldn't understand him. You can land here." Again he pointed to the vacant spot.

In order to keep **Sol Seaker** from swinging around in the current, we dropped a stern anchor a few yards upstream from our proposed landing site. As the bow touched shore, Dee pulled the anchor line tight and scurried to the bow, handing a line to the older man, which he attached to a cable on shore. The landing was picture perfect, and with a sense of pride we stepped off on a wide board provided as a gangplank.

And thus we met the Moreau Family of Melville, Louisiana. The Grandfather, Trapani Moreau, is a fisherman. He has lived his entire life here on the banks of the Atchafalaya. "What kind of fish do you catch?" we asked, after climbing the steep bank.

"Goo, catfish and buffalo, mostly."

"Goo? What's a goo?" I asked.

"Goo. Well some folks call't a drum, but here we call't goo."

"Goo's good," said one of the younger ladies who turned out to be a daughter-in-law. "Downriver you know how them Cajuns fixes goo? They puts a lil' oil inter a pot. Then they puts in the goo. They adds all them spices 'n peppers 'n tomatoes 'n onions. Then they simmers it 'n eats it with rice. Some folks up north don't eat rice. They eats grits in Missouri. They puts gravy over grits. I doan see how they kin eat gravy over grits. Rice, thet's the onliest thing to eat gravy on. Good ol' red-eye gravy 'n rice. Thet Cajun goo is good. In a restaurant you pays a lot of money fer it, an I can have it fer free right here at home."

I wondered what she would think if I told her we ate our gravy over mashed potatoes.

"Fishin's not good right now," Trapani told us. "River's too low. We shore need some rain fer to git the river up a little so's the fish'll start movin'. Fish don't move whils't the river's down 'n you doan ketch fish lessen they's movin'."

The Moreaus offered to take us to town but we declined. It had been a day and a half since we walked

283

and we really needed the exercise. "We'll shore look after yore boat whils't yore gone. It'll be safe."

We were sure it would be.

As we walked along the dirt road past modest houses and mobile homes, we noted with interest that here and there small channel buoys had been used as fence posts; and that almost every building had a sign "Fresh Fish - Catfish, Buffalo, Goo."

We passed between two small taverns, then turned right, and suddenly realized that this tiny village was separated from the main part of Melville by a high levee. "They're at the mercy of the river and the Army Corps of Engineers," said Dee, remembering that any water released from the structure would come down the Atchafalaya.

We stopped at the small Napoli Market to get a pocket sized notebook - we had left ours on the boat. We then found the post office and mailed postcards we had purchased in Natchez. "Where's a good place to eat?" Dee inquired of the postal clerk.

"Jessie's," she replied without hesitation. "Jist go down and under the railroad tracks, then go left a couple of blocks and turn right. You cain't miss it."

As we were walking toward Jessie's, one of the Moreau women came by in the car. She had just picked up her daughter from school. When she offered us a ride to Jessie's we accepted. On our way, I asked the girl how she liked school.

"I hates it."

"She gits into some trouble," the mother admitted. "Lots of kids seem to play hooky, but I tell her she's gotta stay in school."

"It must be hard for a ten year old to see much relationship between a formal education and life in this isolated village," Dee said as we sat in Jessie's.

"I know what I'm having," I exclaimed as soon as I read the specials on the blackboard. "Red beans, rice and sausage." I had heard about this traditional dish, but had never tried it. Dee chose pork steak, rice, gravy, candied yams, greens and cornbread.

On our return to the boat, we stopped again at Napoli's for lettuce, tomatoes, cucumbers, salad dressing and a small molasses cake.

We found the two elder Moreaus on the front porch catching the warm rays of the afternoon sun. Mrs. Moreau was seated in an old fashioned porch swing. "I've

284

always wanted one of those swings," Dee confided as we approached.

"Here, sit with me," said Mrs. Moreau. "Lotsa people jist have them for show, but I like to use mine. We got one out back we use when the sun's on t'other side of the house."

I caught Dee's smile as she recognized a fellow sun lover.

As we talked Trapani's son came around the house and overheard me saying, "The Atchafalaya is certainly quiet and peaceful compared to the Mississippi."

"Thet 'Chafalaya's a treach'rous river when the water's high!" responded the son. "It's full 'a logs 'n it boils 'n swirls all over. Lotsa peoples drown in thet river. When the river's high we ketch logs 'n sticks 'n our nets 'an bodies. Yep we caught several bodies in our nets. Some no one ever identified. Jist drowned an' no one ever knowed who they wuz. Caught one jist last winter. . ."

The ringing of a phone inside the house brought a pause in the story. In a few moments one of the younger women came out. "Do you have that catfish fer Mrs. Greenley?"

"Didn't ketch none today. Tell her we didn't ketch none," Trapani said to the young woman. Then to us, "We gits a dollar seventy a pound fer most catfish we catch. We gits sixty cents fer goo. We get a good price fer fish now. Course things is slow now so's we don't have much to sell."

"Thet one we caught last winter was a black man," the son continued his interrupted story. "No one ever knowed who he wuz or where he come from."

As the sun dipped lower, we rose to leave, asking if there was a place to stop below the bridge near a service station. "Be glad to take you to the station," said the son, "but car's so full of things they'd be no room fer the cans. You can stop at the ferry landing. Jist make shore you stays out of the way of the ferry."

The ferry dock was vacant as we approached, but the boat was on its way from the opposite landing with a load of cars. Since we didn't know just how the ferry would be docking, we decided to make a bank landing. Fifty yards down from the dock, Dee dropped the stern anchor, and I nudged the bow into the muddy bank. Since there was no one to assist, I moved quickly to the bow, and tossed the bow anchor as far up the dark muddy bank

285

as I could. "It looks solid," I said to Dee as I jumped off the bow.

I hit the mud, and went right in, past my shoes, past my ankles, past my knees, then sat backwards, held fast by the thickest, blackest mud I'd ever encountered. I'd heard about and seen the Mississippi mud, but this Atchafalaya mud had it beat in every category on which mud could be judged.

As I sat helpless and embarrassed, I heard laughter coming from the direction of the landing, where the ferry boat was just docking. I sunk deeper, but not deep enough to hide my embarrassment.

There was nothing to do but try to extract myself. I pulled the anchor line tight using it to help pull myself upright. After some effort, I got one foot out and onto the flat anchor. Eventually I was able, with an assist from Dee, to pull myself aboard, leaving a trail of thick, sticky mud as I beat a retreat to the rear deck.

Dee grabbed the camera and said, "Do it again, I didn't get a picture."

After scraping forty pounds of thick chocolatey mud off my body, Dee helped remove my favorite green boat shoes and wrangler jeans. In my embarrassment I wanted to pull in the anchor and head on downriver - gas or no gas. But Dee's calmer head prevailed.

A man in a pickup called to us, "I'll take you in for gas. Just tie to the end of the landing. You'll be out of the way there."

Clean clothes and time to reflect on the humor of the situation reduced the embarrassment sufficiently to get me to agree to run **Sol Seaker** up to the ferry landing, where the ferry was again returning from across the river. A young man, whom I recognized as the loudest laugher, was tending lines. As I stepped off **Sol Seaker**, I said to him, "That must have looked pretty funny."

"Yeah it shore did," he said timidly.

While I went for gas, Dee stayed on the boat to wash the mud out of my best clothes. Here she relates her experience.

DEE: First I tried to get the mud off by bouncing the pants up and down in the water. The mud stuck fast. I finally resorted to removing the mud with my fingernails. After getting the big pieces off, I rubbed the material together under water, finally reducing the mud

286

to a dark stain, which I hoped would come out in the washing machine.

I then tackled the shoes. The mud was almost dry, and clung like used chewing gum. The people at the ferry landing watched in amusement as I worked on the clothes, but after the initial laughter, they became shy. I think they were as embarrassed for Weldon as he was for himself. Every time I looked up, they would look away. Finally I said to the boy who had laughed the loudest, "Did you see him fall in the mud?"

"Yeah, he fell in da' mud. Over der. It's a wonda he din' go kleen up to his haid."

WELDON: The man who took me for gas showed me a beautiful new Pentecostal Church. "We're proud 'a that," he said. "Jist local people did all the work ourselves. Didn't hire nothin' done."

After expressing our gratitude and stowing our cans of gas, we headed for Krotz Springs. The short run was uneventful, and we found a nice new barge to tie to for the night. When Dee took my sun dried jeans from the railing, they were so stiff that they could stand up by themselves.

Trapani Moreau had said, "You won't find nuthin' but woods 'n Cajuns past Krotz Springs." We found lots of woods, but only a few Cajuns. The character of the river changed as we got below the end of the streamside levee system. Here, at high water, the river could spread freely for miles on each side of the channel. From time to time we would see a Cajun cottage half hidden in the dense woods. One of these was made from old signs that formed a collage of eating places, stores and service stations. Another was built on large barrels so it would float during high water.

We searched in vain for a pirogue, that unique craft of bygone days that were hand carved from a single cypress log. On the Atchafalaya, pirogue's have been replaced by jon boats and runabouts sporting Johnsons, Mercuries, Mariners and Evinrudes.

As we entered the Grand Lakes area, it became more and more difficult to plot our course, due to an absence of navigational aids, our use of topographic maps as navigational charts, an unchanging shoreline, and a lack of current. Except for an occasional shack or fishing boat, we would have had the same feeling of suspended animation we had felt on entering Lake Pepin.

Once, when we were totally unsure of which channel to take, a small towboat with two barges rounded a tree covered spit and headed in our direction. We could see a faint wake extending around the bend. "Let's follow that line," Dee said, "It must be the right channel."

After the guiding wake line disappeared, we were again nearing the point of panic, when a nun appeared, reassuring us that we were still in the main channel.

For miles we traveled through this isolated swampland, then, rounding a bend, we entered a new world - a world of waterway commerce that eclipsed anything at St. Paul, St. Louis or Cairo. Unlike the Mississippi towboats, these boats and barges had derricks, cranes, pipes and tubing, creating massive sculptures all along the waterfront. These were the boats that serviced the off-shore oil platforms that dot the surface of the Gulf of Mexico.

The most unique craft were large flat boats with long "legs" protruding high into the air. In the Gulf, these legs were lowered to the bottom, lifting the boat out of the water to create an instant platform for drilling new wells.

The only boats not related to the oil industry were fish and shrimp boats, but these were definitely in the minority.

"We certainly shouldn't have any trouble getting gas here," I said as I maneuvered through the maze of boats, toward a Conoco sign. Pulling alongside a rough wooden sea wall, I stepped off the boat with line in hand, catching my trailing foot on the bow rail as I did. Thrown off balance, I found myself with one foot on land and the other on the boat, which was slowly slipping away from the dock. I did a rather painful and ungraceful split, then pulled my foot free from the boat coming dangerously close to falling headfirst between boat and sea wall.

A sign on the small Conoco office said "closed." At the bottom was a phone number. I called from a nearby pay phone. A lady's voice said, "They won't be open 'til Monday."

Today was Saturday.

As I swung **Sol Seaker** around and started off in search of another fuel dock, Dee spotted an old wooden boat with three fishermen, about fifty yards away. "Did you ever see a fish like that?" one of the men asked, as we came alongside. "It's a flounder."

We had seen many much larger flounders, but since we were seeking help, we felt it prudent to show the proper appreciation. "That's a nice fish." Dee said. Her mind flashed to the picture of the thirty-eight pound king salmon in her wallet. How she longed to show them what a real fish looked like. "Is there any place to get gas and tie up for the night?" she asked instead.

"Gas is closed 'til Monday. City docks yonder." The man gestured toward some undefined location on the opposite shore.

"Which one's the city dock?" I asked peering in the direction of the gesture.

"Thet one. Yall see thet little black 'n white boat. Right in front of it's the city dock."

As we headed across the channel, a Coast Guard boat pulled in about a hundred yards from the city dock. "They should know where we can get gas," Dee said. "I don't want to sit in this busy harbor until Monday."

A helpful Coast Guard officer called the Rio Fuel Dock. "They'll be open from seven in the morning to five in the evening tomorrow. The Rio Dock is about five or six miles east on the Intracoastal Waterway. You go through the Bayou Boeuf Lock then look for a side channel on the left."

We took a cab to Don's seafood restaurant for dinner, then walked back to the boat, just the exercise we needed to prepare us for a good night's sleep, despite the lights and noise of this twenty-four hour port.

We followed the supply boat **Ventura** through the narrow constriction of the inoperative Bayou Boeuf lock, then followed the Intracoastal until we spotted the Rio Dock. Primarily a fueling station for the large offshore boats, the dock was higher than **Sol Seaker's** flying bridge. We climbed onto a horizontal twenty-inch pipeline, then on to a wooden framework before finally reaching the dock.

The gas hose did not have a hand operated nozzle, but was turned on at the pump. As we were filling our tanks, one of the large supply boats pulled in beside us. The turbulence created by her powerful diesels, as she maneuvered stern in, made it almost impossible to hold the flowing fuel nozzle in the tank opening.

It was with a sense of great relief that we pulled away from the busy fuel dock and turned down Bayou Chene on our way to our first glimpse of the Gulf of Mexico, at the point where, except for man's intervention, Ole

Man River would now be creating a new delta at Atchafalaya Bay.

Bayou Chene was a most pleasant contrast to the busy Intracoastal. The edges of the narrow ribbon of water were lined with large moss covered cypress trees, reminiscent of Reelfoot Lake. Herons and Egrets patiently stalked their finney prey from cypress knees as flocks of tiny terns feasted on minnows churned up in our wake.

High overhead a large dark bird circled. It's slow but steady wing beat indicated that it was not a vulture. As the bird banked toward the morning sun, a flash of pure white at head and tail provided positive identification. "It's an eagle," we gasped together.

For two thousand miles we had been on the alert for a glimpse of America's symbol. We had seen wild turkeys, swallows, ducks, geese, hawks and ospreys. But it wasn't until we were within a few miles of the Gulf that we finally saw the one bird we had most wanted to see. As if guiding our way, the giant bird wheeled out of it's slow circle and flew ahead of us toward the Gulf.

After a few more bends the unending Gulf spread out before us. Suspended in that void where sea and sky meet, we could see the fuzzy outlines of several offshore oil platforms. Here and there moving patches of white indicated the presence of supply boats speeding between platforms. Two tiny mosquito-like seaplanes approached from seaward on course to their home bases.

We were greeted by friendly waves from the crew of a large shrimp boat, returning with her tasty bounty from the sea, then we moved out of the main channel and dropped anchor. Dee disappeared into the cabin below, soon reappearing with our two desert rose stem glasses filled with wine. I set my camera on automatic so we could both be in the picture. As we sipped our wine, and basked in the warm sunshine, I remembered that I still had some bait in the refrigerator. I baited a hook and cast out from the stern. I didn't have to wait long. First there was a gentle movement of the rod tip as some unknown fish nudged the bait. Finding it to his liking, the fish took another nibble. This time the rod tip dipped downward twice. On the third bite, the rod bent over in an arc and stayed there as the hooked fish fought to free himself.

After a short struggle, I lifted aboard a catfish, which looked much like the ones I had caught on the

Mississippi, Kaskaskia, and Tennessee Rivers. We laughed, tossed the fish and the rest of the bait into the water and sat watching the gentle movements of the sea.

CYPRESS AND EAGLE - BAYOU CHENE

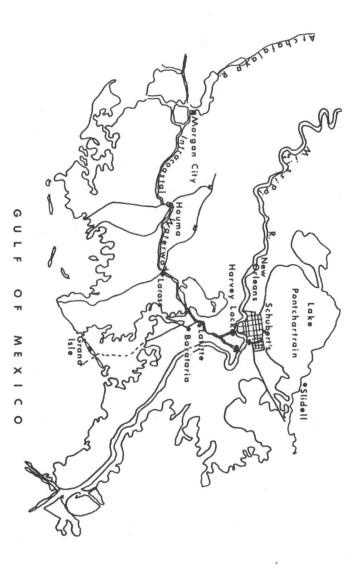

29

LAFITTE - LA FEAT

After a crewboat roared by at full speed, we reluctantly pulled anchor and turned back up the Atchafalaya outlet, then eastward into the Intracoastal on our way toward Houma, Lafitte, and New Orleans.

On the Mississippi there had always been a current and navigational aids to assure us that we were headed in the right direction. Here on the Intracoastal Waterway there was no current and few markers. There were; however, many side channels and a dense jungle to confuse our senses. Each time we had to make a decision between two or more channels, we would carefully check depths on each and choose the deepest one, keeping our fingers crossed until a boat or barge appeared to confirm our choice.

Channel 13, the working channel for towboats, was like listening to a cage of excited magpies. Fishing boats, commercial boats, barges, locks, home bases and draw bridges all tried to use the radio at the same time. In addition to the ever present slow Southern drawl, were the excited sounds of Creole, Cajun, Texan, and several other unidentifiable foreign languages. None of these gave us a clue as to how far we were from Houma. After several tries, Dee contacted a small towboat coming toward us. The Cajun pilot, with some language difficulty, confirmed that we still had eight miles to go.

Darkness came suddenly. In the moonless night we could barely discern the wooded edges of the channel. The black water was dotted with clumps of floating hyacinth reminiscent of the San Joaquin River. When our engine began to make a strange sound, Dee calmly shifted to neutral, and I pulled a clump of pesky hyacinth from the propeller. We moved on, but more slowly.

Rounding a slight bend, we were relieved to see the sparkle of lights in the distance. "There's Houma," I declared, much of the tenseness leaving my body.

The lights grew closer and closer, then passed by, attached to the barges and superstructures of a string of six towboats. They rounded the bend behind us plunging us into a more severe darkness than before. "I'm going to have to use the spot light," I said. "I hate to because it closes the pupils and destroys the night vision."

"Don't," Dee answered. "I can still see well enough to stay in the channel."

It was after ten when lights again appeared, and moments later we spotted two men on a docked supply boat. "Is there any place we can tie up for the night?" we asked.

"Sure, right next to our boat, the **Lady Neva**," replied one of the men as both stood ready to receive our lines. "Come on in and have some coffee."

On board were Captain Rick Weber, from Seattle, Washington and mate Richard Stevens and his wife Marsha, from Bethel Island, California. "I only have a tenth grade education," Rick confided as we relaxed in the boat's small, but adequate, living room-galley combination. "I had to work and study hard to get to be a captain. When I passed that Coast Guard test, I was the happiest man alive. Would you like to see the boat?"

"Sure."

"They don't design these boats very well," he continued. "They put the fuel and water tanks in the wrong place. As long as they are both full or both empty it's okay, but when one or the other gets near empty, the boat is hard to handle. I'm designing a boat that will be balanced even when one of the tanks is empty."

As we talked, we learned that Rick was separated from his wife, who couldn't stand his being gone so much of the time. At Rosedale we had learned from Jerry that the twenty-eight days on and twenty-eight days off schedule put a great strain on family life. It had apparently been too much for Rick's wife.

When I noticed Dee's eyes becoming heavy, we excused ourselves and returned to **Sol Seaker**. We had just snuggled deep into our welcome bed when a towboat came around the bend, its sternwash rocking us violently and banging us hard against the side of the **Lady Neva**. Glasses, bottles and books toppled and rolled. "We can't stay here." Dee said. "By morning we'll be sunk."

We solved the problem by tethering **Sol Seaker** between two anchors on our starboard and two lines, to the

Lady Neva, on our port. We continued to bounce violently each time a towboat passed, but remained secure until
a welcome dawn ended the bumpiest night of our voyage.

After leaving our mooring, we were sandwiched in a
line of towboats waiting for two drawbridges. On the
other side another line of towboats waited. When the
bridges opened, we moved quickly through the maze into a
broad turning basin. Ahead and to our left we spotted
several tiny seaplanes. Some were on the bank near a
ramp, and others were moored like boats at a dock. "We
need to get fuel," I said. "I'll bet we can get it
where those planes are. I see gas pumps."

"You wouldn't want this gas," a man chuckled when I
pulled up by the pumps. "This is airplane fuel. It's
too powerful for your boat engine. Did you see a little
canal between the two drawbridges?"

"No," I said. "We were too busy dodging towboats
and barges."

"Well, you go back through the first bridge then
turn right. There's a place you can get gas."

"Thanks," I replied, not overly thrilled at the
prospect of re-entering Louisiana's towboat version of
the Santa Monica Freeway.

As we turned away from the seaplane dock and headed
back toward the drawbridge, a small plane came roaring
down the middle of the channel. A few yards before
reaching us he lifted, turned sharply to his right, and
headed toward the Gulf. Almost before we had released
our held breaths, a second plane dropped from the sky
and touched down in the spot just vacated by the first.
"I think we're in the middle of the runway!" Dee exclaimed. "Let's get out of here."

We turned right on the narrow channel, searching
both sides for a fuel pump. When we came to a low bridge
marking the end of navigation, I said, "We must have
missed it."

After jockeying around in the channel which, in
addition to being narrow, was liberally littered with
old household appliances, bed springs, logs, limbs and
boxes, I stopped at a tenuous tie up behind a service
station. "I used to have a pump back there," the owner
said, "but it didn't pay. There's a wholesale distribu-
tor where the canal joins the barge waterway. It's on
the left. I think he still sells to boats."

We found the fuel dealer and filled **Sol Seaker** with
the cheapest fuel we found - $1.08 a gallon.

On the next leg of our journey, we passed through a swinging pontoon bridge, crossed Bayou Lafourche, and turned right into Barataria Seaway, once the stronghold of the infamous pirate Jean Lafitte, and now filled with South Louisiana's fishing fleet.

A few petroleum boats and barges use this seaway, but by far the greatest volume of traffic consists of fish, shrimp and oyster boats, ranging in size from tiny cypress pirogues to large ninety foot drag boats. One of the latter, **Macho Man** was moored with us at a rough wooden dock behind a fish processing plant. It took several old tires to fender us against the splintery, bolt and nail infested pilings of our unprotected mooring. As large and small boats sped by, I wondered what had happened to the rule about "no wake."

"So this was the stronghold of Jean Lafitte," Dee said, as we walked along the single street. "I can see how he could elude capture in this swampy country."

"You know he started out as a blacksmith," I said recalling facts from a book I had read about the Battle of New Orleans. "When he came from France he set up a blacksmith shop in New Orleans. I think the building is still standing. After the Louisiana Purchase, the Gulf of Mexico became the center of a profitable pirating business. The war between France and Spain paved the way for Lafitte to attack Spanish ships, steal the cargo, and sell it in New Orleans."

"When Lafitte and his cohorts extended their privateering to English and American ships, a United States Grand Jury indicted him. To save his own skin, Lafitte warned the United States of a planned British attack, then threw the support of his men and weapons to the side of the United States, thus preventing the British from capturing New Orleans. That's how he got the name 'pirate patriot.'"

"After New Orleans was saved, Lafitte's stronghold was attacked by the United States. The pirates that weren't arrested and thrown in jail, were scattered, and great quantities of valuable goods were seized and taken to New Orleans."

"Lafitte fled to Galveston, and built a small town, living in the center in a well fortified bright red house. From his new stronghold he returned to pirating. The United States tolerated Lafitte for awhile, then complaints of attacks on American vessels became so numerous, a navel force was dispatched to persuade him to leave United States waters. Lieutenant Kearney was entertained royally by Lafitte at the red house. Bowing to the wishes of the United States, Lafitte ordered the town burned and sailed away on his favorite vessel, **Pride**. He relocated on the island of Mujeres, off the Coast of Yucatan, where he died in 1826."

"I remember reading somewhere that he left a wife - and a tomb full of turtle shells - to honor his memory," Dee added.

"That's right," I said, "Men always die first leaving widows to enjoy their hard earned money."

I dodged a well aimed kick, and we entered a small take-out restaurant for shrimp and fried oysters.

The next morning we were greeted by a bright sunny sky, and left early for what we had been told was a twenty mile ride to Grand Isle. As we moved slowly along the Dupree Canal, we were continually being passed by boats speeding to and from the gulf. The dense growth of trees gradually gave way to low salt marshes. Here and there side channels led to small clusters of houses accessible only by water.

A loud noise came from the outdrive. I shifted to neutral then to reverse. A flat cardboard box floated to the surface.

When I calculated that we had gone more than twenty miles, I slowed near two sport fishermen in a runabout. "How do we get to Grand Isle?" I asked.

"Straight ahead. You see that water tower in the distance? That's Grand Isle. When you get in the bay, just stay between the markers. Take you right there."

"Thanks," I said to the fisherman, then to Dee, "I'd better speed up if we're ever going to get to Grand Isle and up to New Orleans today."

We were running full-speed between low marshy banks when suddenly a fast, large metal boat appeared in a hidden side channel on our left. According to the Rules of the Road we were the "stand on" vessel and he the "give way." It was our duty to ". . .Maintain course and speed." Unfortunately someone forgot to tell the captain of the other boat about that rule, for he was also maintaining course and speed to the exact spot we would be occupying in a very few moments.

Immediately I invoked the "General Prudential Rule" which states: "In obeying and construing these rules, due regard shall be had to all dangers of navigation and collision, and to any special circumstances, which may render a departure from the above rules necessary in order to avoid immediate danger..."

I jerked back on the throttle. **Sol Seaker** stopped dead in her wake, throwing Dee and I hard against the steering console. As we recovered from this sudden jolt, the first in a series of our own wakes hit us from behind, pushing us forward and jerking our heads backwards.

No sooner had I moved the throttle forward to clear the intersection into which our wake had pushed us, than a second boat sped by in pursuit of the first. "Where the hell did they come from?" I gasped.

"They didn't miss us by more than a few feet!" Dee shouted, shaking her fist at the retreating boats.

"What rules of the road were they following?" I wondered. "We were the 'stand on' and they were the 'give way'."

"I'd like to give them a piece of my mind," Dee growled.

We looked back at the blind intersection and noted a sign on the side-channel that read, "This channel is the private property of Texaco Oil Company."

"They must also think they own the whole damn waterway!" I said, still fuming.

After several more comments about the lack of intelligence, and the probable obscure ancestry of the crew, we found ourselves in open water, in a well marked channel.

A strong easterly wind almost succeeded in pushing **Sol Seaker** outside the safety of the dredged channel. Dee's alert eye spotted the tell-tale signs of sand rising in our wake, and alerted me in time. "We didn't touch," I commented. "But that was too close for comfort."

As we passed Pelican Point, Dee gestured ahead and to our left. "According to our chart, that's Grand Terre Island. Isn't that where Lafitte kept his pirate fleet?"

"That's the place. I wonder if there's any buried treasure there?"

A few minutes later we turned off the main channel and followed the harbor markers to Raoul's Marina, where we met the Priest who was intrigued by the name **Sol Seaker**.

After lunch we headed back up Barataria Bay, stopping once to drink another toast to our adventure.

"Did we find the **Sols** and **Souls** we were seeking?"
I asked aloud.

"Yes", Dee replied, as she leaned back to catch the
full rays of the early afternoon sun.

We rode in silence for more than an hour, each in
our own thoughts and feelings, re-living this dream
journey. We had made the trip together. We had shared
elation, fear, sadness, compassion, courage, anger, joy
and determination. But within the uniqueness of our
innerselves, we each experienced the journey indepen-
dently. It was this combination of the shared and the
unique that would cause our first boating adventure to
live on in our memories as long as God deemed it worthwhile to keep the breath of life within us.

We didn't make New Orleans that night. In fact, we
ran aground attempting to fish in one of the channels
that led to a tiny fishing village. Fortunately the
strong wind blew us off the muddy bottom and back into
deep water. During the process, I caught one fish. Yep,
a catfish.

Back at Lafitte, we found a dock with shore power,
and for the first time in several days had a hot shower
and a chance to re-charge our television batteries.
After shrimp, oysters and crab at Bouttes, we settled in
for the last night before the end of our cruise.

The next morning, with full fuel tanks, we headed
for New Orleans. "Some year let's come back here and
spend two or three months," I said. "This is a fascin-
ating place."

"Sounds good to me," came Dee's answer. "I'm always
ready to travel."

After returning enthusiastic waves from the passengers aboard two of New Orlean's excursion boats, the
Voyager and the **Jean Lafitte**, we headed up the Harvey
canal, which would take us through one of the busiest
most congested waterways in the country, through Harvey
Lock and into the Mississippi River. We kept the radio
on hoping to overhear calls that would give us some
clues about locking through this busy lock. We caught
the end of a conversation, ". . .he's still over there
working on the **Patricia B.**

"I wonder if that's Norm and Patti," Dee said.

We then heard the **Voyager** call the lock, "We'll be
there at 2:10. We have fifty-three people aboard."

"We'll be looking for you. Give us another call
when you're closer."

298

We looked back to see the tour boat gaining on us. "I'll call the lock and see if we can lock through with them," Dee said, making several unsuccessful attempts.

The **Voyager** was getting closer. She called the lock again. "I'm about a half mile out. Have fifty-three passengers aboard."

"Okay skipper. As soon as this small tow leaves the lock you can come in."

Dee tried to call the lock again. Still no answer. "Try calling the **Voyager**," I said to Dee. "We need to check this radio."

"**Voyager** this is the pleasure craft **Sol Seaker**, over."

"Yes, **Sol Seaker**. This is the **Voyager**."

"We've been trying to get through to the lock, but no answer, Do you think we can lock through with you."

"**Voyager**, this is the Harvey Lock. "Tell that pleasure craft they can follow you in. There's a string of barges blocking the lock, but a tow is pushing them aside to make room."

A quarter of a mile from the lock Dee took over the helm. As she started to move to her right to give **Voyager** room to pass, we heard the roar of an engine behind us. I spun around. "Don't turn!" I yelled to Dee, "An airplane is landing next to us."

It seemed incredible, but one of those little seaplanes was landing among the barges, towboats, sightseeing boats and pleasure craft that choked this narrow waterway. If Dee had made her move to the right a few moments earlier, we would have been directly in the path of the plane.

"That was close," Dee said almost too nonchalantly.

While the plane was holding our attention, **Voyager** slipped by on our port. Ahead a towboat pushed on the side of several connected barges, moving them slowly to the right. Out of the lock came a large yacht, followed by a two-barge tow. We moved behind **Voyager**, following her slowly past the emerging craft and into the lock. We looped a short line over a stationery pin and set ourselves for the one-foot lift that would bring us once again into our Mighty, Magical, Mississippi.

At first the river didn't seem mighty at all. A south-easterly breeze created a slight cross chop, but the **Voyager** smoothed the bumps as we followed in her wake toward the end of Canal Street where she docked. We moved on past the French Quarter, then swung across·the river to get a better view of a New Orleans' skyline that has changed dramatically in the last few years, with the addition of numerous high-rise buildings and, of course, the famous Superdome.

Cruising slowly along the right side of the river, we came to a sharp bend to the right. The shore here was lined with parked barges. Occasionally a small towboat would emerge with a single empty, adding it to a string of connected barges. Soon these empties would be fastened to the front of a towboat and begin the long, ponderous journey upriver.

As we rounded the bend two tows, that were beginning their long voyage, blocked our way, preventing us from crossing the river to the Industrial Canal. We moved closer to the parked barges, to give the tows more room. Rounding the end of a long string of moored barges, we found ourselves directly in front of a third upriver tow. We spent several anxious moments pinched between the parked barges on our starboard and the moving tow on our port. I began to understand what that tow captain had meant when he said, "I'm all behind and elbows." We rolled and bounced for several minutes in the sternwash before realizing that the waves were not all from the tow. In rounding the bend we had turned bow into a strong south-east wind.

"This is as bad as the Ohio," Dee commented.

In fact it was worse than the Ohio, for here were boats, barges, and ocean going ships to add a variety of new agitations to the wind driven surface. "Let's get out of here," I said, moving as quickly as possible to the entrance of the Industrial Canal

Dee called the lock. "There are three barges ahead of you," came the reply. "You can go through in about an hour."

We moved close to a row of army barges looking for a quiet place to wait. A fast military boat emerged from behind the barges and streaked past. As we rocked and rolled in her wake, a tow emerged from the canal turning her bow upriver toward us. We moved toward the center of the river, only to encounter two freighters, one coming upriver just below us, and the second heading down. The two ships would meet near our present location. ". . .Well, you are a little small for the Mississippi," the words echoed in my mind.

Turning back toward the canal, we moved downstream to give the emerging tow plenty of room to complete its

300

turn against the current. "This is ridiculous," Dee said. "There must be some safe place to wait." She called the lock again. "Is there any place we can wait other than here in the river?"

"You can come in and go behind the **Blue Dolphin** on the east side. Just be sure you're well out of the path of tows leaving the lock."

"Thanks," Dee said, as I headed **Sol Seaker** past the waiting towboats and toward the quiet waters of the Industrial Canal. As we reached the demarcation line between the swift flowing, agitated river and the calm canal, a particularly large wave slapped our stern pushing us roughly into the calm water.

"He's still master isn't he," I said, as I turned slowly for a last look at the Magical River. "That slap on the tail was to remind us that, even though he gave us safe passage, we shouldn't forget who's boss."

"He really was good to us," Dee added. "He turned our heads in time to see uncharted wing dams. He kept logs out of our propeller. He guided us through the shallows at Buffalo City. He stopped a towboat in front of us at Lansing so we could meet the Leichtmans and Smiths. He brought us to Tony and JoAnn at Quincy. He gave us places to stop at Cottonwood Point, Osceola and Tomato. He even cleared the river of towboats and sent a fast rescue boat when our motor stopped at Memphis. And. . ."

"Whoa!" I shouted. "Next thing you'll be saying he even held our fan belt together until we got to Memphis so we would be close to help, and that he made our belt break so we'd have to return to Mud Island to go to Blues Alley with Norm and Patti from the **Patricia B**, and. . ."

"Well. . .?"

"The **Blue Dolphin**," I said, changing the subject. "That sounds like an elegant yacht."

As we approached the lock, we searched in vain for the boat we were to go behind. Suddenly we both burst into laughter.

"How soon we forget," I mused, as I headed toward a cove behind a large concrete pillar used to moore tows waiting to enter the lock. Here and there on this mooring "dolphin" were faint traces of the blue paint that once covered it's entire surface.

While we waited our turn to lock through, two more pleasure craft joined us, **Sun Chaser**, a cruiser a little larger than **Sol Seaker** and **Rachel B**, a houseboat. All, like us, were headed for Schubert's Marina.

After an interminable wait, the lock master's voice came over the radio. "We've had some trouble with a drawbridge. Now it's fixed. I have a barge going in now. As soon as it's in, the **Sun Chaser** and that little boat can go in and tie off to the barge."

"There's a third boat here," Dee said.

"They can come in too."

We followed **Sun Chaser** in, with **Rachel B** behind us. In a few moments we were lowered one foot to the level of the canal and Lake Pontchartrain. Over the radio came the lockmaster's voice. "The three pleasure craft will leave the lock first if there's room to fit."

We followed **Sun Chaser**, through the narrow space between barge and lock wall without any problem. Last, **Rachel B** edged up to the opening. Her skilled captain brought her through without a scratch although there were only inches to spare on each side.

We had entered the Harvey Lock at 2:10, as we emerged from the Industrial Lock, the sun was getting very close to the western horizon, and we still had five miles of canal, with several drawbridges, and six miles of lake, before we would reach Schuberts. Unless things went smoothly, it would be dark before the end of our journey.

"This is the **Sun Chaser** calling the second bridge. We have three boats coming through." There was no answer.

We called the bridge, with the same results.

Rachel B called, still no answer.

Sun Chaser gave a signal with her loud air horn - still no response from the bridge.

"What should we do?" came a radio voice from the **Rachel B**.

As we milled around, waiting, the sun dropped below the horizon. In the growing darkness **Sun Chaser** switched on a bright spotlight and flashed it in the window of the control room, high on the bridge. Suddenly the radio came to life. "You can toot, flash and honk all you want, but this bridge isn't opening until 5:45."

Later we learned that all highway drawbridges on the canal were closed during the rush hour traffic. Having been in rush hour traffic, we understood and appreciated the need for this schedule. But we didn't understand the lack of consideration shown by the unknown bridge tender who could have graciously explained the situation when we first called, almost an hour earlier.

At 5:47 the bridge opened. In total darkness we followed **Sun Chaser** against a strengthening tidal flow, groping our way along the Industrial Canal. Like three blind mice, we approached the next in the series of drawbridges. Horns, lights and radio calls got no response from the bridge tender.

As this bridge was higher than the previous ones, **Sun Chaser** inched forward hoping to go under the closed bridge, she stopped and drifted back on the current. We moved ahead slowly, making a successful passage. **Sun Chaser** followed, but **Rachel B** was too big.

The two of us continued to grope our way along the dark channel. Ahead the Intracoastal veered to the right toward Mobile Alabama and points east. We stayed left. At the next bridge we had to wait several minutes for a train to arrive and cross. Just as the bridge opened, the **Rachel B** caught up with us. We were three again.

The tidal current had become very strong when we reached the final drawbridge. We called, tooted and flashed for ten, fifteen, twenty, thirty minutes, to no avail. Holding our boats in place in the current was both difficult and expensive. Our fuel gage was steadily dropping between the quarter and empty marks.

Sun Chaser tied to one of the wooden guide walls, and captain John Hall climbed up the wall, trying to find a way to reach the control room, to make our presence known.

Dee continued to call on the radio, "To the bridge between the lock and the lake. Please anyone. Radio check. Anyone out there?"

Finally an answer came, "That's the Seabrook bridge. Call the Seabrook bridge."

"Seabrook bridge. There are three boats that need to get through."

"This is the Seabrook highway bridge. You'll have to call the Seabrook railroad bridge."

John, finding no way to reach the control room was now back on his boat, once again shining his powerful spotlight on the window of the control room.

Dee continued to call. Suddenly a voice said, "Out to lunch," and simultaneously the bridge swung upward.

We hurried through, finding ourselves in the broad

303

black expanses of Lake Pontchartrain. The three of us stayed together, maintaining a safe distance from the row of street lights that lined the lakeshore.

As we skirted a swimming area, I spotted the running lights of a moving boat. The high, white light identified her as a sailboat, and the red said that she was moving from our starboard toward our port. Soon the red disappeared. The boat had turned and was moving ahead of us in the same direction we were traveling. Assuming that she was headed toward the marina, we followed. Our assumption was correct and soon we were safe inside the harbor, after having run in total darkness for more than three and a-half hours.

Unknown to us, our arrival was witnessed by Patti and Norm Bork. The conversation we heard while in the Harvey Canal had, in fact, been about their yacht the **Patricia B.**

Over the next few days we renewed our friendship with Norm and Patti, took a bus to Memphis to pick up our car, trailer and a Calhoun boat at Reelfoot Lake, then hauled, cleaned and stored **Sol Seaker**.

Still full of our experiences, we headed our jeep west toward home. "I hear there are beautiful rivers in Florida," Dee said as we were driving across the endless plains of Texas. "Let's do those next."

"Great!" I exclaimed. "Suppose we can find Ponce de Leon's Fountain of Youth?"

"Why not! We found the **Sol** and **Soul** we sought this time. They say you see what you seek," Dee whispered, as she leaned her head on my shoulder and squeezed my hand."

LA FEAT

30

POST SCRIPTS

On the Mississippi we sought both physical and spiritual "sunshine." We saw what we sought! But some of the events we considered "sunshine" were not viewed in the same way by others.

Several experiences were omitted from the narrative in order to protect the anonymity and integrity of our river friends. Two of these experiences are added here. The facts are accurate, the names are changed and the locations remain unidentified.

EXPERIENCE #1

As we walked along the misty street of one river town, we took refuge in a gift shop whose sign stated: Mississippi River Artist's Association. We were met at the door by Ginny Keene, broom in hand and talking ninety miles a minute.

"Saturday cleaning," she said in a booming voice. "Don't know why I clean on Saturday 'cause I get such crowds on Sunday, they just mess the place up again. Come on in! You from St. Louis?"

"No, San Jose."

"Oh, California. I'm from Hermosa Beach. First time home in years. I came home because this lawyer is bilching my crippled aunt out of $179,000. I'm the only one in the family that came home to help. I bought this whole complex for $19,000. I was making $300,000 a year in California, so you know this had to be something good to leave that. I'm gonna have eighty artists here all workin' on their special things. Look at these (holding up leather sculptures) and them quilts. They wanted to sell them for $40.00. I said, 'no way you gonna sell them for $40.00.' Do you know Southern California."

"Yes. . ."

"Do you know Western Town in Hermosa Beach?"

"Yes, my sister. . ."

"Then she's seen me," she continued as she led us around the shop. "I was the Indian at the artists corner. I danced. I'm part Indian. My aunts were smart. They didn't tell anybody, but they invested in real estate and insurance. I was in that will all the time but I didn't know it. I stand to lose a quarter-million dollars if I move back to California. When I visited out there for three weeks I was out of the inheritance. This lawyer was selling $125,000 houses for $14,000 and buying them himself. I handed him $15,000 and said, 'You get out of here and leave my aunt alone.' This state is like California was in 1938."

"I got me a priest to help. He's a Franciscan. There ain't none of them here. Now he's my partner." She handed each of us an apple.

"I got me a big lawyer from St. Louis and went to the other lawyer and said, 'I'm from California and I know about people like you! The lawyer was Catholic, so I got me a priest an' said, 'How you gonna fight the Catholic Church?' One of my aunts is deceased and the other is crippled."

"When I lived on the reservation there was lots of vandalism. Two boys, that had been drinking, set fire to my car. I converted to be a Catholic. It's gonna take me one-to-five years to straighten out this mess. I got five kids, one at home. Someday I want four hundred artists here. I'm gonna buy a big showroom. Right now I can't get a loan to pay off the building because I've only been here two years."

"Two men own this whole town. Johnson up this way (she pointed upriver) and Sweeney down this way I'm right in between and they're both backing me. I just fell in love with this place. It took me two years to get used to the climate, the cold and the humidity. When I was out in California for a wedding, I sewed up Knott's Berry Farm. Gonna send them crafts made right here. The priest went with me to marry my daughter. He took his golf clubs. The Japanese are buying up all the golf courses; paid cash for them, that's more'n a million dollars at a crack."

"I'd like to buy that house across the street. I can get it for $10,000. Then I could bring my furniture here and be close to my shop. They used to raise peaches here. Every year there's a Peach Festival, but they don't raise peaches anymore."

We had returned to the front door.

"Thank you," Dee said as we hurried out the door and down the street.

"What was that?" I asked.

"That," replied Dee, "was Ginny Keene."

EXPERIENCE #2

In several marinas there were "live-a-boards" who assisted the marina owners and managers by watching boats, dispensing fuel and assisting transients. One such individual, Jim, shared his assessment of sailboaters on the Mississippi:

"I hate sailboaters. They give us all kinds of trouble. They steal things. They'll pick up anything that's loose. They even cut the ends off the water hoses. I don't know what they do with them pieces of hose unless they put them on their bilge pumps. They come in here and dump their garbage, buy a little bit of gas, then expect everyone to wait on them. They're a different breed. Howie (marina owner, Bud Howe) hates sailboaters too!"

Just at that moment in Jim's tirade, we spotted a sailboat about a half-mile upriver. "Damn, there's a sailboat comin' now," he exclaimed. "He's got his mast down 'cause the river's too winding here to sail."

As the sailboat came abreast of the marina, it appeared that it would keep going. Suddenly it slowed and turned upstream toward the gas dock. "Damn, they're comin' in," declared Jim. "I better call Howie."

He stepped aboard **Sea Breeze**. Suddenly the air was split by the powerful speakers of his hailer. "Oh Howie, better hurry down. We've got a sailboat coming in." His voice was dripping with contempt. "Howie! Howie! A sailboater coming. Bring your cash box and get down here on the double."

There was no response from Howie.

Jim helped the sailboat dock. Two men and a woman (all in mid-thirties) and two boys about four and seven were on the deck. "Do you need fuel?" Jim asked.

"A little."

Jim gave me an, "I told you so," look.

"And some ice," said one of the men. "Do you have a cigarette machine?"

"I'm not sure," answered Jim in a less than amiable tone of voice.

307

"How about milk?" queried the woman.

"I don't think so," Jim responded.

Once again Jim tried the hailer. Still no answer. "He must be eatin' breakfast. I guess I'll hafta phone him."

"Didn't you hear me on the hailer?" inquired Jim when Howie answered the phone.

"No"

"We've got a sailboater here, needs a **little** gas, some ice, cigarettes and milk."

"We don't have milk."

"Bring your cash box down."

As Howie serviced the boat, the lady asked, "Do you have milk?"

"No, sorry."

Jim looked at the kids. He knew there wouldn't be a place to buy milk for more than a hundred miles. He disappeared into **Sea Breeze** and emerged in a few seconds with a box of powdered milk which he tossed to one of the men. "That's for the kids."

"Thanks, they drink a lot of milk."

Jim noticed that a long piece of the rubber rub rail was hanging out of its track along the boat's port side. When he called it to the attention of the men, one of them said, "Yeah, it was that way when I got it."

I said to Jim, "Maybe I should go get a screwdriver and put it back in for him."

"Don't bother," came the whispered reply.

Dee joined in, "Maybe he has a screwdriver you could borrow."

"Don't bother," repeated Jim, insistently.

It was then we noticed that Jim was watching the woman scolding and spanking one of the children down by the phone booth.

I didn't bother.

As the boat pulled away, Howie sat down with us and began to talk about sailboaters. "We have some good ones come in here, but there's enough bad ones that give them all a bad reputation. All the marina owners feel the same way. A lot of them will anchor just out from the docks then come ashore in a dinghy with all their garbage. Then they'll come in for $5.00 worth of gas and fill up with free water. They'll use toilets and showers, but never spend any money."

"When they come in here they expect to tie up for a **couple** of dollars. We don't have much space **so we** ʰ⁻

to charge by the foot. When a sailboat comes in with its mast down, the mast is five to ten feet longer than the boat. It takes up that much more space. We try to be fair but some of them will argue over a few inches.

"Ruth (Howie's wife) was really unhappy with one yesterday. She asked how long he was. He answered in a smart-alecky tone of voice, 'twenty-nine feet seven inches if you want to get technical.' Not to be outdone, Ruth replied, 'With that mast down you're thirty-four feet, if **you** want to get technical.' She charged him for only twenty-nine feet, but she wanted him to know that he was really using more space than he was charged for."

While working on our manuscript - DOWN THE MAGICAL MISSISSIPPI - we continued to correspond with many of our new friends. Included below are brief POST SCRIPTS about some of them:

John Filkins: Retired as Prescott's, "keeper of the ramp," and according to John, "I fell in love again."

Vi and Bob Reader: Enjoying their Oquawka home overlooking the Mississippi, even when it becomes completely frozen over for a few days in winter. Wood ducks still nest in their special bird house.

Jan Griffith: Has completed her fifth year at the Lansing Marina. She earned a degree in computer programming at business school and does computer related payroll work in the off season. She says, "I really miss the marina and people. . . I just may be back again next year. Blackie's tumors returned. . ."

Darlene and Vernon Leichtman: Summer at Lansing, then travel to Arizona and Florida in the winter.

Bob and Jo Smith: Summer at Lansing and winter in South Texas, where they have just purchased a 14 x 56 mobile to use as a winter home in Brownsville. Bob continues to write poetry and work on his book.

Edith and Al Lippert: Started remodeling the old pontoon boat in April and completed it by the fourth of July - christened **The Sandpiper.**

Ray and Elaine Lippert: Still enjoy sandbar parties at Sabula. Took a long houseboat trip with friends
- down the Illinois River and up the Mississippi to
Sabula. On the trip they, ". . .sunk an island, talked
to the **Calypso**, and rafted to a barge one foggy night."
Ray supplied the photograph of **Sol Seaker** on the cover
of our book.

Tony and JoAnn: These two very special people are
still in Quincy. Tony doesn't get to fish much. In a
recent letter he wrote: "I have been down most of the
time since you saw me. I had a very hard time passing
this driving test, my bad eyes, my bad hands, and my bad
truck worried me almost to death; but, I passed with a
great big A. I'll be driving for a while anyway."

Judee and Gary Brone: Still have Our Own Hardware,
but its a struggle. Judee says, "The money doesn't keep
rolling in." But they stay busy. Gary coached a high
school cross-country team to the state championship, and
Judee directed an anti-nuclear allegorical play called,
"Alice in Blunderland."

Harold Kennedy: Curetor at the Buffalo Bill Museum,
Le Claire, Iowa is still teaching valuable and interesting lessons to "fifth-graders" of all ages.

Joe, Cindy, Fern and Hoppie: In April, 1984 we
stopped to visit at Hoppie's. All were well. The river
was about to flood so the Hoppie's were on alert to move
their possessions. The river retreated before flooding
the marina store. We invited Joe and Cindy to dinner -
Joe sneaked away from the table and paid for the meal
without my knowledge - then refused my offer to pay. We
got an irate phone call after we returned home - when
Joe found the money I left under his coffee maker aboard
Cloud Nine.

Floyd Ligons: The old man with the artificial leg
died some months after we rescued him where he had fallen at the edge of the street. On the nearby vacant
lot, where Ray "rescued" us from Floyd, a convenience
food market now stands.

Ray and Lucille: When we spent the night with them
in the spring of 1984, they had bought another new car.

Pops: Left Hickman in his repaired boat. Spent some months at Greenville, Mississippi. By January of 1984 he had made it to Natchez, where his old dog died. Local people gave him two puppies.

Emily and Robert Lee: Still hold on to what reality is left at Tomato, Arkansas. The church is gone, the store is gone, but as long as there are good "folks" like Emily and Robert, Tomato, Arkansas will continue.

Steve and Rita: We stopped for a brief visit in January, 1984. Rita was busy bailing rainwater out of boats and trying to figure out a graceful way to get rid of "Pops.

Patti and Norm Bork: After getting engines repaired at New Orleans, continued to Fort Myers, Florida where they live aboard the **Patricia B.** In 1983 we spent a month aboard **Sol Seaker** in the same marina, and visited them again in 1984. "We are loving every moment of 'live aboard' life," they say.

Walt and Maxie Votaw: Took **Doublerun** to California (Dee was correct). They entertain friends and cruise, "back and forth to Catalina."

Trapani Moreau Family: They have a beautiful new grandchild. In December, 1984 we received a letter stating, "It got so cold around Red River until the river froze up, and when it started to melt we had big, huge ice blocks to come down our river. Some of them were 8 feet thick and about 10 feet square."
"My son, Roger, caught two catfish, one 30 lb. and the other one 53 lb. My other son, Paul, that was telling you about the drowning of different people, he gotten marry and built him a house across from us."
"Our new grandbaby, the one you took a picture of, will be one year old Dec. 20, 1984.
"Melville is so bad, it is just a stop-off for Coonass Frenchmen!"

John and Irma Hall: Ran into rough seas after leaving New Orleans - almost lost their 50 gallon fuel barrel. When they finally got **Sun Chaser** to Cape Coral, Florida, they sold her. They miss their home up north.

Dee and Weldon Parker: That's us! After two months at Clearlake, we returned to **Sol Seaker,** stored on her trailer at Slidell, Louisiana. The leaks that occurred at Cassville and Hickman hadn't been completely repaired. Heavy rains at Slidell had flooded the cabin and bilge with three inches of water. It took days to dry the interior and defeat the mildew.

During the winter of 1983 and 1984 we worked on: DOWN THE MAGICAL MISSISSIPPI, and began our next series of cruises aboard **Sol Seaker**: ON THE RIVERS OF FLORIDA.

SOL SEAKER ON THE ST. JOHNS RIVER FLORIDA.